Getting Started

With

Lotus 1-2-3 5.0

For Windows

Getting Started With Lotus 1-2-3 5.0 For Windows

Barbara Farrell CPA Ed.D
Lubin School Of Business
Pace University

Babette Kronstadt
David Sachs
Series Editors
Pace Computer Learning Center
School of Computer Science and Information Systems
Pace University

JOHN WILEY & SONS, INC.
New York / Chichester / Brisbane / Toronto / Singapore

ISBN 0-471-12067-7

Printed in the United States of America

10 9 8 7 6 5 4 3 2 1

Preface

Getting Started with Lotus 1-2-3 5.0 for Windows provides a step-by-step, hands-on introduction to *Lotus*. It is designed for students with basic PC and Windows skills who have little or no experience with *Lotus 1-2-35.0 for Windows*. Basic skills are taught in short, focused activities which build to create actual applications.

Key Elements

Each lesson in *Getting Started with Lotus 1-2-3 5.0 for Windows* uses eight key elements to help students master specific worksheet and *Lotus 1-2-3 5.0* concepts and skills and develop the ability to apply them in the future.

- **Learning objectives**, located at the beginning of each lesson, focus students on the skills to be learned.

- **Project orientation** allows the students to meet the objectives while creating a real-world application. Skills are developed as they are needed to complete projects, not to follow menus or other artificial organization.

- **Motivation** for each activity is supplied so that students learn *why* and *when* to perform an activity, rather than how to follow a series of instructions by rote.

- **Bulleted lists of step-by-step general procedures** introduce the tasks and provide a handy, quick reference.

- **Activities with step-by-step instructions** guide students as they apply the general procedures to solve the problems presented by the projects.

- **Screen displays** provide visual aids for learning and illustrate major steps.

- **Independent projects** provide opportunities to practice newly acquired skills with decreasing level of support.

- **Feature reference** at the end of the book allows students to have a single place to look for commands to carry out the activities learned in the book.

Stop and Go

The steps for completing each *Lotus 1-2-3 5.0 for Windows* feature introduced in this book are covered in two ways. First they are described clearly in a bulleted list, which can also be used for reference. Then the steps are used in a hands-on Activity. Be sure to wait until the Activity to practice each feature on the computer.

Taking Advantage of Windows

Getting Started with Lotus 1-2-3 5.0 for Windows provides a balanced approach to using a Windows application. The use of the mouse, buttons, and icons is emphasized. However, familiarity with the menus is developed so that students can take advantage of the greater options often available in menu commands. Shortcut menus and keys are introduced when appropriate. The convenient **Feature Reference** at the end of the book summarizes menu commands and mouse and keyboard shortcuts for each of the features covered in the lessons. Students can use this both to review procedures or learn alternate ways of carrying out commands.

Flexible Use

Getting Started with Lotus 1-2-3 5.0 for Windows is designed for use in an introductory computer course. As a "getting started" book, it does not attempt to cover all of the features of the software. However, the topics included in later lessons allow instructors to provide opportunities for individualized or extra credit assignments or use the book in short courses focused specifically on *Lotus 1-2-3 5.0*. While designed to be used in conjunction with lectures or other instructor supervision, basic concepts are explained so that students can use the book in independent learning settings.

Data Disk

Data disks are provided to the instructors for distribution to the students. Many of the projects use files from the data disk so that the focus of the lesson is on the new skills being learned in each project. Initial projects require that students develop applications from the beginning, while later projects mix developing new applications with editing existing applications. Enough explanation and data entry is always included so that students understand the full application that they are building.

Acknowledgments

Getting Started with Lotus 1-2-3 5.0 for Windows was written by me, but it represents the work and effort of many individuals and organizations. Special thanks go to Elizabeth LoSacco for her careful editing, testing and expansion of the book. Nancy Treuer, Joe Knowlton, and Matthew Poli worked miracles with the layout and text formatting. Babette Kronstadt provided energetic leadership and orchestrated the production of not only this book but all of Pace's books in the Getting Started Series.

We received enormous institutional support from Pace University and the School of Computer Science and Information Science (CSIS). In particular, much personal support and personal leadership for our work has come from the Dean, Dr. Susan Merritt.

From another perspective, this book is also a product of the Pace Computer Learning Center, under the direction of Dr. David Sachs, which is a loose affiliation of approximately 15 faculty and staff who have provided more than 7,000 days of instruction to over 60,000 individuals in corporate settings throughout the United States and around the world during the past nine years. Our shared experiences in the development and teaching of these non-credit workshops, as well as credit bearing courses through the Pace University School of Computer Science and Information Systems, was an ideal preparation for writing this book.

We have received many invaluable comments and suggestions from instructors at other schools who were kind enough to review earlier books in the *Getting Started* series and offer their suggestions for the current books. Our thanks go to Jack D. Cundiff, Horry-Georgetown Technical College; Pat Fenton, West Valley College; Sharon Ann Hill, University of Maryland; E. Gladys Norman, Linn-Benton Community College; and Barbara Jean Silvia, University of Rhode Island.

Our thanks also go to the many people at Wiley who provided us with the support and assistance we needed. Our editor, Beth Lang Golub, and editorial program assistant, David Kear, have been very responsive to our concerns, and supportive of all of the Pace Computer Learning Center's writing projects. Andrea Bryant was invaluable in her management of all aspects of the production of this book.

Last but not least, I would like to thank my husband Jim and my son Brandon for their patience and support throughout the long writing process.

Barbara Farrell

March, 1995
White Plains, New York

Contents

4 USING FUNCTIONS AND FORMULAS

5 ABSOLUTE AND RELATIVE CELL ADDRESSING

6 MULTIPLE WORKSHEETS

7 CREATING CHARTS 133

8 DATABASE BASICS 161

Students and Instructors
Before Getting Started Please Note:

WINDOWS INTRODUCTION

Getting Started with Lotus 123 5.0 for Windows assumes that students are familiar with basic Windows concepts and can use a mouse. If not, instructors may consider using the companion book, *Getting Started with Windows 3.1*, also published by Wiley. Windows has a tutorial which can also help students learn or review basic mouse and Windows skills. To use the Windows Tutorial: 1) turn on the computer; 2) type: **win** or select Windows from the menu or ask your instructor how to start Windows on your system; 3) press the **ALT** key; 4) press the **H** key; 5) when the **Help** menu opens, type a **W**; and 6) follow the tutorial instructions, beginning with the mouse lesson if you do not already know how to use the mouse, or going directly to the Windows Basic lesson if you are a skilled mouse user.

STUDENT DATA DISKS

Most of the projects in this book require the use of a Data Disk. Instructors who have adopted this text are granted the right to distribute the files on the Data Disk to any student who has purchased a copy of the text. Instructors are free to post the files to standalone workstations or a network or provide individual copies of the disk to students. This book assumes that students who use their own disk know the name of the disk drive that they will be using it from. When using a network, students must know the name(s) of the drives and directories which will be used to open and save files.

SETUP OF WINDOWS AND LOTUS 123 5.0 FOR WINDOWS

One of the strengths of Windows and *Lotus 123* is the ease with which the screens and even some of the program's responses to commands can be customized. This, however, can cause problems for students trying to learn how to use the programs. This book assumes that Windows and *Lotus 123 for Windows* have been installed using the default settings and that they have not been changed by those using the programs. Some hints are given about where to look if the computer responds differently from the way it would under standard settings. If your screen looks different from those in the book, ask your instructor or laboratory assistant to check that the defaults have not been changed.

VERSION OF THE SOFTWARE

All of the screenshots in this book have been taken using Version 5.0 of Lotus 123 *for Windows*. If you are using a different 5.0 version, the appearance of your screen and the effect of some commands may vary slightly from those used in this book.

Introduction; Creating A Worksheet In 1-2-3 For Windows

Lotus 1-2-3
Release 5

Objectives

In this lesson you will learn:

- The Capabilities of 1-2-3 for Windows:
- Starting 1-2-3 for Windows;
- The 1-2-3 for Windows Screen;
- How to Use HELP;
- Moving Around the Window;

- How to Create a New file;
- How to Open Existing files;
- How to Save your file.
- How to Close Files.

THE CAPABILITIES OF 1-2-3- FOR WINDOWS

1-2-3 Release 5 for Windows is a spreadsheet package that will permit you to calculate and analyze data in the Windows environment. Release 5 offers spreadsheet, charting, drawing, scenario and database capabilities.

The spreadsheet organizes information in columns and rows. Once data is entered, formulas can be entered to perform calculations based upon the numbers entered. When numbers are changed, the new results are automatically calculated. 1-2-3 for Windows also provides over 220 built-in functions (preconstructed formulas) for calculations

Database functions can also be accomplished with 1-2-3 for Windows. You may sort by alphabetic or numeric orders using different columns of data. Finding data in the 1-2-3 database and querying data are two other database functions.

Once the information in the spreadsheet is created, it can be used to create charts. Charts are useful when creating presentations and reports.

Using 1-2-3 in the Windows environment allows the user to transfer information between 1-2-3 for Windows and other software applications easily. The information being shared between 1-2-3 for Windows and the software packages can be linked. Whenever the data in the Lotus 1-2-3 file changes, the file in the other software package is also updated automatically.

STARTING 1-2-3 FOR WINDOWS

Before you can use 1-2-3 , you must install it on the hard disk.

To start 1-2-3:

1. Start Windows.

2. Open the Windows Program Manager (if it is not already open).

3. Open the Lotus Applications Window by double clicking on it (your Lotus applications may be in a different group window).

4. Select the 1-2-3 Icon by double clicking on it.

1-2-3 displays the program title screen and then the 1-2-3 window with a worksheet window inside it. The Welcome to 1-2-3 dialog box will allow you to choose whether you want to create a new worksheet, work on an existing worksheet, or start the 1-2-3 tutorial.

If you do not want the Welcome display to appear again, select **Don't Show this Screen Again** by clicking on it.

THE 1-2-3 FOR WINDOWS SCREEN

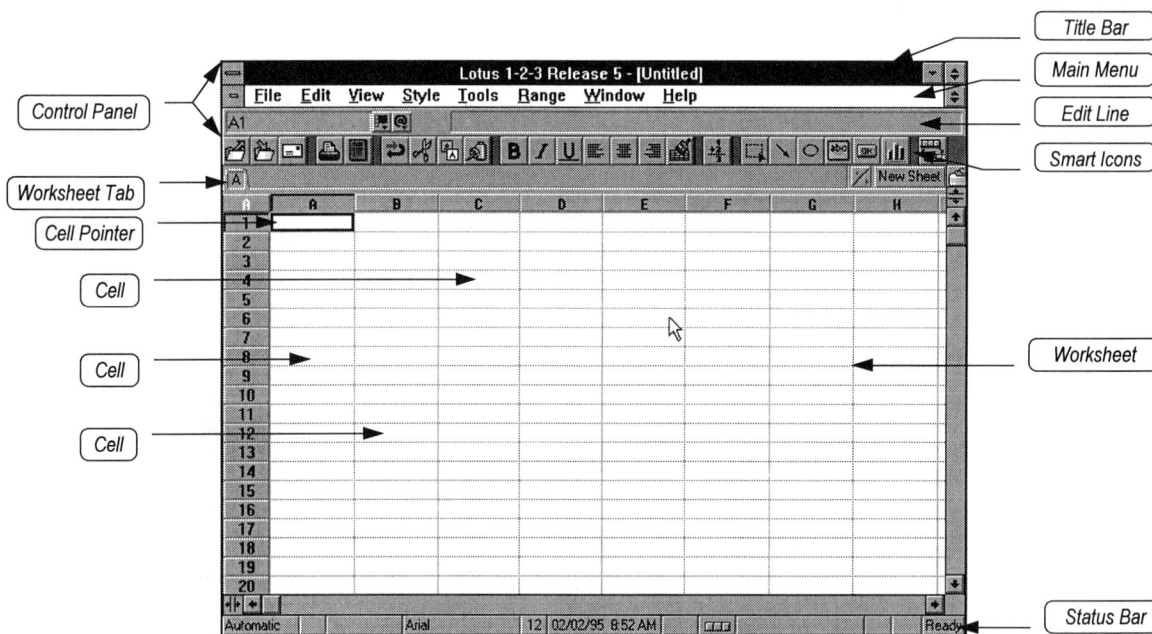

Figure I - 1

There are many parts of the 1-2-3 for Windows screen. Lets take a look at what appear on the screen before you.

The Worksheet

A large portion of the screen contains the worksheet. The worksheet is a grid composed of **columns, rows**, and **sheets. Columns** are named by the letters of the alphabet: A, B. C, etc. **Rows** are named using numbers: 1, 2, 3, etc. Each worksheet contains 256 columns and 8,192 rows (2,097,152 cells per worksheet).

The intersection of a row and a column is a **cell.** Every cell has is addressed by using the column first, followed by the row (i.e.: A1, Q192, etc.) A cell is highlighted on you screen. This cell is A1. The highlighted box surrounding cell A1 is called the **cell pointer.** It identifies the **current cell.** When a cell is current, you may enter data, change the contents, or choose a command to affect the cell

Initially, the worksheet file has one worksheet open. You can add up to 255 more sheets to each worksheet file (536,870,912 cells per file). Each worksheet it identified by a letter , A, B, etc.. The worksheet letter is displayed at the top left corner of the worksheet.

The Control Panel

The **Control Panel** displays information about 1-2-3 and the active window. It contains information about the **Title Bar,** the **Main Menu** and the **Edit Line.**

Title Bar

The **Title Bar**, located at the very top of the screen, contains the Control menu box, the program name, the file name, the Minimize button and the Maximize or Restore button.

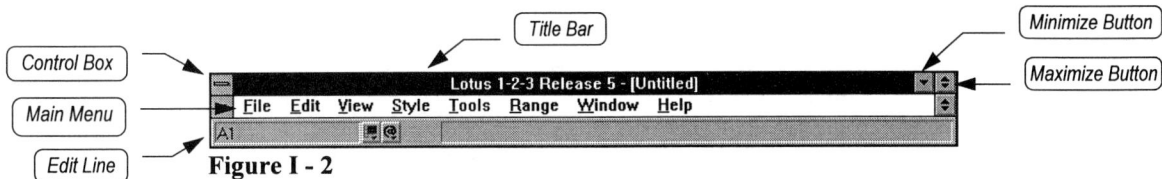

Figure I - 2

When a command from the menu is selected, the title bar displays a description of the command. Occasionally, if you choose a command, the title bar will display instructions to help you complete the command. For example, instructions appear when you are drawing a chart.

The Main Menu

The **Main Menu** contains the commands that will be used with 1-2-3 for Windows. Commands on the main menu can change depending on the users selection.

The Edit Line

The **Edit Line** contains the selection indicator, the navigator, the @function selector , the Cancel and Confirm buttons and the contents of the box

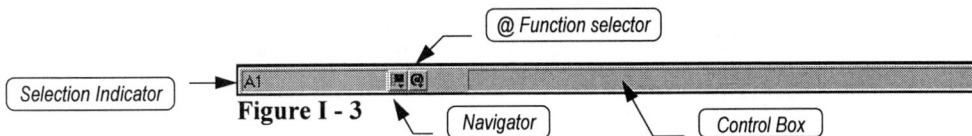

Figure I - 3

The **selection indicator** displays the current cell address or the name of the current selection (i.e.: range, chart,). If you click on the **Navigator,** a list of range names in the current file will be displayed. While in Ready mode, you can move to a range name by selecting it from the list. By clicking on the **@Function selector**, a list of @ functions available in 1-2-3 will be displayed. When data is entered such as values, labels,, etc., 1-2-3 will display the data in the **contents box**. Also, the Cancel and Confirm buttons appear. Select the Confirm button to enter the data or the cancel button to cancel the entry.

SmartIcons

Figure I - 4

SmartIcons are shortcuts for the menu commands. The SmartIcons displayed will change depending on the menu item selected.

The Status Bar

The **Status Bar** is located at the bottom of the window. This bar displays formats for the selected cell, time and date, SmartIcon selector, Status Indicator, and the Mode Indicator. You can use the Status bar to perform many tasks with the mouse.

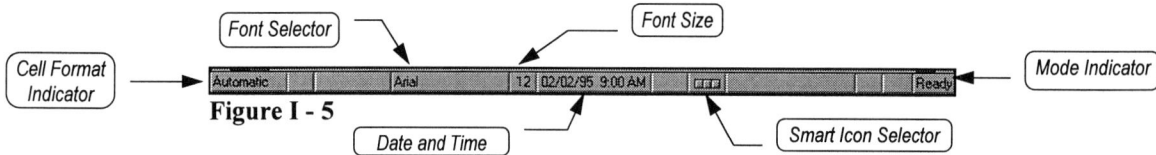

Figure I - 5

USING HELP

1-2-3 for Windows makes use of an on-line **Help** feature that may be accessed many ways. You may select Help by:

> The steps for completing each *Excel* feature introduced in this book are covered in two ways. First, they are described in a **bulleted** list, that can also be used for reference. The steps are used in a hands-on *Activity*. Be sure to wait until the **numbered** instructions in the *Activity* to practice each feature on the computer.

- From the menu commands;

- By pressing **F1**.

- By selecting the Question Mark in the top right corner of every dialog box.

Help is context sensitive. If you are in the middle of an operation and select Help, information about that operation appears. Help appears in a window that can be sized or moved. There are buttons and a menu in the Help window. Topics within the Help menu show as green and underlined. Help terms appear as green with dashed underlines.

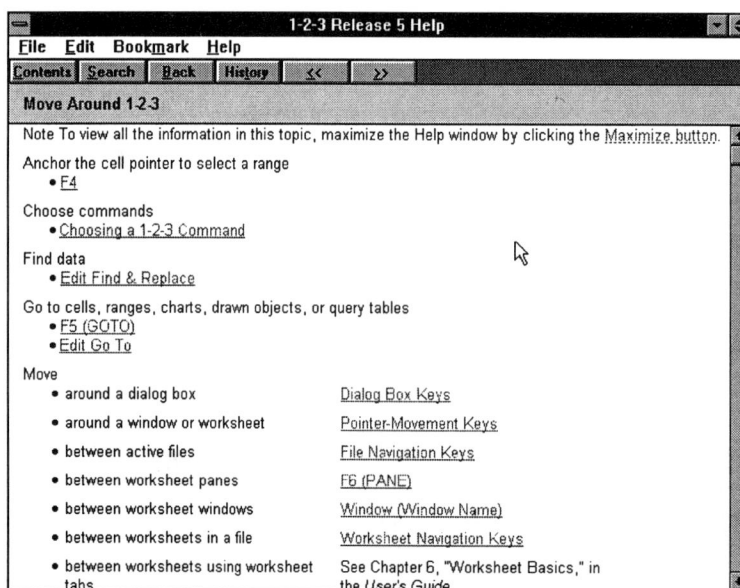

Figure I - 6

Activity I.1: Using Lotus 1-2-3 for Windows Help

The F1 HELP in 1-2-3 for Windows is context sensitive.

1. Click on **HELP** from the menu.

2. Click on **SEARCH.**

3. Type in **FORMULAS.**

4. Click on **SHOW/Topics**.

5. Select **@FUNCTION CATEGORIES** by clicking on it and pressing **ENTER** or selecting **GoTo**.

6. In the second row of the dialog box that appears there is a tern, *edit line*. Click on *edit line* and read the definition.

7. Click a second time to make the definition of edit line disappear.

8. In the center of the dialog box is the term **financial.** Click on **Financial**. A list of financial @ functions will appear.

9. When you are ready to end **HELP**, click on **CLOSE**. Then select **FILE/Exit**.

MOVING AROUND THE WINDOW

To enter data, the cell pointer must be placed in the correct location. There are many ways to move the cell pointer by using either the mouse or the cursor.

To Change Cell Positions using the Mouse

All of the following methods can be used to change cell positions using the mouse:

•	Click on the cell	This makes the cell active
•	Click on scroll bar arrow	Moves the screen in the direction of the arrow: one row or column for each click
•	Click on scroll bar	Moves the entire screen up, down, left or right
•	Drag scroll bar	Moves up, down, left or right quickly
•	Edit, Go To	Go to a cell specified by the user (**F5**)

To Change Cell Positions using the Keyboard

All of the following methods can be used to change cell positions using the keyboard:

•	Right Arrow	Right one column
•	Left Arrow	Left one column
•	Up Arrow	Up one cell
•	Down Arrow	Down one cell
•	Home	To cell A1 of the current sheet
•	Ctrl-Home	To cell A:A1 (beginning of the file)
•	**F5** and cell location	**GO TO** specific cell within the worksheet
•	End-Home	End of the file
•	Page Up	One Screen Up
•	Page Down	One Screen Down

- Tab or Ctrl Right Arrow   Right one screen
- Shift-Tab or Ctrl-Left Arrow   Left one screen

Activity I.2: Cursor Movement

To get some practice moving around the worksheet, complete the following Activity:

1. Select **FILE/New**.

2. Press **HOME** to place your cursor in cell **A1**.

3. Press the Right Arrow → to move to **B1**.

4. Press the Down Arrow ↓ to move to **B2**.

5. Press the Left Arrow ← to move to **A2**.

6. Press **PGDN** to move the cursor to cell **A22**. Notice the screen has scrolled down 20 rows.

7. Press **TAB** (or CTRL-Right Arrow) to move to cell **I22**. Notice that the screen has scrolled across 8 columns.

8. Press **F5** to bring up the **GoTo** prompt. The **F5** key is used to specify the cell location that you want to move you pointer to. A dialog box will appear.

9. Type **P200** and press **ENTER**. Now your cursor (or pointer) is in cell **P200**.

10. Press **HOME** to return to cell **A1**.

CREATING A NEW FILE

When you start 1-2-3, you have a choice of creating a new file or opening an existing file. If you are working in 1-2-3, you would choose **FILE/New** to open a new file or **FILE/Open** to open an existing file.

Activity I.3: Creating a New File

1. Choose **FILE/New**.

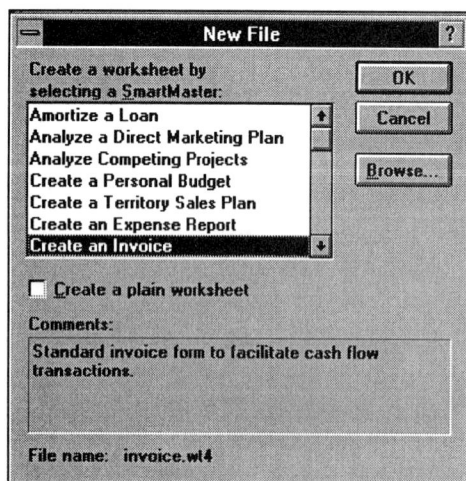

Figure I - 7

2. A dialog box appears. You may select a SmartMaster template or you may select the "**Create a plain worksheet**" check box. We want to start a blank worksheet so make sure there is an X in the check box before "**Create a Plain Worksheet**".

3. Choose **OK**.

1-2-3 creates a new file and gives it a default name. The default name is displayed in the Worksheet window. The first default name is **FILE0001.WK4**, the second is **FILE0002.WK4**, etc.. The number in the file name increases for each new file that uses the default name.

OPENING EXISTING FILES

Files already created and saved can be accessed by selecting **FILE/Open** or by clicking on the icon ![icon]. The dialog box that appears contains information about the file names, the file types, the directory, and the drive. To see how we would use this information to select a file, lets perform the following Activity.

Activity I.4: Opening a File

1. Select **FILE/Open** or click on the **FILE/Open** SmartIcon.

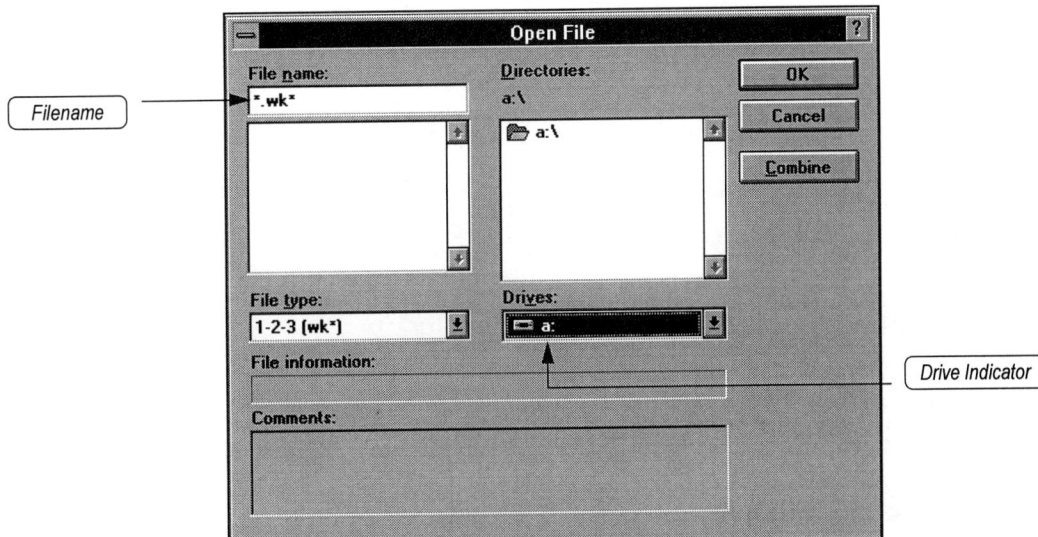

Figure I - 8

2. If the incorrect disk drive is selected, click on the arrow to the right of **drives.** To select the correct drive, simply click on the appropriate letter. Your Activity disk will likely be the **A** drive. Select **A**.

3. To see a list of files of a specific type, use the *File drop down* box. Click on the arrow to the right of File type.

4. A list of file names are now displayed in the File Name List box. Select the file **PRACTICE.**

5. Choose **OK**.

1-2-3 will open the file in the Worksheet window and make the last opened file the active window. Other windows will remain open. Later we will explore how to move from one window to another.

SAVING YOUR FILES

When using any software package, saving your work is one of the most important steps you can perform. It is always suggested that you save your work on a regular basis, about every 30 minutes. If you do not save your work, data will be lost when you close your files, end 1-2-3, or shut off the personal computer. Also, saving you files will prevent a considerable amount of duplicate effort in the event of a power failure or other accidents.

In the **FILE** menu, two options are **SAVE** and **SAVE AS**. **SAVE AS** will be used if you are saving a file for the first time, if you are modifying the file name, or saving the file to a different drive or directory. **SAVE** is used when you want to save the file under the same name on the same drive.

To save the current file under the same name:

There is another method of saving the file under the same name. There is a SmartIcon which will **Save the Current File.**
There are DOS rules that must be followed when saving files:

- File names are limited to eight characters.

- No spaces are permitted within the file name

- Lotus will automatically assign the extension of WK4.

Activity I.5: Saving your files

In this Activity, we will get some practice saving files under the existing name and under a new file name.

1. The file **PRACTICE** should be the active file on your screen.

2. Select **FILE/Save** or click the **FILE/Save** SmartIcon.

3. The file will automatically be saved under the existing file name.

4. Select **FILE/Save As.**

5. When the **SAVE AS** dialog box appears, the old file name appears in the File Name list box. Press the **BACKSPACE** key once. The old file name disappears. Type the new file name: **NEWFILE**.

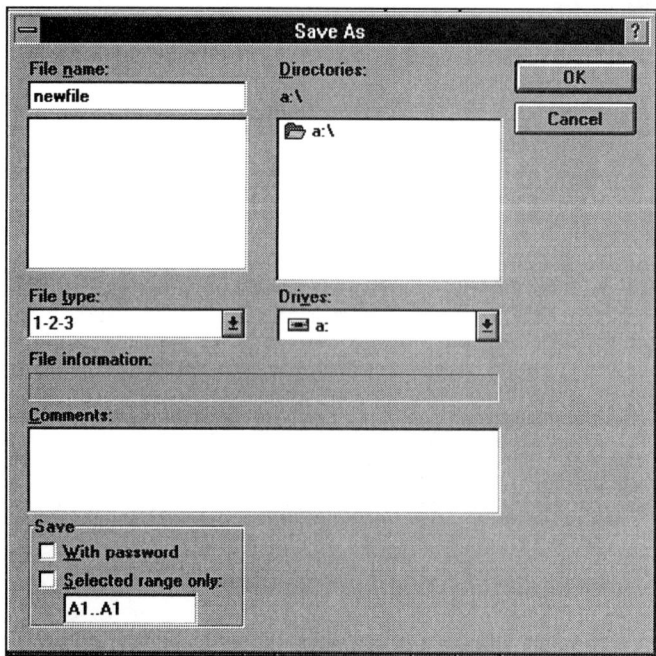

Figure I - 9

6. Select **OK** or press **ENTER.**

7. Notice the new file name, **NEWFILE,** now appears in the Title Bar.

CLOSING FILES

In 1-2-3- for Windows, several files may be open at the same time. Each open file is contained in a window. For the beginning user of 1-2-3, it is suggested that you close a file when you have finished working on it.

1-2-3 is designed so that you can never accidentally lose your work by closing the file if the file is not saved first. A **Close** dialog box will appear asking if you need to save the file before closing it.

When a file is closed, if any other files are currently open, one of the open files is displayed on the screen. When the file is closed and no other files are open, a window with a new file is displayed.

To close a worksheet file:

- Select **FILE/Close** or double click the control menu box for the worksheet

- **SAVE** the file if necessary.

Activity I.6: Closing all open files

1. Select **FILE/Close.** The file **NEWFILE** will be closed.

2. **If any other files are open, again select FILE/Save**.

3. If all files are closed, the Title Bar should say: **LOTUS 1-2-3 RELEASE 5-[UNTITLED]**.

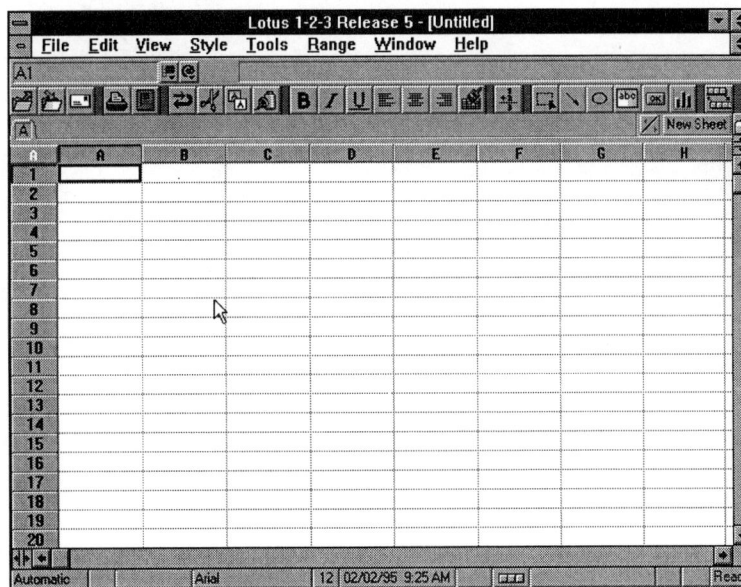

Figure I - 10

Creating a Worksheet in 1-2-3 for Windows

Objectives

In this lesson you will learn how to:

- Distinguish between a label and a value
- Enter labels
- Enter values
- Correct errors

- Enter formulas
- Change column width
- Save, close and retrieve a worksheet
- Print a worksheet.

PLANNING THE WORKSHEET

Before entering any data into the worksheet, you must first decide what the general objectives of the worksheet are and how it will be designed to meet those objectives. The general steps in planning a worksheet and how they are applied to our first project are listed below:

To plan a worksheet:

- Define the general objectives of the worksheet.

- *You need to create a budget for your clothing store for the first quarter of 1995. The budget will estimate the sales for the quarter, the expenses for the quarter, and the net income for the quarter.*

- Define the specific results you want the worksheet to provide.

- *The worksheet must provide: Monthly sales estimates in each of the departments (Men's, Ladies, and Children's), a total of all sales monthly, monthly expenses for the quarter, a total of all expenses monthly, a calculation of the monthly Net Income, and totals of all categories of data for the quarter.*

- Specify and obtain the data needed to obtain the results.

- *The required data are: estimates of the monthly sales data from the accounting department, a breakdown of the categories of expenses, and estimates of the monthly expenses by category.*

- Specify the calculations to be performed on the data:

RESULT	CALCULATION
Total Monthly Sales	Add the sales in the Men's, Ladies and Children's departments for each month
Total Monthly Expenses	Add the expenses in each category for each month
Monthly Net Income	Subtract the Expenses for the month from the Sales for the month
Quarterly Total	Add the data for each category of item for the months of January through March.

- Organize the worksheet on paper. Determine which data will be in each column and row. Select a title for the worksheet and for each column and row. Indicate where calculations are to be performed. See the Sample Worksheet in Figure 1 - 1.

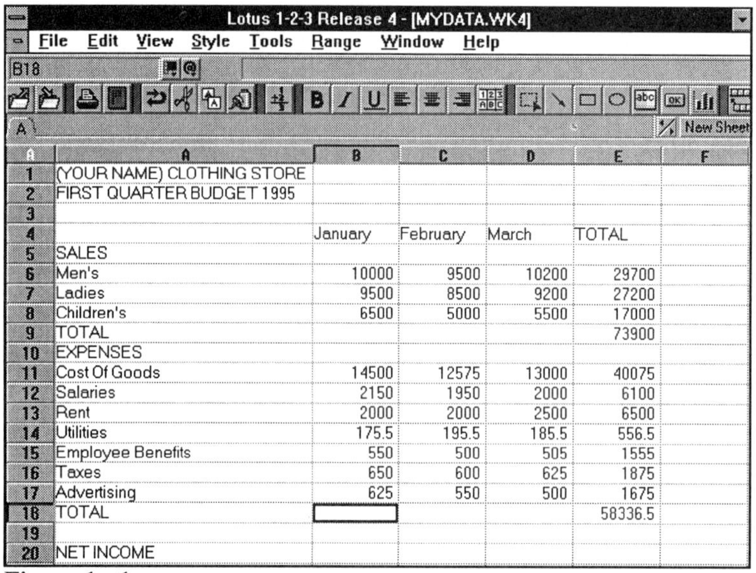

	A	B	C	D	E	F
1	(YOUR NAME) CLOTHING STORE					
2	FIRST QUARTER BUDGET 1995					
3						
4		January	February	March	TOTAL	
5	SALES					
6	Men's	10000	9500	10200	29700	
7	Ladies	9500	8500	9200	27200	
8	Children's	6500	5000	5500	17000	
9	TOTAL				73900	
10	EXPENSES					
11	Cost Of Goods	14500	12575	13000	40075	
12	Salaries	2150	1950	2000	6100	
13	Rent	2000	2000	2500	6500	
14	Utilities	175.5	195.5	185.5	556.5	
15	Employee Benefits	550	500	505	1555	
16	Taxes	650	600	625	1875	
17	Advertising	625	550	500	1675	
18	TOTAL				58336.5	
19						
20	NET INCOME					

Figure 1 - 1

PROJECT DESCRIPTION

Worksheets consist of headings (also known as titles), data (which includes text and numbers), and formulas. In order to create a worksheet, we will perform some very simple tasks such as entering data, entering labels which explain the data, performing calculations on the data, saving the worksheet and printing it out.

In this first lesson, you will create the quarterly budget for your clothing store. You will enter data projecting the sales, enter the classifications of expenses, and enter formulas to calculate the expected net income for the period. Your results at the end of lesson 1 will look like Figure 1 - 2.

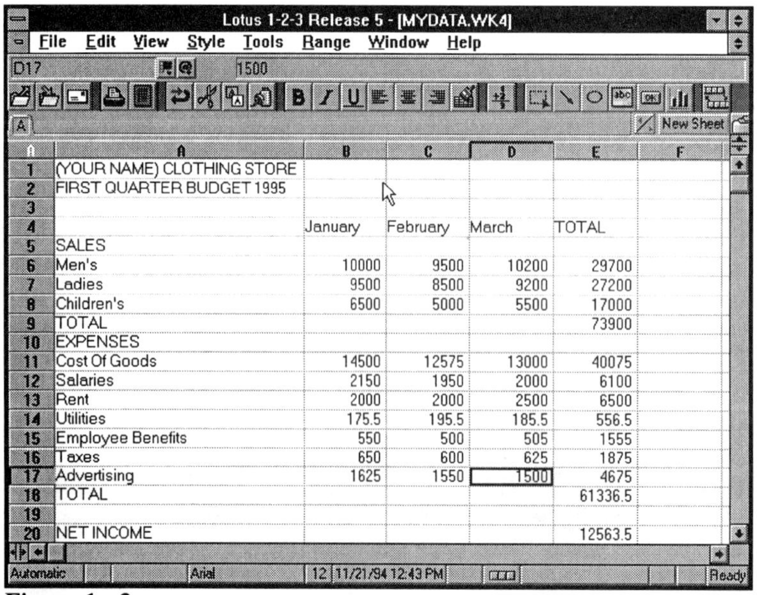

	A	B	C	D	E	F
1	(YOUR NAME) CLOTHING STORE					
2	FIRST QUARTER BUDGET 1995					
3						
4		January	February	March	TOTAL	
5	SALES					
6	Men's	10000	9500	10200	29700	
7	Ladies	9500	8500	9200	27200	
8	Children's	6500	5000	5500	17000	
9	TOTAL				73900	
10	EXPENSES					
11	Cost Of Goods	14500	12575	13000	40075	
12	Salaries	2150	1950	2000	6100	
13	Rent	2000	2000	2500	6500	
14	Utilities	175.5	195.5	185.5	556.5	
15	Employee Benefits	550	500	505	1555	
16	Taxes	650	600	625	1875	
17	Advertising	1625	1550	1500	4675	
18	TOTAL				61336.5	
19						
20	NET INCOME				12563.5	

Figure 1 - 2

In Lesson 2 you will improve the appearance of the worksheet by changing the alignment of the labels, formatting the numerical data with dollar signs and commas, and using text enhancements to make different parts of the worksheet stand out.

ENTERING LABELS AND VALUES

When creating a worksheet, the first step is to enter the headings (or titles) which describe the contents of the worksheet. Once the labels are entered, the data (which can be either text or numbers) are entered. Last, the formulas are placed into the worksheet so the computations can be performed. All these entries can be classified as either labels or values.

Entering Labels

Labels are usually referred to as text. They are used to identify the data being placed into the worksheet. Usually label entries are found across the top of the worksheet and down the left side of the worksheet. Remember however, you are not limited to using labels only in this manner. Labels are text entries and they can be used anywhere within the worksheet. In this lesson you will use labels as column headings at the top of the worksheet and as row headings on the left side of the worksheet.

If you want to enter a label into a cell, you begin by selecting that cell either by clicking on it or using the **ARROW** keys on your keyboard to move your cell pointer to that cell. Next, you type in your label. Finally, by pressing **ENTER**, an arrow key ($\rightarrow,\leftarrow,\uparrow,\downarrow$), clicking on the **Confirm** button on the Edit Line or clicking the mouse pointer on a different cell, the data is entered and *left aligned* (or left justified) within the cell. (You will be taken through this procedure step-by-step in the first activity.) Data that is left aligned within a cell is placed starting at the left edge of the cell location. You will also notice that there is an apostrophe (') placed before the label you just typed. This is called a *Label Prefix*. A label prefix denotes the alignment of the entry. In this case, the apostrophe means the label is *left aligned*. In lesson 2 you will learn how to change the alignment of entries.

Entering Values

A value is an entry which is a *number* or a *formula*. Values can be used in all mathematical calculations such as addition, subtraction, multiplication or division. To enter a value, simply type the value without any numerical formatting characters (dollar signs, commas, percents, etc.) using the same steps as entering a label. Later you will learn to use Lotus' formatting commands to improve the appearance of the data. Values are automatically *right-aligned* in the cell. Entries are considered to be numbers if they contain only numerical digits and any of the following characters:

.	a decimal place
,	a comma to separate the number into thousands; if you type commas in the wrong place, Lotus will not accept the entry as a number
+	a plus to indicate the number is positive
-	a minus to indicate the number is negative
()	brackets to indicate the number is negative
/	a slash to indicate the number is a fraction
%	a percent to indicate the number is a percentage
E ^e	to indicate the number is an exponent

Numbers or values can also be called *constants*. Constants (e.g. 45, -988) cannot change unless they are retyped or edited. Changing entries will be discussed later in this lesson. Also later in this lesson, formulas will be entered to perform calculations within the worksheet.

Entering Data

You are now ready to start creating your own worksheet.

To enter data:

- Select the cell to contain the data by clicking on the cell or using the **ARROW** keys
  ($\rightarrow,\leftarrow,\uparrow,\downarrow$) to move the cell pointer to the cell location.

  The selected cell is enclosed in a dark rectangular outline, known as the cell pointer. It is now the ACTIVE cell.

- Type the data. If you notice any errors while you are typing, press the **BACKSPACE** key until the error is removed and finish typing.

- Press **ENTER** or click on the **Confirm Button** ✓ to enter the data. You may also click on another cell or press an **ARROW** key to enter any data.

Activity 1.1: Entering Labels

In this activity, you will enter all the labels necessary to start the worksheet. When you initially enter some labels, they will not fit neatly in the cell location. Later we will explore how to change the width of the columns to improve the appearance of the labels.

1. Start *Lotus*. Follow the instructions in the Introductory chapter if necessary.

   A blank worksheet will be displayed. Cell A1 should be enclosed in a dark rectangular outline, known as the cell pointer. This indicates that A1 is the selected cell and that any data you type will be entered into that cell.

2. With **A1** selected, press the **CAPS LOCK** key and type: **(YOUR NAME) CLOTHING STORE**

   (YOUR NAME) should be typed as your first name and last name without the parenthesis.

   *As soon as you begin typing, two icons appear on the Edit line below the menu bar: the **Cancel** Button and the **Confirm** Button. As you type, the data entered is visible both in A1 and in the Contents Box, also located on the Edit Line to the right of the **Cancel** and **Confirm** Buttons. (See Figure 1 - 3).*

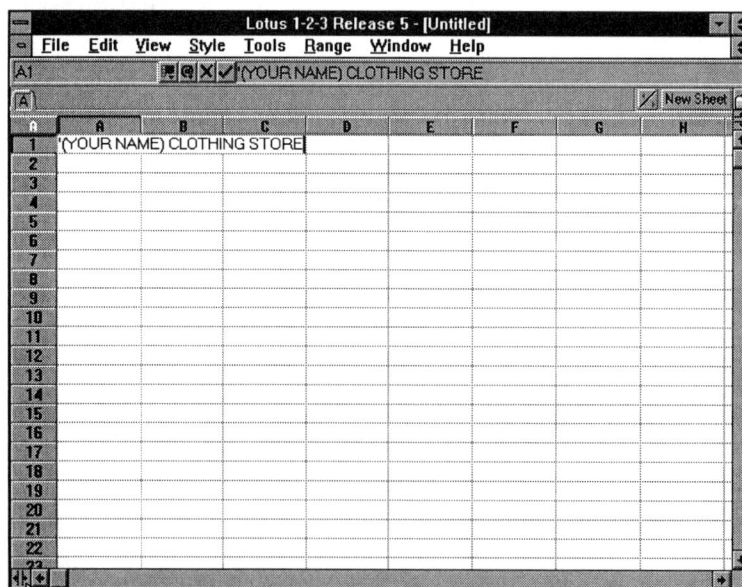

Figure 1 - 3

3. Press **ENTER** or click on the **Confirm** Button to the left of the **Contents Box**.

*Clicking on the **Confirm Button** or pressing **ENTER** will leave the cell pointer in cell **A1**. If you want the cell pointer to move to an adjacent cell, press an arrow key ($\rightarrow$,$\leftarrow$,$\uparrow$,$\downarrow$) or click on that cell.*

*Since (**YOUR NAME) CLOTHING STORE** is too wide for cell **A1**, it will overflow into the adjacent cells. We will fix cell overflows at the end of this lesson (see Figure 1 - 4).*

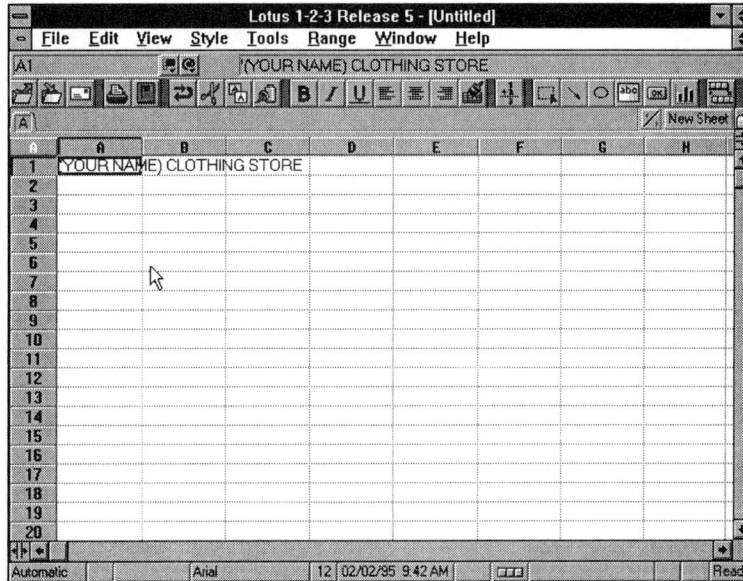

Figure 1 - 4

4. Click on cell **A2** or press the **DOWN ARROW** key to move the cell pointer to cell **A2**.

5. Type : **FIRST QUARTER BUDGET** and press **ENTER** or click on the **Confirm Button**.

6. Click on cell **A5** or press the **DOWN ARROW** key three times to move the cursor to cell **A5**.

7. Type : **SALES** and press **ENTER** or click on the **Confirm Button.**

*Since SALES is a label, it left-aligned in the cell (see Figure 1 - 5). An apostrophe is placed before the word SALES in the **Contents Box**. The cell pointer also remains in cell **A5**.*

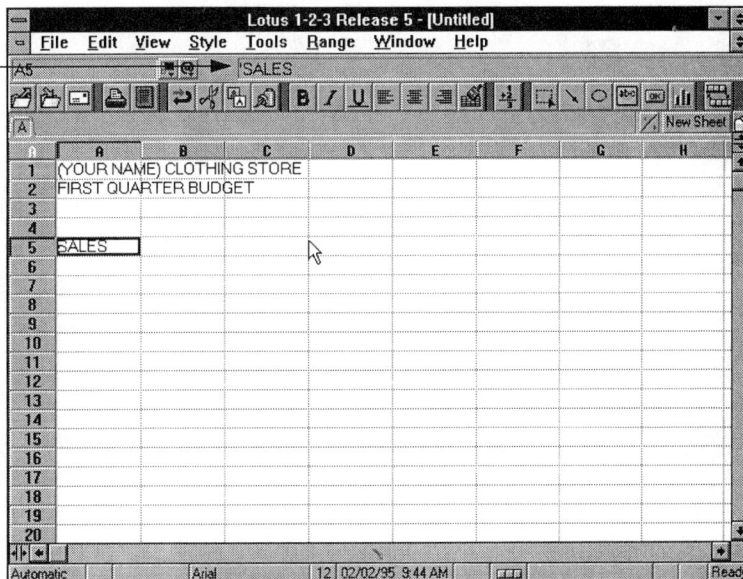

Apostrophe placed at beginning of SALES

Figure 1 - 5

8. Press the **DOWN ARROW** to move to cell **A6.**

9. Press the **CAPS LOCK** key if necessary, and type: **Mens.**

10. Press the **DOWN ARROW**($\downarrow$).

11. The cell pointer moves to cell **A7.**

12. Continue to enter the data in the **A** column. Listed below is the data to be entered and the cells it will be entered in. Type the data exactly as it appears below. If the entry listed below is in all CAPS, you should enter the same. Do not worry if you make typing errors. We will correct them in the next lesson.

A7	**Ladies**
A8	**Childrens**
A9	**TOTAL**
A10	**EXPENSES**
A11	**Cost of Goods**
A12	**Salaries**
A13	**Rent**
A14	**Utilities**
A15	**Emp Benefits**
A16	**Taxes**
A17	**Advertising**
A18	**TOTAL**
A20	**NET INCOME**

*Some of the data entered will overflow into the **B** column. At the end of this lesson, we will correct the width of the A column to allow enough room for the entries within the column.*

Problem Solver: *If you have entered data into a cell that should be blank, click on that cell and press the **DELETE** key to erase the data. If a cell contains wrong information, click on the cell, retype the entire entry and press **ENTER**.*

Your worksheet should resemble Figure 1 - 6.

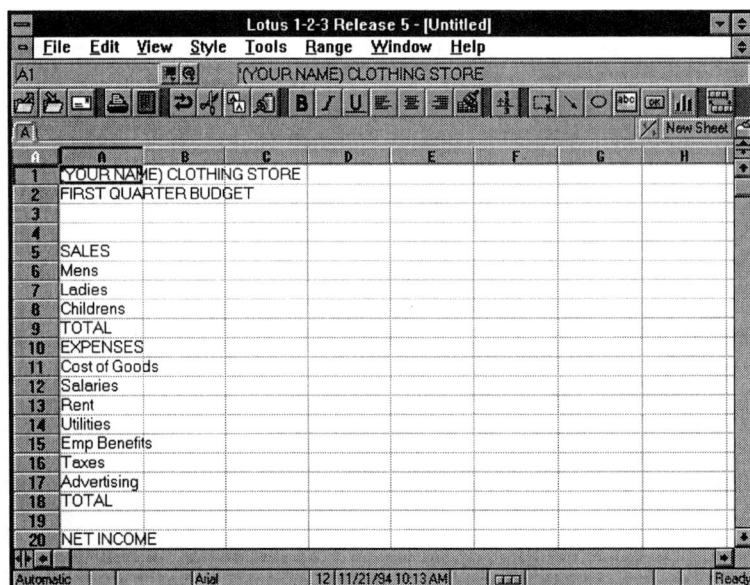

Figure 1 - 6

13. Move the cell pointer to cell **B4**. Next you will enter data across the top of the worksheet. There will be four additional entries made across row four in columns **B** through **E**.

14. In cell **B4**, type: **January**.

15. Press the **RIGHT ARROW** key (→). This will place the cell pointer in cell **C4**.

16. In cell **C4**, type: **February**.

17. Press the **RIGHT ARROW** key (→). This will place the cell pointer in cell **D4**.

18. In cell **D4**, type: **March**.

19. Press the **RIGHT ARROW** key (→). This will place the cell pointer in cell **E4**.

20. In cell **E4**, type: **TOTAL**. (Make sure the entry is in all CAPS).

21. Press the **UP ARROW** key (↑). This will place the cell pointer in. cell **E3**.

22. In cell **E3**, type: **FIRST QTR** and press the **ENTER** key or click on the **Confirm Button**. (Make sure the entry is in all CAPS**).**

Your worksheet will now resemble Figure 1 - 7.

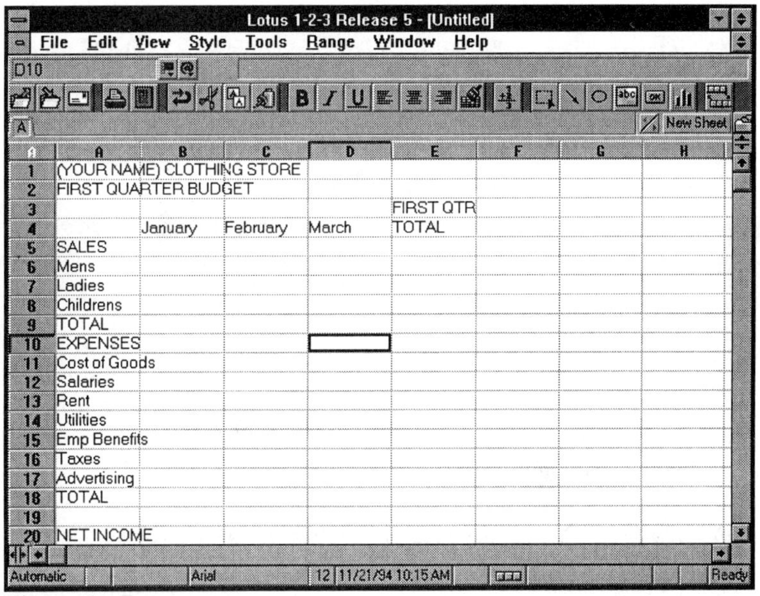

Figure 1 - 7

CORRECTING ERRORS

There are several methods you may use to correct errors using 1-2-3. The appropriate procedure to use depends on when you discover the error and how incorrect the data is that you typed.

To correct errors:

- To correct an error before you enter it into a cell (by pressing the **ENTER** key, or by clicking on the **Confirm Button** ✓) use the **BACKSPACE** key to erase the incorrect data. Then type the remaining contents of the cell correctly and press **ENTER** or click on the **Confirm Button**.

  When you are entering data, you cannot use the ARROW keys to move the insertion point and correct an incorrect entry. Pressing any of the ARROW keys, as you saw in the previous activity, moves the cell pointer to the next cell in the direction of the ARROW pressed and enters the data you have typed up to that point.

- To correct a <u>major</u> error after you have pressed the **ENTER** key, select the cell that contains the error by moving the cell pointer to that cell. Retype the entire contents of the cell and press **ENTER** or click on the **Confirm Button**.

  *When you retype the entry and press **ENTER**, the data you retype replaces the previous data.*

To correct a data entry error that contains only a few wrong characters, or to add to the contents of a cell, it is more efficient to EDIT the contents of the cell by using one of the methods below.

To edit cells:

- Double click on the cell containing the data you want to edit.

  *When you enter **EDIT** mode, there are some noticeable changes to the screen. First, the word **Edit** replaces the word **Ready** in the bottom right of the status bar. Second, the insertion point appears in the cell. Third, the **Confirm Button** and **Cancel Button** reappear.*

- Click to the left of the character to be changed or use the **RIGHT** or **LEFT ARROW** keys to move the insertion point to the left of the character to be changed.

- To delete characters, press the **DELETE** key once for each character to be deleted. To **INSERT** characters, type them. To type over characters that appear within the cell, press the **INSERT** key. Your insertion point will then appear with a blue rectangle highlighting the first letter which will be typed over. Now just type the characters. The characters typed will replace the existing characters.

- When editing is completed, press the **ENTER** key or click on the **Confirm button**.

KEYBOARD ALTERNATIVE: *Select the cell to be edited. Press **F2** to enter edit mode. The insertion point will appear in the cell at the end of the data. Move the insertion point to the characters to be changed and edit the data as described above.*

ALTERNATE METHOD: *To edit the data in the Edit Line (directly underneath the menu bar; the line on which the Confirm and Cancel Buttons appear), use the mouse or keyboard to enter Edit mode for the cell to be edited. Then click in the Contents Box to the left of the characters to be changed, inserted or deleted.*

Activity 1.2: Correcting Errors

There are some corrections you will need to make to the data entered. The second line of the title should state: **FIRST QUARTER BUDGET 1995**; the sales categories should be **Men's** and **Children's**; and the expense category in cell **A15** should appear as **Employee Benefits**. To make these corrections:

1. Make sure that your mouse pointer is in the shape of an arrow and double click on cell **A2**.

   This is the first step in correcting the second line of the title. Compare your screen to Figure 1 - 8.

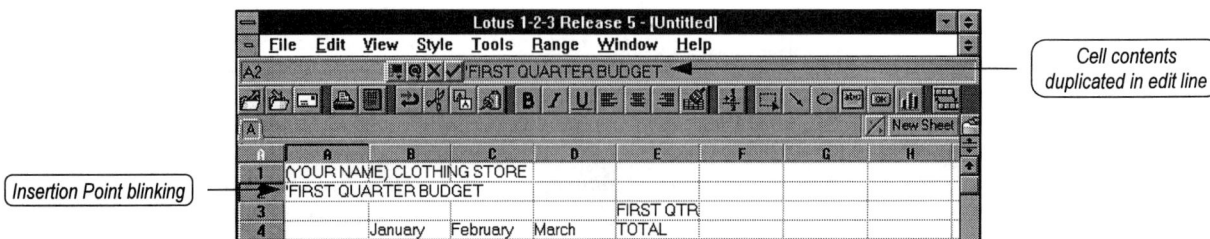

Figure 1 - 8

PROBLEM SOLVER: *Make sure the Selection Indicator on the Edit Line indicates that the selected cell is **A2**. Since the title **FIRST QUARTER BUDGET** overflows into cells **B2** and **C2**, if the mouse points to the end of the name when you double click, you will be editing cell **B2** or **C2**, both of which are empty. To solve this problem, press **ENTER**, move the mouse pointer to cell **A2** and double click.*

2. Notice that the insertion point is blinking just to the right of the **T** in **BUDGET** in cell **A2** (refer back to Figure 1 - 8). Press the **SPACEBAR** once, then type: **1995** and press **ENTER** or click on the **Confirm Button**.

3. To change **Mens**, double click on cell **A6**. Click to the left of the **s** in **Mens** in cell **A6**. Type an apostrophe and press the **ENTER** key or click on the **Confirm** button.

4. Use the same procedure to change **Childrens** to **Children's**.

5. Follow the same procedure to change **Emp Benefits** to **Employee Benefits**. Your worksheet should now look like Figure 1 - 9.

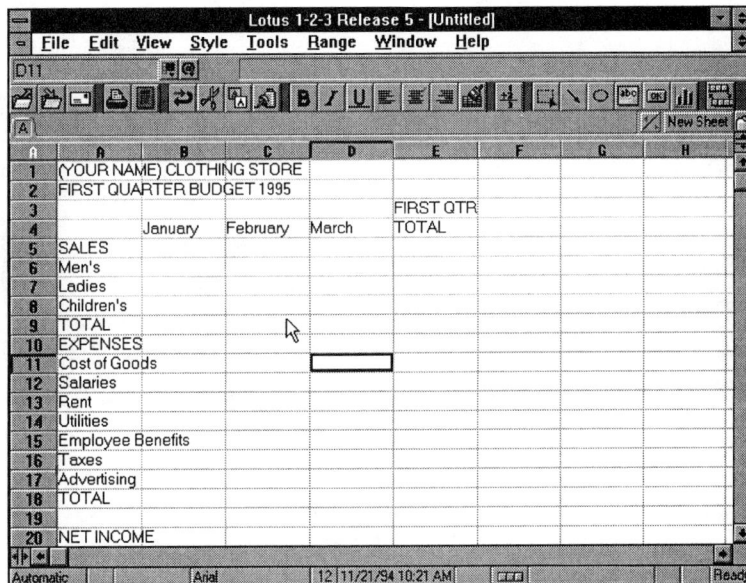

Figure 1 - 9

KEYBOARD SHORTCUT: *When you are in Edit mode, pressing **END** moves the insertion point to the end of the cell and pressing **HOME** moves the insertion point to the beginning of the cell.*

Clearing The Contents Of A Cell

There are times when you will want to clear the entire contents of a cell. The easiest method of clearing a cell is to make the cell active and press the **DELETE** key.

To clear the contents of a cell:

- Click on the cell to make it active.
- Press the **DELETE** key.

Activity 1.3: Clearing the Contents of a Cell

After entering the data you realize that the **FIRST QTR** portion of the title over the **E** column is redundant. The title should read only **TOTAL**, not **FIRST QTR TOTAL**.

1. Click on cell **E3** to make it active.

2. Press the **DELETE** key.

    *Cell **E3** should now be empty.*

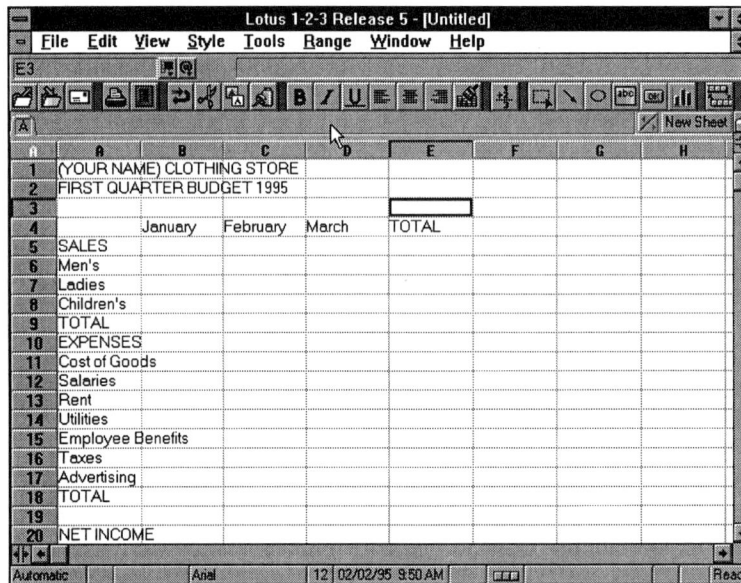

	A	B	C	D	E	F	G	H
1	(YOUR NAME) CLOTHING STORE							
2	FIRST QUARTER BUDGET 1995							
3								
4		January	February	March	TOTAL			
5	SALES							
6	Men's							
7	Ladies							
8	Children's							
9	TOTAL							
10	EXPENSES							
11	Cost of Goods							
12	Salaries							
13	Rent							
14	Utilities							
15	Employee Benefits							
16	Taxes							
17	Advertising							
18	TOTAL							
19								
20	NET INCOME							

Figure 1 - 10

UNDOING ACTIONS

Lotus will permit you to undo many commands if you realize you have made a mistake immediately after making it.

To Undo an action:

- Open the **EDIT** menu by clicking on the word **EDIT** on the Control Panel menu bar.

    *The top command on the **EDIT** menu will indicate whether you can Undo the command or whether you cannot undo the command. Press the **DOWN ARROW** once so you can see the color of the letters in the word **UNDO**. If the word **UNDO** appears in Black, you can Undo the command. If the word **UNDO** appears in gray, you cannot Undo the command.*

- Select **UNDO** by clicking on it or by using the **ARROW** keys to move the highlight to **UNDO** if it is not already highlighted, and pressing **ENTER**.

Activity 1.4: Undoing an Action

After you have deleted the label First Qtr, you decide you want it back.

1. Click on **EDIT** on the Control Panel menu bar. See Figure 1 - 11.

    *The first menu choice is **Undo.***

2. Click on **Undo.**

```
┌─────────────────────────────────┐
│ Edit  View  Style  Tools        │
│ Undo              Ctrl+Z         │
├─────────────────────────────────┤
│ Cut               Ctrl+X         │
│ Copy              Ctrl+C         │
│ Paste             Ctrl+V         │
│ Clear...          Del            │
│ Paste Special...                 │
│ Paste Link                       │
├─────────────────────────────────┤
│ Arrange                      ▶   │
├─────────────────────────────────┤
│ Copy Down                        │
│ Copy Right                       │
├─────────────────────────────────┤
│ Insert...         Ctrl +         │
│ Delete...         Ctrl -         │
├─────────────────────────────────┤
│ Find & Replace...                │
│ Go To...          F5             │
├─────────────────────────────────┤
│ Insert Object...                 │
│ Links...                         │
└─────────────────────────────────┘
```

Figure 1 - 11

3. **FIRST QTR** should reappear in cell **E3**.

4. To see if you can clear **FIRST QTR** again by using **EDIT/Undo** again, select **EDIT** on the Menu bar. This time you will notice that Undo is in gray. If you attempt to click on it, nothing happens. There are rules about what actions you can and cannot Undo. In *Lotus*, you cannot Undo the Undo. We will explore more rules about Undo later.

5. To get back to **Ready** mode (the mode in which you can enter data or choose a command), press the **ESCAPE** key twice.

6. To again delete the contents of cell **E3,** click on cell **E3** if it is not active.

7. Press the **DELETE** key.

   Cell E3 should now be empty.

Entering Values

The process of entering values is similar to that for entering labels. However, Lotus aligns values on the right side of the cell rather than on the left. The reason numbers are right aligned is so the columns of ones, tens, hundreds, etc., appear correctly aligned for adding. Also, when you enter values, you have some additional choices regarding how you enter them. For example, when you type a number such as 1000, the dollar sign and comma can be entered so the data appears as $1,000. *Lotus* gives you the option of entering *formatting characters* such as the dollar sign and commas when you enter the data or waiting until all the values are entered and adding all these formatting characters at once. When you enter the data in this activity, enter only the data with decimal places but without the formatting characters. We will enter formatting characters later.

Activity 1.5: Entering Values

1. Select cell **B6.** Type **10000.** You do not need to type the decimal point now because the 10000 is a whole number.

2. Press the **DOWN ARROW.** In cell **B7,** type **9500.**

3. Press the **DOWN ARROW.** In cell **B8,** type **6500** and press **ENTER** or click on the **Confirm Button.**

   Your screen should resemble Figure 1 - 12.

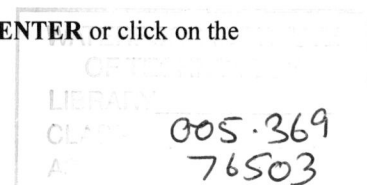

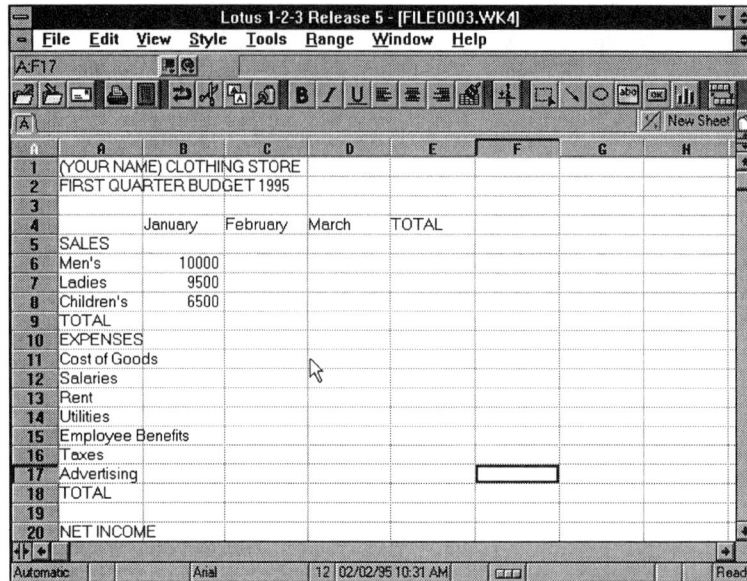

Figure 1 - 12

4.   Select cell **B11**. Type: **14500**

*As soon as you start typing in cell **B11**, part of the label Cost Of Goods that has overflowed into cell **B11** will disappear. Do not worry. Lotus remembers the entire entry in cell **A11**. The entry is just too wide for the A column, and the overflow is now concealed by cell **B11**. We will fix this problem later by increasing the width of the A column.*

5.   Move the cell pointer to cell **B12**. Type: **2150**

6.   Move the cell pointer to cell **B13**. Type: **2000**

7.   Move the cell pointer to cell **B14**. Type: **175.50** and press **ENTER** or click on the **Confirm Button**.

*As Figure 1 - 13 indicates, Lotus enters **175.50** as **175.5**. Lotus' "default," or preselected option, is to ignore insignificant digits. This will be changed later when we format all the entries within the worksheet.*

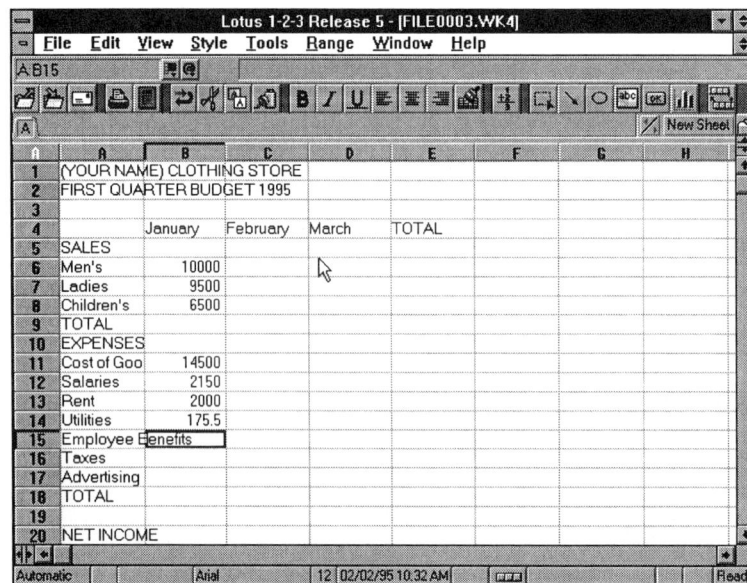

Figure 1 - 13

8. Type the remaining data into the cells indicated.

B15	**550**
B16	**650**
B17	**625**
C6	**9500**
C7	**8500**
C8	**5000**
C11	**12575**
C12	**1950**
C13	**2000**
C14	**195.50**
C15	**500**
C16	**600**
C17	**550**
D6	**10200**
D7	**9200**
D8	**5500**
D11	**13000**
D12	**2000**
D13	**2500**
D14	**185.50**
D15	**505**
D16	**625**
D17	**500**

When you are completed, you work should resemble Figure 1 - 14.

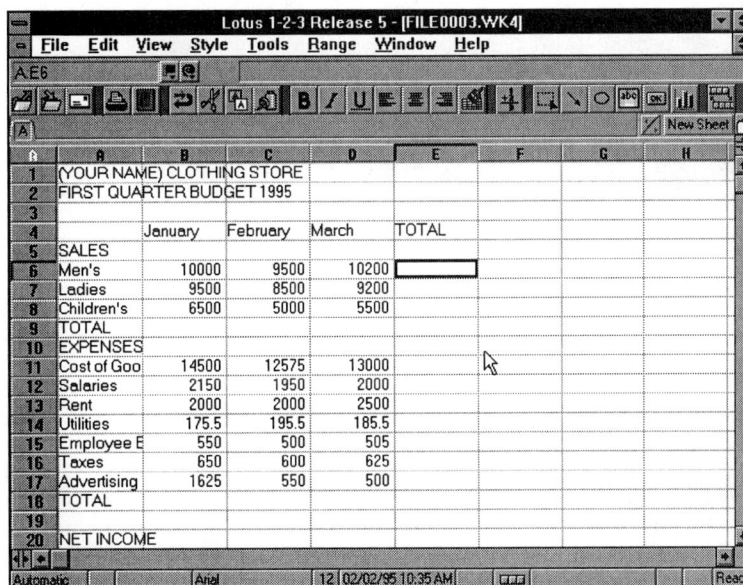

Figure 1 - 14

SAVING A WORKSHEET

It is important that you save your work frequently. It is usual to save your files every 15 to 20 minutes. Therefore, it you make a serious mistake or if the power fails, you only lose a few minutes of your work.

The general procedure for saving files was covered in the introductory chapter.

Activity 1.6: Saving your worksheet

1. If you are saving your file on a floppy disk, place the disk into the drive.

2. Click on **FILE** on the menu bar.

3. Click on **Save As**.

    *You have selected the **FILE/Save As** command and the **Save As** dialog box is displayed. The default name, **file0001.WK4**, is displayed in the File Name box.. If, however, a file has previously been saved with the name **file0001.WK4**, you will be supplied with the default name **file0002.WK4**. If another file has previously been saved, with the name **file0002.WK4**, you will be supplied with the default name **file0003.WK4**, and so on. See Figure 1 - 15.*

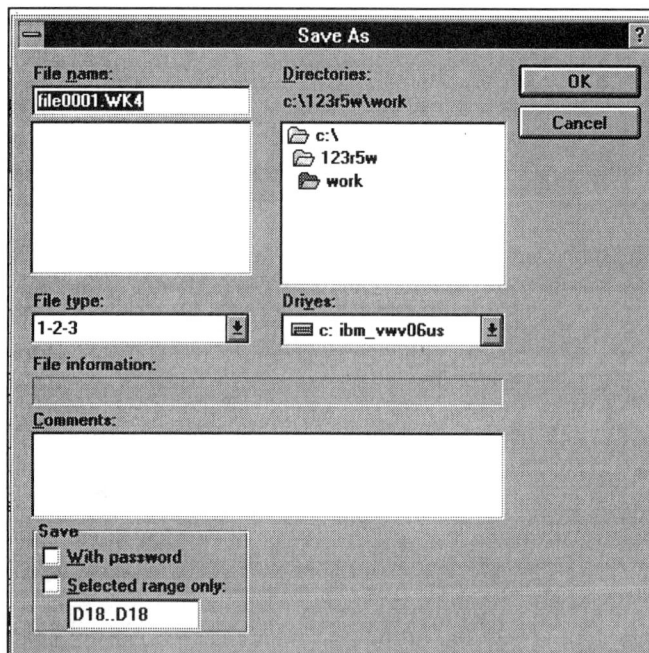

Figure 1 - 15

4. Type: **MYDATA.**

    *As soon as you begin to type, **mydata** should replace **file0001** in the **File name** text box. You do not need to type the extension, .wk4. Lotus will place the extension automatically at the end of the file name.*

    Problem: *If any letters remain from the old name, **file0001**, use the **backspace** or **delete** keys to remove them.*

5. Look at the drive and the directory listed in the right side of the **Save As** dialog box (refer back to Figure 1 - 15). If both the drive and directory are correct, go on to step 8. If the drive listed is not the one on which you are saving your file, click on the arrow to the right of the **Drives** drop-down list box.

6. Click on the letter representing the drive containing your data disk. For floppy disks, this will be **A:** or **B:**.

7. If you have been instructed to save your files on a network, click on the network drive. Ask your instructor for the name of the drive and directory to which your files will be saved. If the correct directory is not currently listed as the active directory, click on it in the **Directories** list box.

    PROBLEM: *If the directory for which you are looking is not visible, click on the arrows of the Scroll bar on the right side of the **Directories** list box. This will scroll the entries. When the directory you want is visible, click on it.*

8. Click on **OK** to save the file.

    PROBLEM: *If Lotus produces a message stating that the name of the file is invalid, click on the OK button in the message box. Retype the file name **mydata**. Click on **OK** again.*

TAKING A BREAK

In this book, you may take a break whenever it is convenient for you. You do not have to finish an activity before taking a break. Just save the worksheet and exit from *Lotus 1-2-3*. When you are ready to continue to work, open the worksheet and continue from where you left off.

The general procedures for exiting from 1-2-3 and opening files were included in the introduction.

Activity 1.7: Exiting from 1-2-3.

1. Select **FILE/Exit.**

    Problem: *If you have made any changes to **mydata.WK4** since you saved it, or if you have any other open worksheets that have not been saved, Lotus will display a warning box similar to Figure 1 - 16. Click on **Yes** to save the worksheet or click on **No** if you do not want to save the worksheet. If you do not know whether you want to save the worksheet, click on **Cancel**, take a look at the worksheet and make your decision.*

Figure 1 - 16

Activity 1.8: Returning to Lotus and your worksheet.

1. If you have just completed Activity 1.7, Program Manager is probably displayed and the program group containing *Lotus* is likely visible. If this is not the case, switch to Program Manager and open the program group containing Lotus 1-2-3.

2. Double click on the *Lotus 1-2-3* icon.

3. Select **FILE/Open.**

    *The **Open** dialog box will be displayed (see Figure 1 - 17). The **Open** dialog box in Figure 1 - 17 may differ from yours, depending on which drive and which directory are currently selected.*

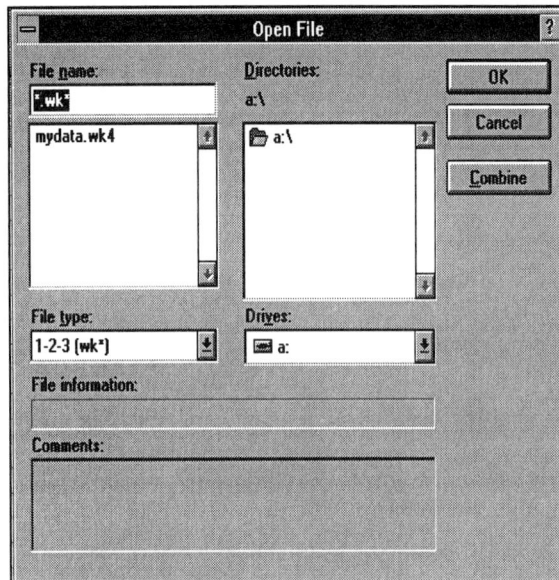

Figure 1 - 17

4. Look at the drives listed on the right side of the **Open** dialog box. If both the drive and directory are correct, go on to step 7. If the drive listed is not the one on which you are saving your files, click on the arrow to the right of the **Drives** drop-down list box.

5. Click on the icon representing the drive containing your data. If you are using a floppy disk, it will likely be **A:** or **B:**.

6. If your files have been saved on the network, click on the network drive. Your instructor will be able to tell you the name of the network drive and directory.

7. Look at the list of files under the **File name** list box. If **mydata** is visible, click on it. If it is not visible, click on the ↓ of the **File name** list box scroll bar until the name is visible and then select it.

8. Click on **OK** to open the file.

CHANGING COLUMN WIDTH

Lotus sets a default column width for all columns within a Lotus worksheet. The default column width is 9 characters. Some of the labels you placed in the **A** column are too wide to fit in the nine character spacing allowed. Therefore, they overflow into the **B** column. Once we entered text into the **B** column, the labels in **A** were truncated on the screen; the data still remained in the cell, but you were and are unable to see it. In order to make the full text of all of the labels appear, we must increase the width of the **A** column.

Fit Widest Entry

Lotus can automatically calculate the best width of the column based upon the widest entry in that column.

To Use Fit Widest Entry:

• Click on the column heading to select the entire column:

• Select **Style/Column Width/Fit Widest Entry** from the menu bar; or

• Double click on the right border of the column heading.

Changing the column width manually

There are times when you want to select a different column width than that selected with Fit Widest Entry. For example, in your worksheet, Fit Widest Entry selects a very wide column width for column **A** because of the titles in cells **A1** and **A2** of the worksheet. Nevertheless, you will allow Lotus to set the column width for column **A** for you based on the widest entry.

Activity 1.9: Using Fit Widest Entry to change the column width

1. Place the mouse pointer at the **A** column heading and click.

   Column A is selected. (Figure 1 - 18)

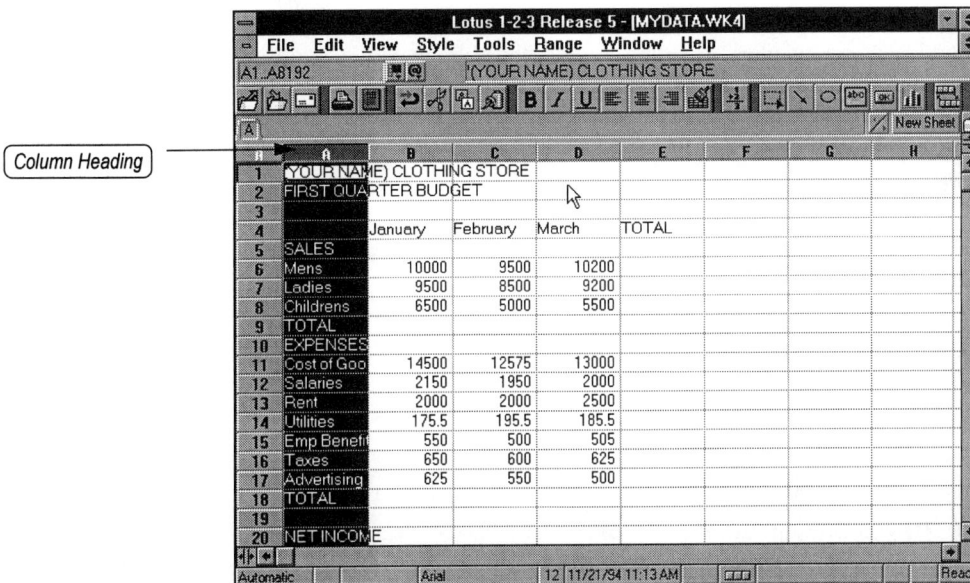

Figure 1 - 18

2. Select the **STYLE/Column Width** command by first clicking on **STYLE** on the menu bar and then clicking on **Column Width.**

   *Since **Column Width** is followed by three dots, a dialog box is displayed.*

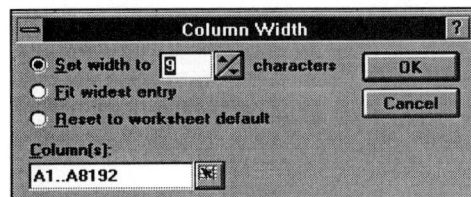

Figure 1 - 19

3. Select **Fit Widest Entry** by clicking on it. The **Fit Widest Entry** option button is filled.

4. Click on **OK.**

   The Column automatically increases so that all of the names are now visible.

ENTERING FORMULAS

The correct use of formulas releases the power of spreadsheet packages. Spreadsheets are designed to provide up-to-date information about the data included in a worksheet. For example, in your worksheet you want to know the total sales in the men's department for the first quarter. Therefore, in cell **E6** you want to enter a formula that will add the sales in the men's division for January,

February, and March. If any of the sales figures are later revised, the total sales will be automatically recalculated to reflect the revision as soon as the new figures are entered.

Formulas contain several components. All formulas in Lotus must start with one of a particular set of characters. The plus (+) or the open parenthesis (are commonly used. If you use the open parenthesis as the start of a formula, you must use a close parenthesis) later in the formula. The plus sign or the open parenthesis tell Lotus that you will be entering a formula. Formulas may contain numbers, cell addresses and mathematical operators (such as the plus or minus sign). If the number you want to use in a formula appears within the worksheet, you should never use that number in the formula. Instead, you should use the cell address where that number is located. By doing so, if the number within the cell changes, the formula will automatically recalculate.

It is possible to enter formulas by typing in the cell locations or by pointing to the cells. While mathematical operators must be typed, it is preferable to point to the cell locations by using either the mouse or the arrow keys. Pointing is better than typing cell locations because you can see exactly what data are being used in the formula, and you are therefore less likely to make an error in entering the formula.

To Enter a formula using pointing:

- Select the cell to contain the formula.

- Type the plus (+) sign.

- Click on the first cell containing the data that should be part of the formula.

- Type a mathematical operator. The symbols for the mathematical operators are:

Operator	Used For:
+	Addition
-	Subtraction
*	Multiplication
/	Division
^	Exponentiation

- Repeat the last two steps until the formula is complete. **DO NOT** type a mathematical operator or an equal sign after the last cell location.

- Press **ENTER** or click on the **Confirm Button.**

Activity 1.10: Creating Formulas:

You will enter a formula to calculate all the total sales and total expenses for your organization.

1. Select cell **E6.**

    *Notice that selecting cell **E6** automatically removes the selection from column A., if it was still selected from the previous activity.*

2. Type: +

    *The word **Value** now appears in the mode indicator on the status bar, indicating that you are about to enter a formula into the cell.*

3. Now you will select the first cell to be included in the calculation: **B6**. Either click on cell **B6** or press the ← **ARROW** key three times.

    Notice that:

    - *the cell pointer has moved to cell **B6**;*

    - *the beginning of the formula, +**B6**, now appears in the Contents Box;*

    - *the mouse pointer has changed from a plain arrow to an arrow pointing at a rectangle with a dotted outline below it, and;*

- *the word Point appears on the status bar because you are pointing at the cells to be included in the formula. See Figure 1 - 20*

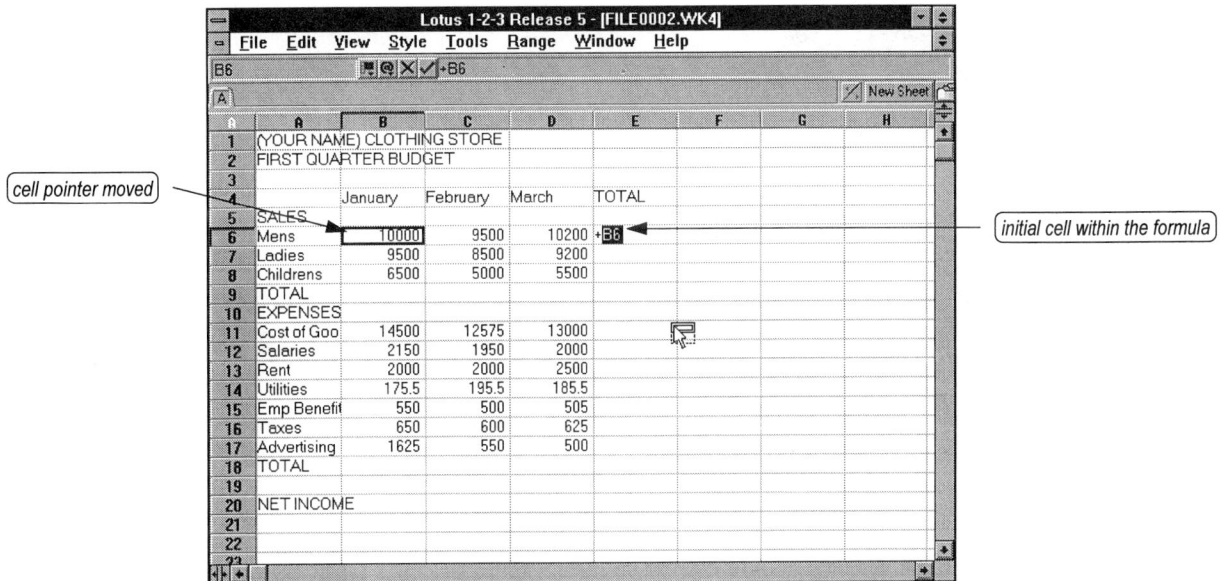

Figure 1 - 20

4. Type the plus (+) sign indicating you want to add the contents of another cell.

   *As soon as you type the plus sign, the cell pointer is removed from cell **B6**.*

5. Click on cell **C6**.

   *The contents of cell **E6** should now be +**B6+C6**. The formula now needs one final entry.*

6. Type the plus (+) sign indicating you want to add the contents of another cell.

7. Click on cell **D6**.

   The formula is now complete (see Figure 1 - 21).

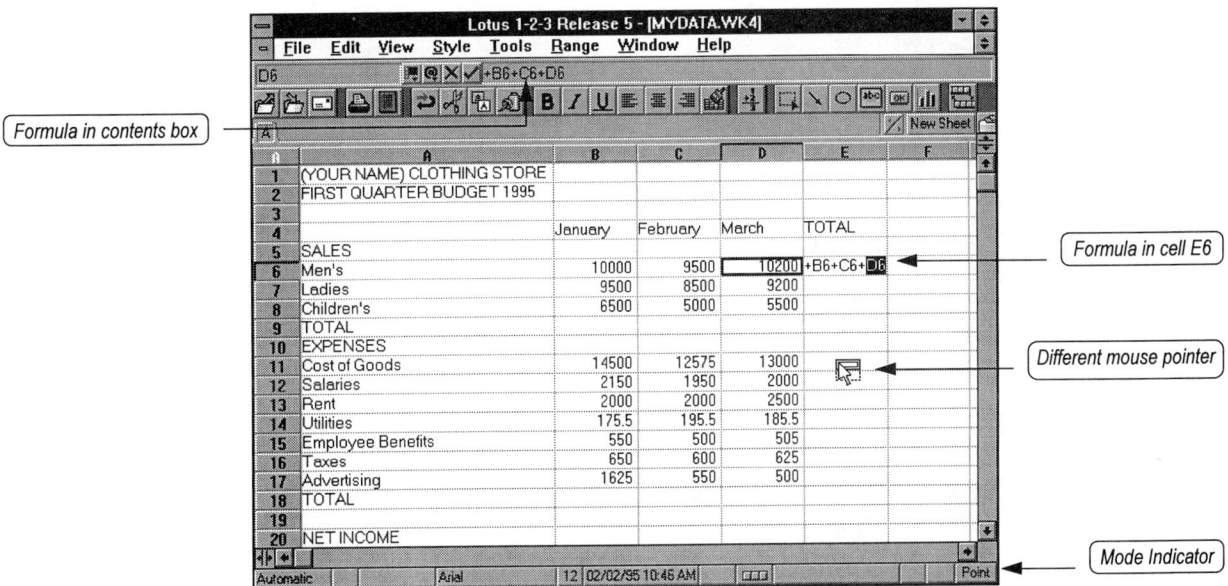

Figure 1 - 21

8. Press **ENTER** or click on the **Confirm Button**.

   The formula, +B6+C6+D6 remains visible in the Contents Box, but the value of that formula, 29700, appears in cell E6.

   Problem? *If you have made an error in the syntax of the formula, Lotus will display the message **ERR** in cell E6. Compare your formula to the one shown in Figure 1 - 21 and make any necessary corrections.*

9. Click on **E7**.

10. Type: +

11. Click on **B7**.

12. Type +.

13. Click on **C7**.

14. Type: +

15. Click on **D7**.

16. Press **ENTER** or click on the **Confirm Button**.

17. The formula in cell **E6** is the same as the one in **E7** except that they are adding up different rows; the formula in cell **E6** is adding values in row **6**, and the formula in **E7** is adding values in row **7**. You are now going to enter formulas to calculate the remainder of sales and expenses figures for which you entered labels earlier.

    When you are finished, your worksheet should resemble Figure 1 - 22.

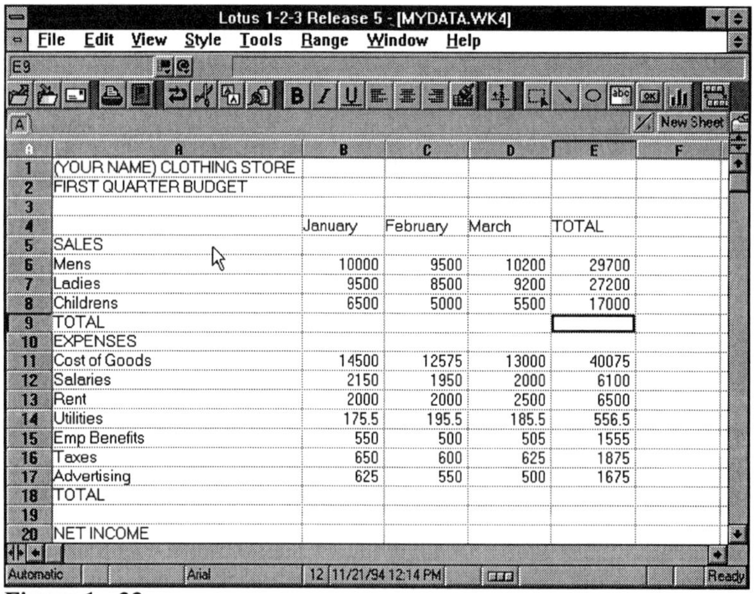

Figure 1 - 22

18. Click on cell **E8**.

19. Use pointing to enter the formula **+B8+C8+D8** and press **ENTER**.

    The results of the formulas you have entered thus far should be the same as those in Figure 1 - 22.

20. In cell **E9**, you want to enter a formula that will total all the sales for the first quarter. This formula will be **+E6+E7+E8**. Use pointing to create the formula.

Your results should look like Figure 1 - 23.

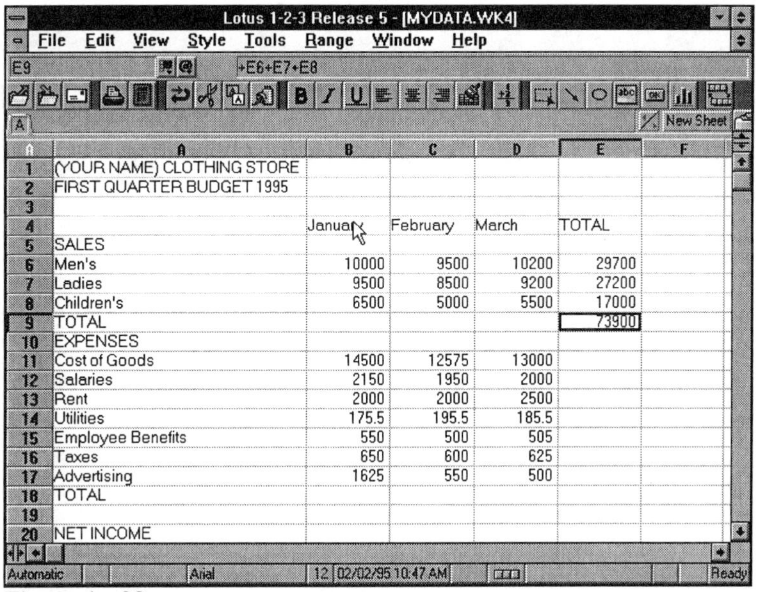

Figure 1 - 23

21. Use pointing to enter similar formulas to total all of the expense categories. In addition, enter a formula to calculate total expenses for the first quarter. When you are finished, your worksheet should resemble *Figure 1 - 24*.

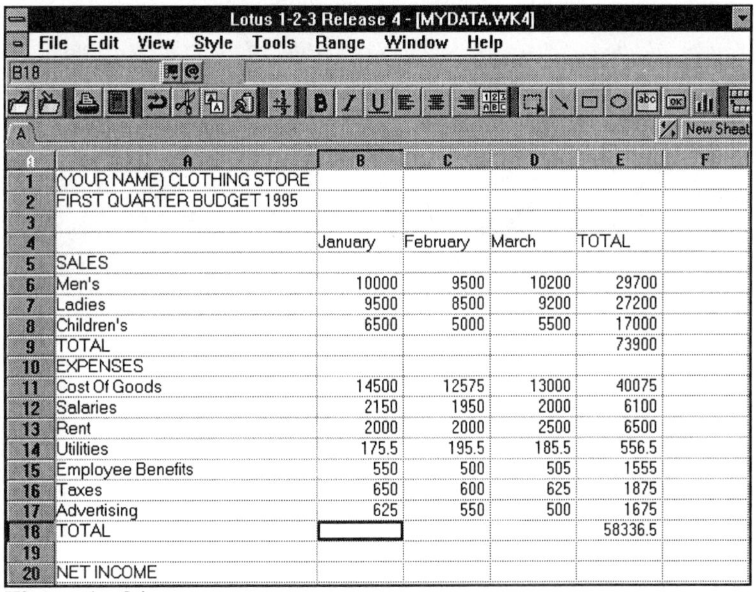

Figure 1 - 24

22. In cell **E20**, you want to use pointing to create a formula to calculate Net Income. Net Income is Total Sales minus Total Expenses. The formulas should be **E9-E18.**

23. When you are finished, your worksheet should look like *Figure 1 - 25*.

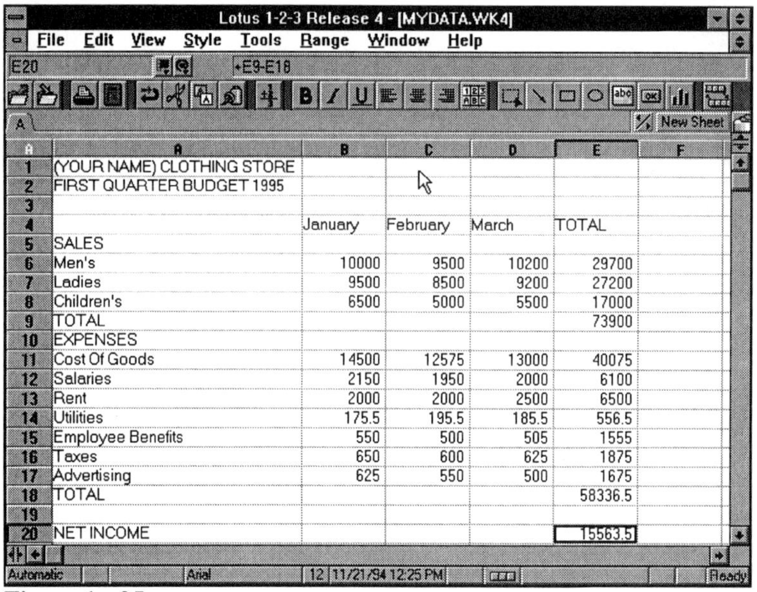

Figure 1 - 25

Activity 1.11: Letting formulas recalculate automatically

The advantage of using formulas within the worksheet is that whenever a value within a cell changes, any formulas referring to that cell will be recalculated automatically, and the new results displayed. In looking at your budget, you realize that two advertising contracts for newspapers were overlooked. Advertising costs should be $1,000 per month more than that included in the budget. In this activity, you will correct this error.

1.   Position your mouse pointer on **B17** and double click.

   You should be in Edit mode. Hint: Look at the status bar. The mode indicator should say Edit. See Figure 1 - 26.

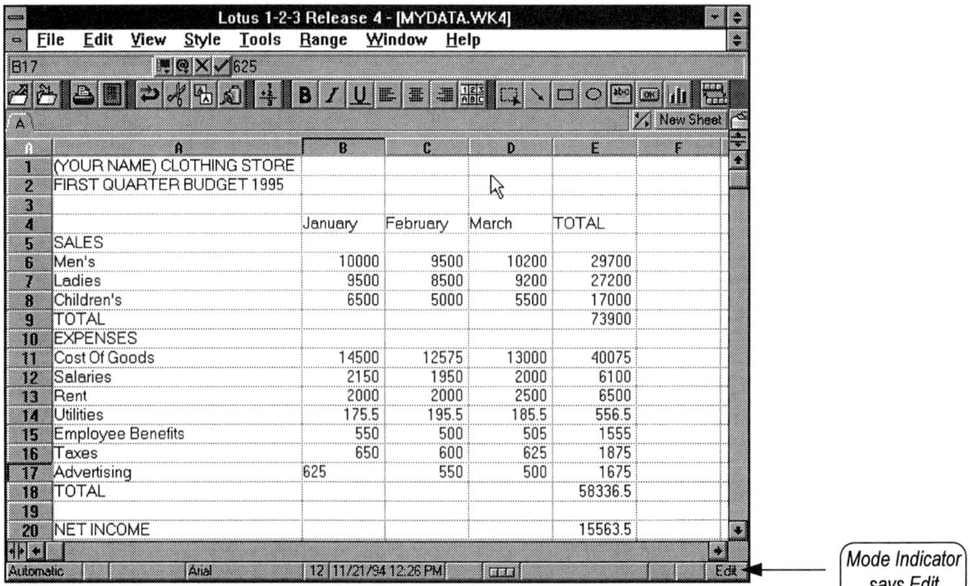

Figure 1 - 26

2.   Click to the left of the **6** in cell **B17** and type a **1**.

3. Press **ENTER.**

4. Compare your screen with Figure 1 - 25, which shows the worksheet before you changed the value of the advertising. What other values changed?

5. Click on each cell with a changed value and look at the formula bar. The value in each of these cells changed because the formula contains the address of a changed cell or references a total which includes a changed cell.

6. Change the contents of **C17** to **1550** and the contents of cell **D17** to **1500**.

	A	B	C	D	E	F
1	(YOUR NAME) CLOTHING STORE					
2	FIRST QUARTER BUDGET 1995					
3						
4		January	February	March	TOTAL	
5	SALES					
6	Men's	10000	9500	10200	29700	
7	Ladies	9500	8500	9200	27200	
8	Children's	6500	5000	5500	17000	
9	TOTAL				73900	
10	EXPENSES					
11	Cost of Goods	14500	12575	13000	40075	
12	Salaries	2150	1950	2000	6100	
13	Rent	2000	2000	2500	6500	
14	Utilities	175.5	195.5	185.5	556.5	
15	Employee Benefits	550	500	505	1555	
16	Taxes	650	600	625	1875	
17	Advertising	1625	1550	1500	4675	
18	TOTAL				61336.5	
19						
20	NET INCOME				12563.5	

Figure 1 - 27

SAVING A FILE WITH THE SAME NAME

Every time you make changes to a file, you must save it again or the changes will be lost when you close the worksheet or exit from *Lotus.* When you save a file using the same name, the current version of the worksheet replaces the previously saved worksheet.

To save a file with the same file name:

- Select **FILE/Save** or click on the **Save the current file** SmartIcon button .

Activity 1.12: Saving a file using the same file name.

1. This time when we save the file, we are going to use the same file name, **mydata.** To quickly save a file under the same name, use the **Save the current file** SmartIcon instead of the menu bar.

2. Click on the **Save The Current File** SmartIcon.

   *The mode indicator on the status bar will say **Wait** briefly, while the file is saving..*

PRINTING A WORKSHEET

It is likely that you will want to print out your worksheets so you can share the information with others. Your worksheet file, **mydata,** contains much of the data it needs, and so you will print it now. You will learn how to enhance the appearance of the information in Lesson 2. You will use the default print settings to print the data; in a later lesson you will learn how to change these settings.

To Print a worksheet using the default settings:

- Make sure the printer is turned on.
- Select **FILE/Print** from the menu bar.
- Click on **OK.**

Activity 1-13: Printing a worksheet using the default settings

1. Make sure the printer is turned on.

2. Select **FILE/Print** from the menu bar.

    *The **Print** dialog box will appear. See Figure 1 - 28.*

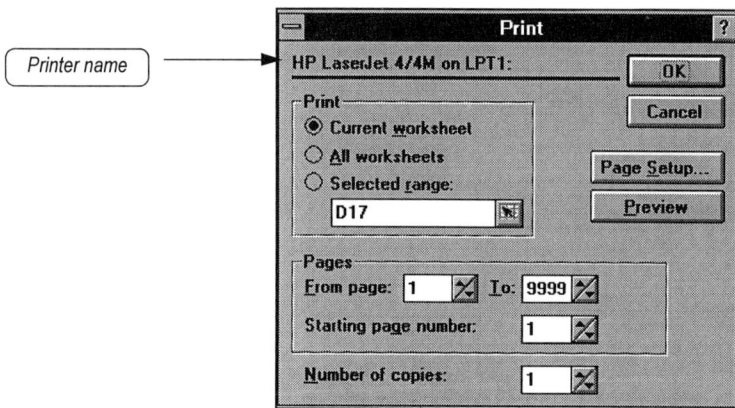

Printer name →

Print	?

HP LaserJet 4/4M on LPT1:

[OK]

Print
- ● Current worksheet
- ○ All worksheets
- ○ Selected range:
  - D17

[Cancel]

[Page Setup...]

[Preview]

Pages
From page: 1   To: 9999

Starting page number: 1

Number of copies: 1

Figure 1 - 28

3. Look at the name of the printer listed on the top left side of the **Print** dialog box. If that is not the one you are using, consult your Laboratory Instructor.

4. Click on **OK.**

    Your worksheet should appear as in Figure 1 - 29. We will learn to add enhancements in lessons 2 and 3.

```
(YOUR NAME) CLOTHING STORE
FIRST QUARTER BUDGET 1995

                       January   February   March    TOTAL
SALES
Men's                   10000      9500     10200     29700
Ladies                   9500      8500      9200     27200
Children's               6500      5000      5500     17000
TOTAL                                                  73900
EXPENSES
Cost Of Goods           14500     12575     13000     40075
Salaries                 2150      1950      2000      6100
Rent                     2000      2000      2500      6500
Utilities                175.5     195.5     185.5     556.5
Employee Benefits         550       500       505      1555
Taxes                     650       600       625      1875
Advertising              1625      1550      1500      4675
TOTAL                                                 61336.5

NET INCOME                                            12563.5
```

Figure 1 - 29

SUMMARY

In this lesson you completed the basic tasks of entering labels, values, and formulas; editing cell contents; changing column width; and saving, retrieving and printing a worksheet. In Lesson 2 you will learn how to improve the appearance of the worksheet. In later lessons you will explore some of the more sophisticated capabilities of *Lotus1-2-3* for Windows. The skills you learned in this lesson are summarized in the following table.

KEY TERMS

Active Cell	Edit cells	Opening a File
Arrow keys	ENTER key	Planning a worksheet
Backspace	File	Pointing
Cancel Button	File name	Printing
Cell	Formula	Right Aligned
Center Aligned	Insert key	Saving a File
Column-width	Labels	Spacebar
Confirm Button	Left Aligned	UNDO
Currency	Mathematical Operator	Values
Delete key	Number	

INDEPENDENT PROJECTS

Independent Project 1.1: Creating a Worksheet of your Family Investments

In this project, you will create a worksheet that contains all of the information about your families investments. Your completed worksheet will look like Figure 1 - 30.

	A	B	C	D	E	F	G
1		FAMILY INVESTMENTS					
2							
3	TYPE	1991	1992	1993	1994		
4							
5	IN BANK	10500	14500	15900	16250		
6	STOCKS	5000	4400	5225	5530		
7	BONDS	2500	2600	2750	2950		
8	IRA'S	13500	13700	14200	14700		
9	MUTUAL FUNDS	3000	3300	3125	3260		
10							
11	TOTAL	34500	38500	41200	42690		
12							
13							
14							
15							
16							
17							
18							
19							
20							

Figure 1 - 30

1. Select **FILE/New**.

2. In cell **B1,** type: **FAMILY INVESTMENTS.**

3. In the **A** column, type the following labels:

Cell Location	Type:
A3	TYPE
A5	IN BANK

A6	**STOCKS**
A7	**BONDS**
A8	**IRA'S**
A9	**MUTUAL FUNDS**
A11	**TOTAL**

4. In row **3,** type the following labels:

Cell Location	**Type**
B3	**1991**
C3	**1992**
D3	**1993**
E3	**1994**

5. Type the following values in cells **B5** through **B9:**

Cell Location	**Type**
B5	**10500**
B6	**5000**
B7	**2500**
B8	**13500**
B9	**3000**

6. Continue to enter the data as it appears in Figure 1 - 30.

7. Click on the column heading for the **A** column. Make the column wider by selecting **STYLE/Column, Fit Widest Entry**.

8. Place your cursor in cell **B11.** You want to create a formula to add up the entries in the **B** column.

9. Type: +

10. Click on cell **B5**

11. Type: +

12. Click on cell **B6**

13. Type: +

14. Click on cell **B7**

15. Type: +

16. Click on cell **B8**

17. Type: +

18. Click on cell **B9**

19. Press **ENTER**

20. Repeat this process for columns **C, D** and **E.**

21. **FILE/Save** your file as **IA1-1**.

22. **Print** your worksheet.

23. **FILE/Close** your file.

Independent Project 1.2: Creating a Monthly Budget Report

In this project, you will create a worksheet that contains all of the information about the monthly budget of the Sales Division of your organization. When you are done, your worksheet should look like Figure 1 - 31.

	A	B	C	D	E	F	G
1		Monthly Budget Report					
2		Sales Division					
3		For the month of January, 1995					
4							
5					% OVER(UNDER)		
6	ACCOUNT	BUDGET	ACTUAL	DIFFERENCE	BUDGET		
7							
8	Salaries	40000	38525	1475	0.036875		
9	Travel	12500	13450	-950	-0.076		
10	Entertainment	3250	4720	-1470	-0.45231		
11	Telephone	1625	1460	165	0.101538		
12	Rent	9250	9250	0	0		
13	Furniture	2500	725	1775	0.71		
14	Supplies	1000	1863	-863	-0.863		
15	Miscellaneous	9000	8426	574	0.063778		
16							
17	Total	79125	78419	706	0.008923		
18							
19							

Figure 1 - 31

1. Select **FILE/New**.

2. In cell **B1,** type: **Monthly Budget Report**.

3. In cell **B2,** type: **Sales Division**

4. In cell **B3,** type: **For the Month of January 1995**

5. In the **A** column, type the following labels:

Cell Location	Type:
A6	ACCOUNT
A8	Salaries
A9	Travel
A10	Entertainment
A11	Telephone
A12	Rent
A13	Furniture
A14	Supplies
A15	Miscellaneous
A17	Total

6. In row **6** type the following labels:

Cell Location	Type
B6	BUDGET
C6	ACTUAL
D6	DIFFERENCE
E6	BUDGET

7. In cell **E5**, above the word **BUDGET**, type: **% OVER(UNDER)**

8. Type the values in the **B** and **C** columns as they appear in Figure 1 - 31.

9. Place your cursor in cell **A15**.

10. To make the A column as wide as the widest entry, select **STYLE/Column Width, Fit Widest Entry**.

11. Click on **OK**.

12. Place your cursor in cell **B17**. Using the + and cell locations, enter a formula that will add up cells **B8** through **B15**.

13. Place your cursor in cell **C17**. Using the + and cell locations, enter a formula that will add up cells **C9** through **C15**.

14. In cell **D8**, create a formula to subtract actual salaries from the budgeted salaries (+B8-C8).

15. Continue this process for all the entries in the **D** column. Make sure you include the total in cell **D17**.

16. In cell **E8**, create a formula that will divide the Difference by the Budgeted values (+D8/B8).

17. Continue this process for all the entries in the **E** column. Make sure you include the total in cell **E17**.

18. **FILE/Save** your file as **IA1-2**.

19. **Print** your worksheet.

20. **FILE/Close** your file.

Independent Project 1.3: Creating a Salary and Profit Report

In this project, you will create a worksheet to calculate the salaries of your employees, the amounts they are to be billed at, and the profit to the firm. When you are done, your worksheet should look like Figure 1 - 32.

	A	B	C	D	E	F	G	H
1	EMPLOYEE BILLING							
2								
3		Consulting	Salary	Total	Billing	Total		
4	Employee	Hours	Rate	Salary	Rate	Billed	Profit	% Profit
5	George Snidowski	32	27.5	880	50	1600	720	0.818182
6	Claire Corbow	41	32.5	1332.5	60	2460	1127.5	0.846154
7	Thomas Henderson	29	42.5	1232.5	75	2175	942.5	0.764706
8	James Dorning	35	30	1050	60	2100	1050	1
9	Susan Claremont	21	25	525	58	1218	693	1.32
10	Eileen Healy	22	45	990	90	1980	990	1
11								
12								
13								
14								
15								
16								
17								
18								
19								
20								

Figure 1 - 32

1. Select **FILE/New**.

2. In cell **A1**, type: **EMPLOYEE BILLING**.

3. In the **A** column, type the labels as they appear in Figure 1 - 32.

4. Type the labels in rows **3** and **4** .

5. Type the values in columns **B, C** and **E**.

6. In cell **D5**, create a formula to multiply the Consulting Hours by the Salary Rate: (+B5*C5).

7. Repeat this formula for all the remainder of the **D** column.

8. In cell **F5**, create a formula to multiply the Consulting Hours by the Billing Rate: (+B5*E5).

9. Repeat this formula for all the remainder of the **F** column.

10. In **G5**, the profit is calculated by subtracting the Total Salary from the Total Billed (+F5-D5).

11. Repeat this formula for the remainder of the **G** column.

12. The % Profit is calculated by dividing the Profit by the Total Salary (+G5/D5).

13. Repeat this formula for the remainder of the **H** column.

14. Make the **A** column wide enough to fit the widest entry.

15. **FILE/Save** your file as **IA1-3**.

16. **Print** your worksheet.

17. **FILE/Close** your file.

Independent Project 1.4: Creating a Travel and Expense Report

In this project, you will create a worksheet to track you travel expenses when you are on business trips. When you are on business trips, you are required to keep track of your weekly expenditures on a daily basis. You are required to submit weekly a spreadsheet compiling all the costs of your trip. Usually, your expenditures while on a business trip include: airfare, hotels, meals, tips, auto rental, parking, and entertainment. When you are done, your worksheet might resemble Figure 1 - 33.

	A	B	C	D	E	F	G
1			Travel Report				
2							
3	Destination:	Los Angeles,	CA		Week of:	July 23	
4							
5			Sunday	Monday	Tuesday	Wednesday	Thursday	Friday
6	Airfare	899					
7	Hotel	149.5	149.5	149.5	149.5	149.5	149.5
8	Meals	32.89	38.98	43.5	45.6	32.45	42.45
9	Tips	7.9335	8.847	9.525	9.84	7.8675	9.3675
10	Auto Rental	19.95	19.95	19.95	19.95	19.95	19.95
11	Misc.			14.9			
12	Total	1109.2735	217.277	237.375	224.89	209.7675	221.2675
13							
14							
15							

Figure 1 - 33

1. Select **FILE/New**.

2. Organize your worksheet so the days of the week (starting with Sunday) are placed across the worksheet. (Hint: start in the B column because in the A column you will need to enter your categories of expenses).

3. Enter the categories of expenses down the A column. You may use the categories we used, create you own, or simply add more categories.

4. Enter the values corresponding to the moneys spent.

5. Total the columns.

6. Total the rows.

7. Save your file as **IA1-4**.

8. **Print** your worksheet.

Lesson 2

Using Ranges within Spreadsheets

Objectives

In this lesson you will learn how to:

- Define a range
- Enhance the appearance of data within the worksheet
- Select a range
- Change fonts in the printed output

- Change the alignment of data within the worksheet
- Format values
- Create named ranges

PROJECT DESCRIPTION

In this lesson, you will continue to use the file **MYDATA** and you will improve the appearance of this worksheet. You will learn how to select groups of cells, add enhancements such as boldfacing, italics and underlining to the data and to assign names to areas of the worksheet. When completed, our worksheet will look like Figure 2 - 1.

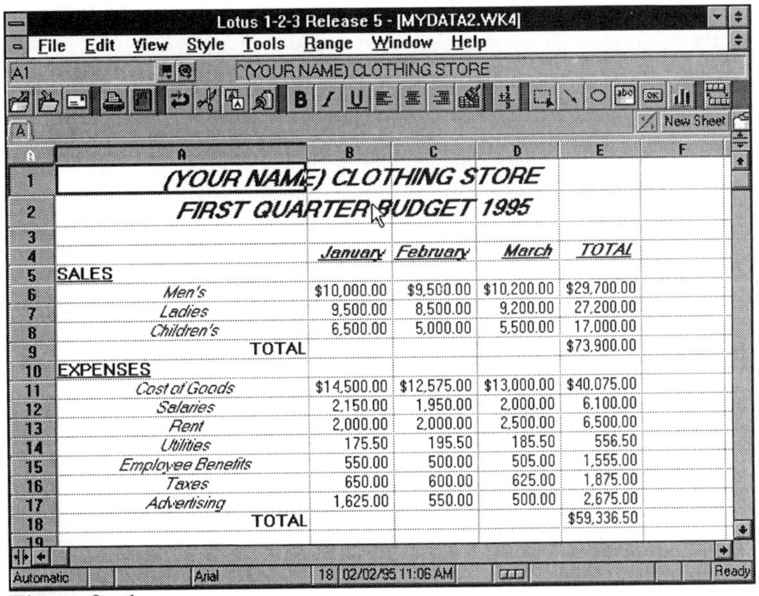

Figure 2 - 1

DEFINING A RANGE

A *range* is a group of adjacent cells within a worksheet. These cells can be in a column, a row, or groups of columns and rows that form a rectangle or a block. When using worksheets, you group similar information together. Therefore, when you perform a command to affect one cell, it is likely that you will want to affect others in the same column or row. For example, if our totals are in cells **C19, D19, E19** and **F19**, you probably want to add dollar signs and commas to all these numbers to highlight the fact that these totals are dollars. Rather than performing the commands to add the dollar signs to each individual cell, we would instead select the range and then tell Lotus to add the dollar signs to all the cells at once. You specify a range by identifying the beginning and ending cells. Ranges can be enclosed in parenthesis ( ) and always contain two periods between the beginning and the ending cell. In the example above, the range for your totals would be *(C19..F19)*.

Selecting Ranges of Data

It is always easier to select the range of cells you wish to work with before you choose the commands you will be performing. You can choose ranges by using either the mouse or the keyboard. First you will look at selecting ranges using the mouse; then you will explore the keyboard alternatives.

To Select a Range of Data using the Mouse:

- Move the mouse pointer to the beginning cell of the range.

- Press and hold down the left mouse button.

- While holding down the left mouse button, drag the mouse pointer across the worksheet to the ending cell within the range.

  Be sure not to release the left mouse button. If you do release the left mouse button simply start again at the beginning cell.

- Release the mouse button when the range you want is highlighted.

Activity 2.1: Selecting ranges using the mouse

In this activity, we will practice selecting various ranges within the worksheet.

1. **Open** the file **MYDATA** if it is not already open.

2. Place your mouse pointer in cell **B6**.

3. Press the left mouse button and hold it down. <u>DO NOT</u> release the left mouse button.

4. Holding down the left mouse button, drag the pointer to the right to the **E** column and down to cell **E8**.

   *When you release the left mouse button, you are indicating that you have reached the end of the range. If you released the left mouse button too soon, or you selected too large a range, simply place your pointer back in the starting cell, **B6**, and start again.*

   *As you are dragging the mouse, the mouse pointer changes to an arrow pointing at a rectangle with a dotted outline below it. Also, the range you are selecting becomes highlighted, or shaded in black, with the exception of the starting cell, which is filled in white. Lastly, the **Mode Indicator** on the status bar says **Point**. See Figure 2 - 2.*

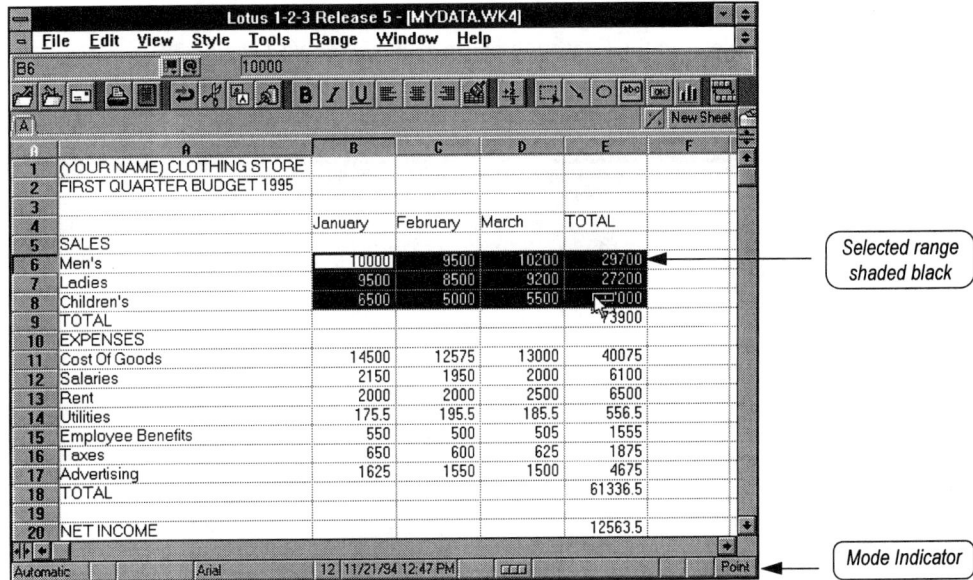

Figure 2 - 2

5. When you reach the end of the range, cell **E8,** release the left mouse button. Your range is now selected. See Figure 2 - 3.

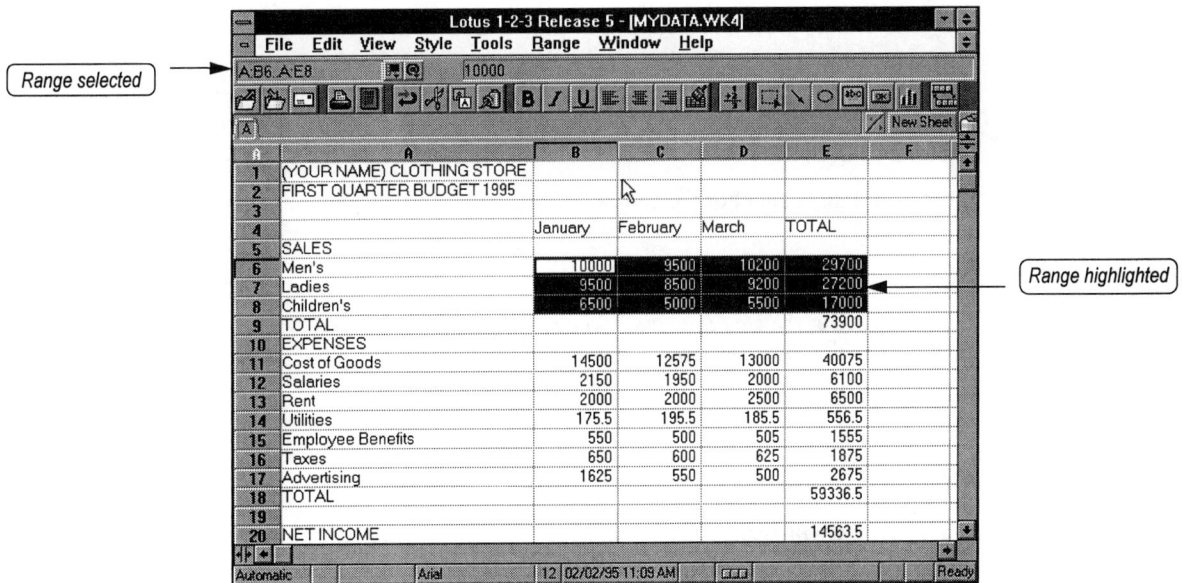

Figure 2 - 3

6. If you decide the range you selected is not correct or you want a different range, simply move your mouse pointer to another cell and click once. Place your mouse pointer in **A9** and click the left mouse button once.

7. Using the same method described above, we are going to select all the expenses: cells **B11** through **D17.**

8. Place your mouse pointer in cell **B11.**

9. Press the left mouse button and hold it down. Holding down the left mouse button, drag the pointer to the right to the **D** column and down to cell **D17**.

10. When you reach the end of the range, cell **D17,** release the left mouse button (Figure 2 - 4).

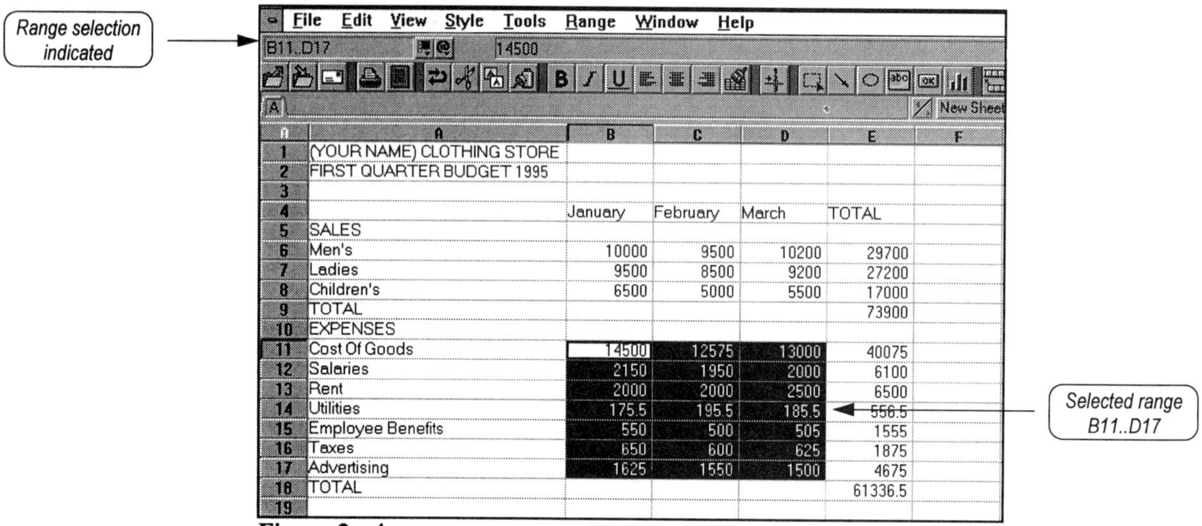

Figure 2 - 4

To Select a Range of Data using the Keyboard:

You may also select ranges of data using the keyboard. To select a range using only the keyboard:

- Press the ←, ↑, →, ↓ keys or other cursor movement keys to move the cell pointer to the beginning cell position.

- Press the **F4** key to anchor the cell pointer and to tell Lotus you will be selecting a group of cells (range).

- Press the ←, ↑, →, ↓ keys to highlight the range you want.

    *The range being selected appears in the **Contents Box** of the **Edit Line**, whether you use the keyboard or the mouse to select a range.*

- Press **ENTER.**

Activity 2.2: Selecting ranges using the keyboard

In this activity, we will again select ranges but this time we will use the keyboard.

1. Place your cell pointer in cell **B6** by pressing the ←, ↑, →, ↓ keys.

2. Press the **F4** key.

    *By pressing the **F4** key, you are telling Lotus that you plan on selecting a range using the keyboard. The Contents Box of the Edit Line now says **B6..B6**. Also, the Mode Indicator on the status bar says Point. See Figure 2 - 5.*

3. Press the ←, ↑, →, ↓ keys until the range **B6..D8** is selected.

4. Press **ENTER.**

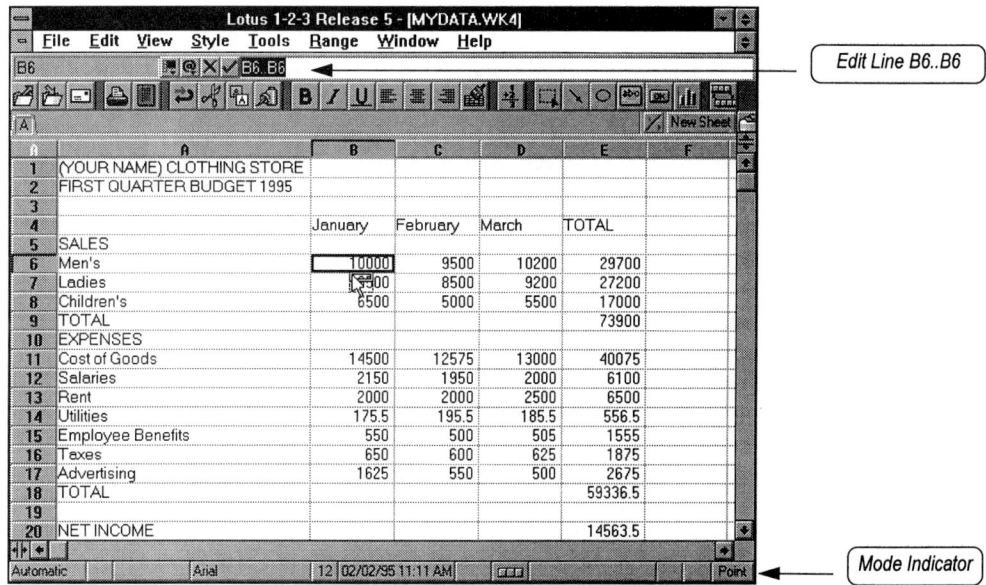

Figure 2 - 5

CHANGING THE ALIGNMENT OF LABELS

In Lesson One, when you entered our labels, Lotus automatically placed the labels against the left side of the cell. If you move your cell pointer to a cell containing a label, you will see that a *label-prefix* character, the apostrophe ('), was placed at the beginning of the label. The label-prefix character controls the alignment of labels within cells. This is only visible in the Contents Box when the cell is active. In this next activity, you will learn how to change the alignment of labels within cells.

However, before you change the alignment of entries in cells, you need to be able to identify the various label prefixes. Label prefixes recognized by Lotus are:

Label Prefix	Alignment
'	Left
"	Right
^	Center
\	Repeat

To Change the Alignment of Data

There are three means of changing the alignment of data: the first method is to edit the cell entry manually; the second is to use the alignment style SmartIcons from the SmartIcon set; the third is to use the Lotus menu bar.

To Edit the data to change the alignment:

- Move the mouse pointer to the cell containing the data.
- Double click on the cell to edit the cell entry.
- Move the insertion point to the beginning of the label, delete the current label prefix and type in the new label prefix.

To Use SmartIcons to change the alignment:

- Move the cell pointer to the cell containing the data.
- Click on the **Center data** SmartIcon ▣ to center the data within the cell; or
- Click on the **Align data to the right** SmartIcon ▣ to right align the data within the cell; or
- Click on the **Align data to the left** SmartIcon ▣ to left align the data within the cell.

  PROBLEM: *If the SmartIcons you need are missing from the SmartIcon set, click on the SmartIcon Selector ▣▣▣ located on the status bar. A list of SmartIcon sets appears. Click on **Default Sheet**. You now should see the alignment style SmartIcons.*

  If you want to change the alignment of an entire group of cells, select the group, and then use the SmartIcons to select the proper alignment.

To Use the menu bar to change the alignment:

- Move the cell pointer to the cell containing the data.
- From the menu bar choose **STYLE/Alignment**
- Click on your choice for aligning the data.

  Horizontal alignment choices are: General - the default alignment; Left - to left justify the entry; Right - to right justify the entry; Evenly spaced - evenly aligns text with both the left and right edges of a selection; Across Columns - aligns text across a range of cells rather than just one cell.

- Press **ENTER** or choose **OK**.

Activity 2.3: Changing the alignment of labels

In this activity, we will change the alignment of data manually and by using the alignment style SmartIcons.

1. Place your mouse pointer in cell **A6**.
2. Double click on cell **A6**.

   Double clicking in a cell allows you to edit the contents of that cell.

3. Place your insertion point to the *left* of the M in Men's.

   You can use the mouse to move the insertion point or you can use the ←, ↑, →, ↓ keys.

4. Delete the apostrophe by pressing the **DELETE** key.
5. Type the caret (^). See Figure 2 - 6.
6. Press **ENTER**.

   *Now your label, **Men's**, should be centered within cell A6.*

   Problem: *If you entry is not center aligned, look at the Contents Box of the Edit Line. If the entry does not say ^Men's, you may have typed the wrong character. Repeat the process from step 1.*

7. Place your mouse pointer in cell **A7**.
8. Double click on cell **A7**.
9. Place your insertion point on the L in Ladies.
10. Delete the apostrophe by pressing the **BACKSPACE** key.
11. Type the caret (^).
12. Press **ENTER**.

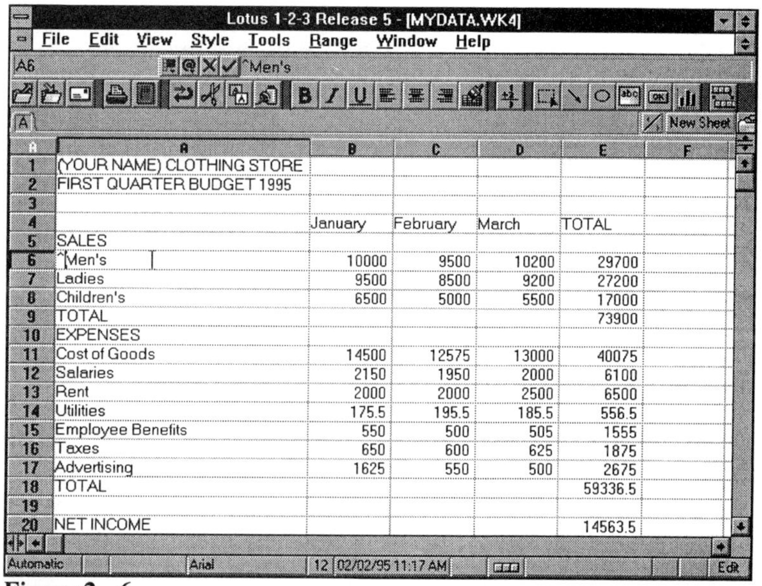

Figure 2 - 6

13. Repeat this process for cell **A8**.

Now the labels, Men's, Ladies, and Children's should all be centered within the A column.

As you can see, the process of editing the data to correct the alignment is time consuming. If there were only a few entries to edit, this would not be of concern. However, when there are numerous entries that need to be changed, using the SmartIcons is significantly quicker.

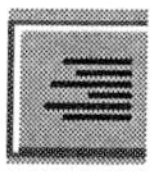

14. Place the cell pointer in cell **A9**.

15. Click on the **Align data to the right** SmartIcon.

*The word **TOTAL** is now right aligned in cell A9. The editing was performed by clicking on the SmartIcon.*

16. Select cells **A11** to **A17**.

If you do not remember how to select a range of cells, see Activity 2.1 or 2.2.

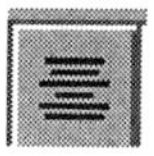

17. Click on the **Center data** SmartIcon. See Figure 2 - 7.

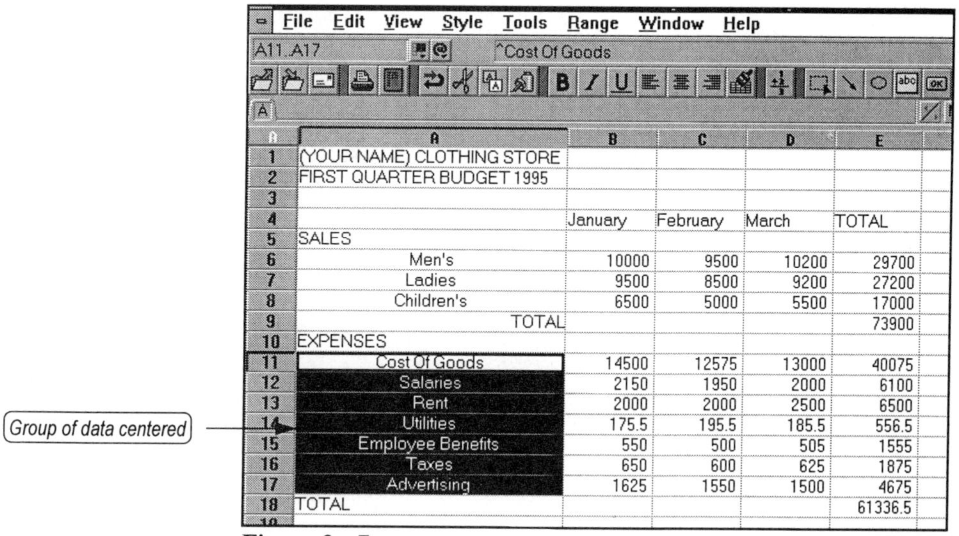

Group of data centered

Figure 2 - 7

This time, you selected a range of labels for which to change the alignment. When a range of labels is selected and an alignment SmartIcon is clicked on, the alignment of all of the labels in the range will change.

You can see how easy it is to change the alignment of labels. For the remainder of this activity, we will tell you how the labels are to be aligned. You may either edit the entries or use the SmartIcons to change the alignment.

18. Change the alignment of the following cells:

Cell address(es)	Alignment
A18	Right
A20	Right
B4..E4	Right

*Click on cell **C3** to remove the range selection. Now your worksheet should look like Figure 2 - 8.*

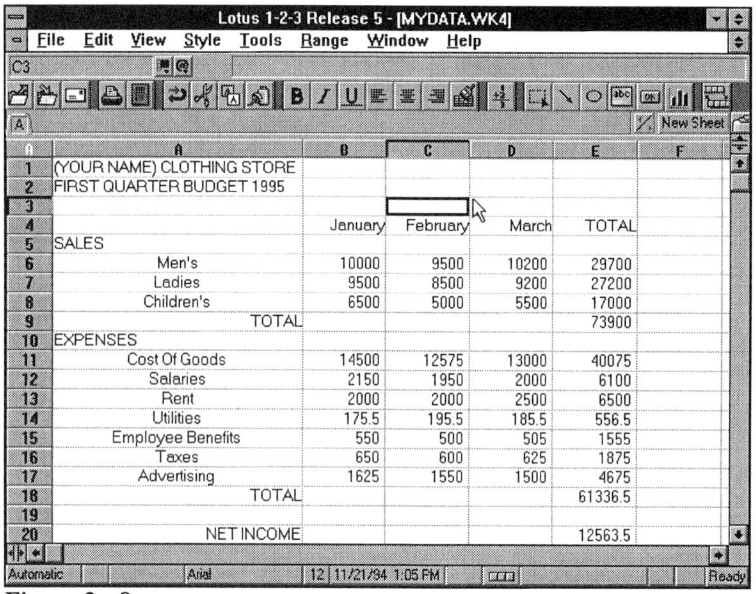

Figure 2 - 8

19. The final labels for which we want to change the alignment are the titles. We want to take the titles in cells **A1..A2** and **center them across** the columns comprising the entire worksheet. We will use the menu bar to make this change.

20. Select the range **A1..E2**.

*We need to select not only the range that contains the data, but also the range that the data will be centered over. Therefore the range must extend across the worksheet from the **A** column to the **E** column.*

21. From the menu bar choose **STYLE/Alignment**.

*The **Alignment** dialog box appears. See Figure 2 - 9.*

22. In the Horizontal Alignment box, click on **Center** AND **Across Columns**.

*The **Center** option button is filled and the **Across Columns** check box is checked. See Figure 2 - 10.*

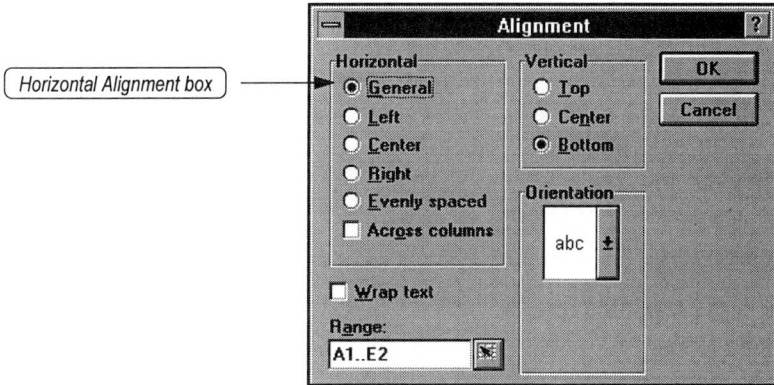

Figure 2 - 9

Horizontal Alignment box

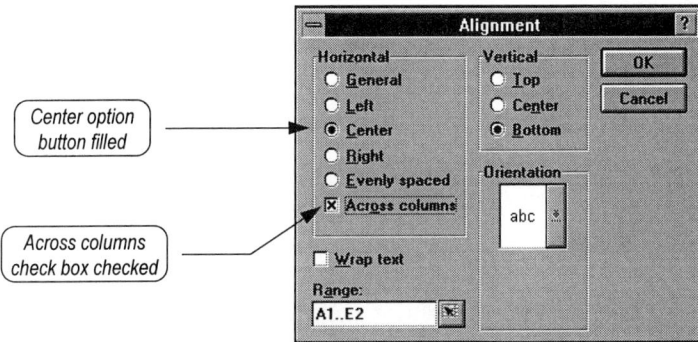

Center option button filled

Across columns check box checked

Figure 2 - 10

23. Choose **OK**. Click on cell **A3** to remove the range selection.

   Your worksheet should now look like Figure 2 - 11.

	A	B	C	D	E	F
1	(YOUR NAME) CLOTHING STORE					
2	FIRST QUARTER BUDGET 1995					
3						
4		January	February	March	TOTAL	
5	SALES					
6	Men's	10000	9500	10200	29700	
7	Ladies	9500	8500	9200	27200	
8	Children's	6500	5000	5500	17000	
9	TOTAL				73900	
10	EXPENSES					
11	Cost Of Goods	14500	12575	13000	40075	
12	Salaries	2150	1950	2000	6100	
13	Rent	2000	2000	2500	6500	
14	Utilities	175.5	195.5	185.5	556.5	
15	Employee Benefits	550	500	505	1555	
16	Taxes	650	600	625	1875	
17	Advertising	1625	1550	1500	4675	
18	TOTAL				61336.5	
19						
20	NET INCOME				12563.5	

Figure 2 - 11

CREATING NAMED RANGES

When working with a spreadsheet, you often refer to the same ranges many times. In the previous activity, you first selected the range, then selected what you wanted done with the range. If it is likely that a range will be used often, a name can be substituted for the cell addresses of that range. Having a name associated with a group of cells makes it easier for the user. Rather than having to select the cells within the range, the user needs only to refer to the name of that range. **Named ranges** can be used in formulas, for printing, in formatting data, and for quick movement throughout the worksheet. We are going to create some named ranges and use them throughout the remainder of this lesson.

To Create a Named Range

- Select the range using either the mouse or the keyboard.

  If you have forgotten how to select ranges, look back to the beginning of the lesson.

- From the menu bar, choose **RANGE/Name**.

  *A dialog box appears. The range you have selected appears at the bottom of the dialog box. Your insertion point is flashing in the **Name** text box.*

- Type a name for the range in the **Name** text box.

  The following guidelines need to be followed when naming ranges:

  - Ranges names cannot exceed 15 characters.

  - You can enter the name in upper, lower, or mixed cases. Lotus will change the name to all upper case.

  - You can use letters, numbers, and underscores in named ranges, but do not start a named range with a number.

  - Do not start named ranges with special characters such as an exclamation point(!).

  - Do not use spaces in named ranges. Use an underscore to show spacing.

  - Do not create named ranges that look like cell addresses.

- Click on **Add**. The name of the range is now placed in the **Existing Named Ranges** list box.

- Click on **OK**.

Activity 2.4: Creating Named Ranges

You are going to create a total of nine named ranges within your worksheet.

1. Using either the mouse or the keyboard select the range **B6..D8**. (See the beginning of this lesson if you do not remember how to select the range.)

   *The range **B6..D8** should now have white text on a black background, with the exception of cell **B6**.*

2. From the menu bar, choose **RANGE/Name**.

   *The Name dialog box appears. The range you have selected appears at the bottom of the dialog box. If this range is incorrect, click on the Range selector Icon to the right of the range text box. This will place you back into the worksheet. Select the correct range. As soon as the range is selected, you will be returned to the **Name** dialog box. If you selected the correct range prior to choosing **RANGE/Name**, your insertion point is flashing in the **Name** text box.*

PROBLEM: *If you returned to the worksheet from the **Name** dialog box to reselect the range, then returned to the **Name** dialog box, your insertion point is not in the **Name** text box. To rectify this, move the mouse pointer to the **Name** text box (it will change from an arrow to an I-beam shape when you are in the correct location, over the text box). Click the mouse, and you will see the insertion point appear in the **Name** text box.*

3. Type: **sales.**

   You do not have to worry about case. Lotus will change the name to all uppercase letters after the range is added to the worksheet.

4. Click on **Add.**

   *The name **SALES** is now listed as an **Existing Named Range**. See Figure 2 - 12.*

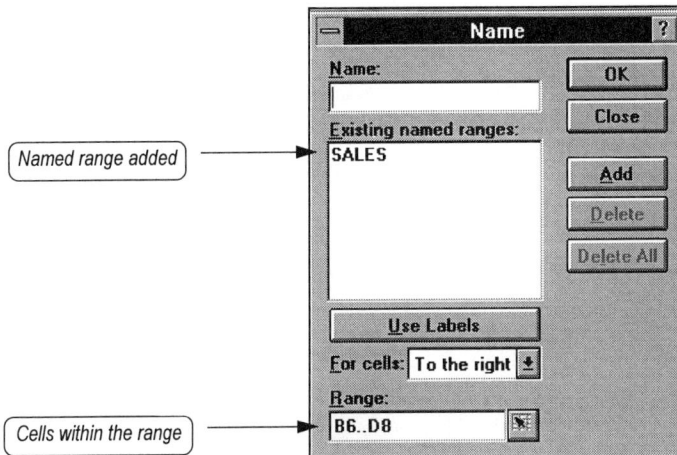

Figure 2 - 12

5. Click on **OK.**

   You now have added one named range to the worksheet. Let's go through this process a few more times to create some additional named ranges.

6. Select the range **B6..B8.**

7. Choose **RANGE/Name.**

8. Type: **Jansales.**

9. Click on **Add.**

   *Now two named ranges appear in the **Existing Named Ranges** list box. Notice that the names are placed in the box in alphabetical order. This will make it easier to find names later.*

10. Click on **OK.**

11. You have created two named ranges. You are going to continue this process to create the named ranges listed below.

    *If this process is easy for you, there is a shortcut you can take add names. Rather than clicking on **OK** after entering each range name, click on the Range selector Icon to the right of the **Range** text box at the bottom of the dialog box. This will place your mouse pointer back into the worksheet, enabling you to select a new range. Once the new range is selected, you automatically bounce back into the **Name** dialog box. Simply click in the **Name** text box* *(this moves your insertion point from the **Range** text box to the **Name** text box), type the next name, and then click on **Add**.*

Use either the first technique or the shortcut method to add the following range names to your worksheet:

Range Name	Cells
febsales	C6..C8
marchsales	D6..D8
janexp	B11..B17
febexp	C11..C17
marchexp	D11..D17
expenses	B11..D17
everything	A1..E20

*When you are done, your **RANGE/Name** dialog box should look like Figure 2 - 13.*

Figure 2 - 13

ENHANCING THE APPEARANCE OF THE DATA WITHIN THE WORKSHEET

In this lesson, you have explored how to select ranges of data, align data in cells and in ranges of cells, and how to name ranges of data. In looking at your worksheet thus far, you decide that you would like to add some boldfacing and italics to some of the labels. You also notice that some values have decimal places and others do not; you would like their formatting to be consistent. Finally, you decide it would be helpful to place some dollar signs before some of the values. In this next section, you will add these enhancements to your worksheet.

Enhancing the Appearance of Labels

When spreadsheet packages were first introduced, they were perfect for performing the calculations you needed, but the output did not look *pretty*. Today, Lotus 1-2-3 contains a worksheet publishing add-in used for formatting the data in the worksheet. **WYSIWYG (What You See Is What You Get)** is this worksheet publishing add-in. It will allow you to change fonts, and add italics, underlining, and boldfacing, shadow boxes, and many other enhancements. You will use some of these capabilities to improve the appearance of your budget.

Changing the Attributes of Labels

As in most Windows packages, there is more than one method of changing the attributes of labels. We will look at three methods.

To change the attributes of labels using the menu bar

- Select the cell or cells that you want to enhance.
- From the menu bar choose **STYLE/Fonts & Attributes**.

  *The **Font & Attributes** dialog box appears. On the right side of the dialog box is a list of the attributes you may choose. **Normal** applies no attributes; **Bold** will boldface the selection; **Italics** will apply italics and **Underline** will permit an entry to be underlined in one of three ways. If you click on the ⬇ to the right of the underline style drop-down list box, a list box will appear. Your may choose a single underline, a double underline or a wide underline style.*

- Choose **OK**.

To use SmartIcons to change the attributes of labels

- Select the cell or cells that you want to enhance.
- Click on the **Bold data** SmartIcon **B** to **bold** the label(s); or
- Click on the **Italicize data** SmartIcon *I* to *italicize* the label(s); or
- Click on the **Underline data** SmartIcon U to underline the label(s).

  PROBLEM: *If you cannot find the SmartIcons you need on the set of SmartIcons, click on the SmartIcon Selector located on the status bar. A list of SmartIcons sets appears. Click on **Default Sheet**. You now should see the attribute style SmartIcons.*

  If you want to change the appearance of an entire group of cells, select the group, and then use the SmartIcons to select the proper enhancement.

To Use the Quick Menu to change the Attributes of Labels

- Select the cell or cells that you want to enhance.
- With your mouse pointer resting somewhere on the selected range, press the ***Right*** mouse button.

  A menu appears on your screen this is a quick menu. The choices contained in the quick menu which appears depend upon what was selected when you pressed the right mouse button.

- Choose **Font & Attributes**.
- Click on the attribute of your choice.
- Press **ENTER** or choose **OK**.

Activity 2.5: Enhancing the Appearance of Labels within the Worksheet

1. Place your cell pointer in **A5**.
2. Click on the **Bold data** SmartIcon.

   Now the label SALES will be in bold.

3. Select the range of cells **A6..A8**.

   If you do not remember how to select a range, look back at Activity 2.1 and 2.2.

4. Click on the **Italicize data** SmartIcon.

   The labels Men's, Ladies and Children's are now in italics.

5. Place your cell pointer in **A9**.

6. Click on the **Bold data** SmartIcon.

7. Continue using the SmartIcons to enhance the appearance of the following labels:

Cells	Enhancement
A10	Bold
A11..A17	Italics
A18	Bold
A20	Bold

   Your worksheet now looks like Figure 2 - 14.

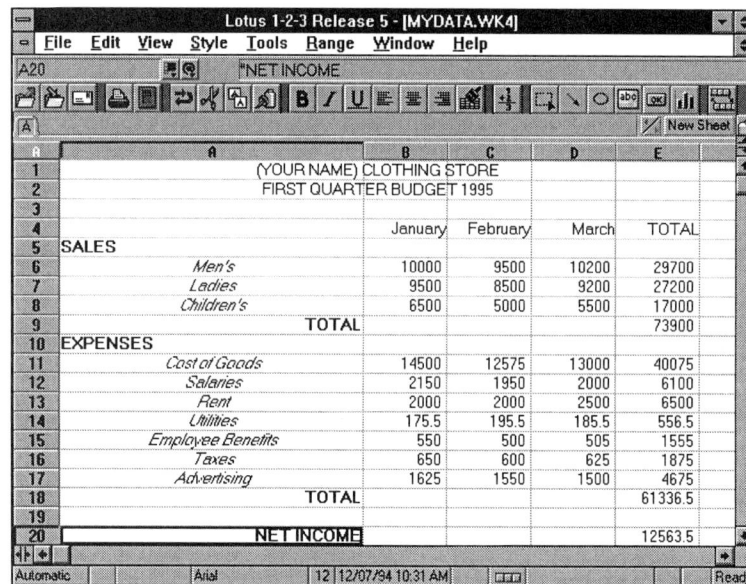

Figure 2 - 14

8. Now you are going to use the quick menus to enhance the worksheet. Select cells **B4..E4**.

9. Make sure that your mouse pointer is resting somewhere on the selected range. Press the right mouse button. A menu will appear. See Figure 2 - 15.

   PROBLEM: *If a menu appears but the correct range is no longer selected, press the* ***ESCAPE*** *key to close the menu. Select the correct range again, make sure your mouse pointer is resting somewhere on the selected range, and press the right mouse button.*

10. Click on **Font & Attributes**.

11. Click on **Bold, Italics** and **Underline**.

12. Choose **OK**.

    You applied all three attributes to the labels. Alternatively, you could have selected multiple attributes by using the SmartIcons. Once the cells were selected, you could have clicked on all three SmartIcons individually.

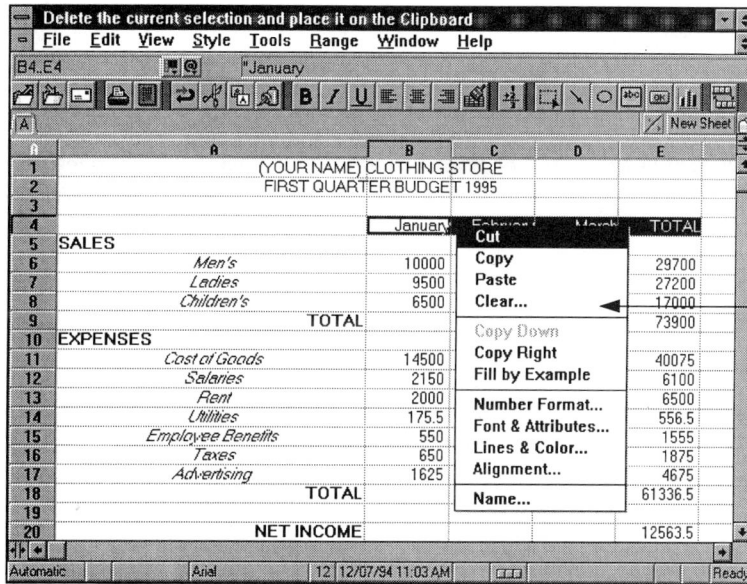

Figure 2 - 15

13. Select cells **A1..A2**.

14. Using the Quick Menu, apply the attributes **Bold** and **Italics**.

15. Move your cell pointer to **A3**. Your worksheet now looks like Figure 2 - 16.

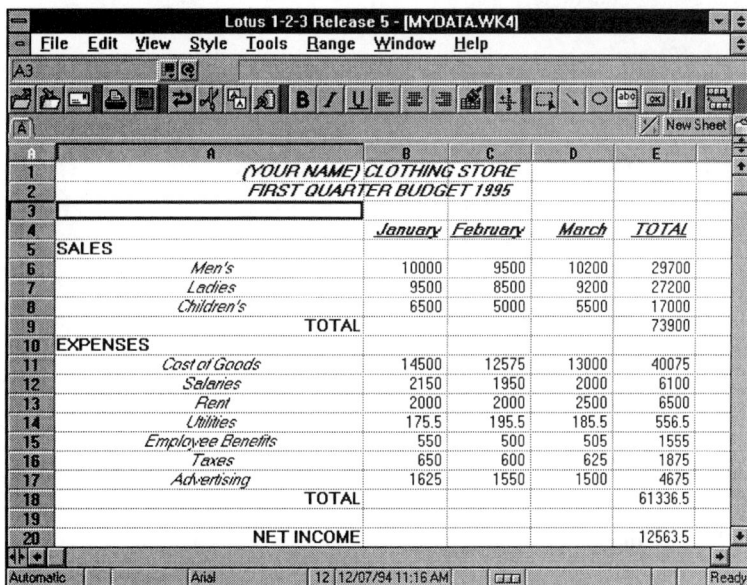

Figure 2 - 16

Changing Fonts

Although your worksheet looks good, you still want to increase emphasis on the titles. The heading on your worksheet should be larger than the remainder of the worksheet. A **font** is a typeface of a particular size (or **point** size). We can change to a larger font (typeface) the same way we changed the attributes.

To change fonts using the menu bar

- Select the cell or cells that you want to enhance.

- From the menu bar choose **STYLE/Font & Attributes**.

  *On the left side of the **Font & Attributes** dialog box is an alphabetical list of available faces. To the right of the **Face** list box is a font **Size** list box. After you choose a typeface and a point size, a sample of what you selected is displayed at the bottom of the dialog box.*

- Choose a **Face**.

- Choose a **Size**.

- Choose **OK**.

Shortcut: Once you have selected the cell or cells that you want to enhance, you can also use the **Font** and **Point-Size Selectors** on the status bar. If you click on the typeface on the status bar (the default is Arial), a list of typefaces appears. You can click on one to choose it. To the right of the typeface is the **Point-size Selector**. Again, you can choose a different size by clicking.

You can also use the quick menu to change the font. You will use the quick menu to change the font in the next activity.

Activity 2.6: Changing the Font Size in the worksheet heading

1. Select cells **A1..A2**.

2. Let your mouse pointer rest somewhere on the selected range. Click the right mouse button.

3. The Quick Menu appears. See Figure 2 - 17.

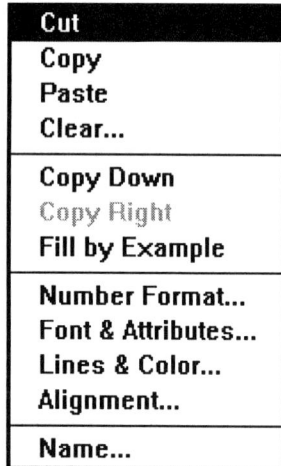

Figure 2 - 17

4. Choose **Font & Attributes**.

5. Increase the **Size** to **18**.

6. You can change the **Face** if you wish.

   Your dialog box now resembles Figure 2 - 18.

7. Choose **OK**.

   *As the size of the titles increased, so did the height of the row. Due to the increased row height, part of row 19 and all of row 20 are no longer visible. Do not be alarmed! They did not disappear! If you press the **Page Down** key you will see the full contents of rows 19 and 20. Press the **Page Up** key to see full lines 1-18 again.*

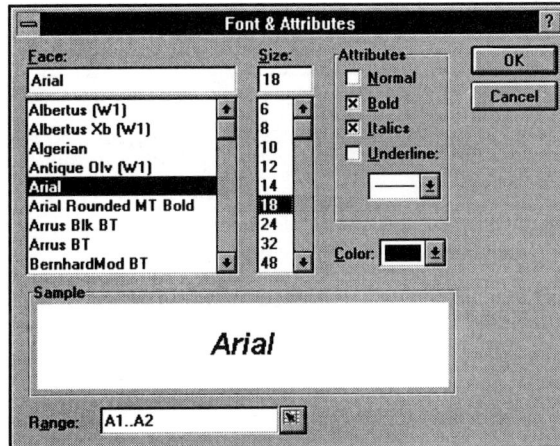

Figure 2 - 18

If you want the title larger or smaller, you can adjust the size (or the face) by repeating the above six steps.

Format Values

Although all the labels in the worksheet are more attractive, the values need enhancements. In this last segment, we will add **formatting** to the values in the worksheet.
Again, there are a few methods of formatting values in the worksheet.

To Change the Appearance of Numbers

- Select the cell or cells that you want to enhance.

- From the menu bar choose **STYLE/Number Format**.

  *On the left side of the **Number Format** dialog box is an alphabetical list of available formats.*

  Alternatively, you could have used the right mouse button (the quick menu) to obtain the dialog box.

- Choose a **Format** from the **Format** list box. A brief description of each follows.

- If you choose **Fixed, Scientific, Currency, Comma, or Percent**, the **Decimal places** box appears. Click the arrows or enter the number of decimal places (0 through 15) you want to display.

- Choose **OK**.

  Shortcut: You can also use the **Format** and **Decimal Selectors** on the status bar. If you click on the **Format Selector** on the status bar (currently showing **Automatic** format), a list of number formats appears. You can click on one to choose it. If your selection allows for decimal places, the **Decimal Selector** becomes available and the default of **2** is selected. If you want to change the number of decimal places, click on the Decimal Selector to the right of the Format Selector and choose a different size. Note, however, that when you use the Format Selector, you do not have a currency option. Use the **US Dollar** selection instead.

Definition of the Most Commonly Used Number Formats:

Although there are many number formats available, the most commonly used formats are defined in Table 2-1.

Number Format	Definition
Currency	Displays numbers with a currency symbol, thousands separators, and up to 15 decimal places. For example: $2,221.45
Fixed	Displays numbers with up to 15 decimal places, a minus sign for negatives and a leading zero for decimal places. For example: 2221.45
Comma	Displays numbers with thousands separators and up to 15 decimal places. Comma is the same as currency without the currency symbol. For example: 2,221.45
Percent	Displays numbers as percentages with a percent sign and up to 15 decimal places. For example: 53.45%.
General	Displays numbers with a minus sign for negatives, no thousands separators, and no trailing zeros to the right of the decimal point. For example: 2221.45

Table 2-1; Commonly Used Number Formats

Activity 2.7: Formatting Values in the Worksheet

1. Select cells **B6..E20**.

   Remember, rows 19 and 20 are not visible. However, if you drag you mouse to the bottom of the screen, it will scroll so the lower rows are visible and can be selected.

2. From the menu bar choose **STYLE/Number Format**. The **Number Format** dialog box appears . See Figure 2 - 19.

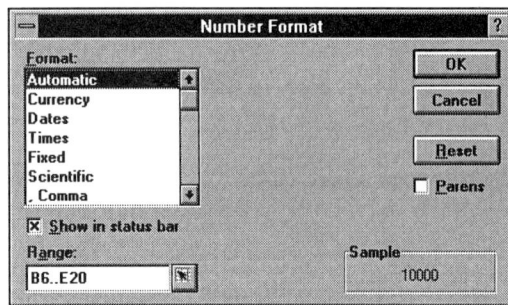

Figure 2 - 19

3. Click on **, Comma**.

4. We want to leave the Decimal places at **2**.

5. Choose **OK**.

6. Now you want to add dollar signs to some of the values in your worksheet. Select **B6..E6**.

   *Note: It is not necessary to select , **Comma** prior to selecting **Currency**. We are changing from , **Comma** to **Currency** in certain cells.*

7. From the menu bar choose **STYLE/Number Format**.

8. Click on **Currency**.

9. We want to leave the Decimal places at **2** and leave **US Dollar** selected in the **Currency** list box. See Figure 2 - 20.

10. Choose **OK**.

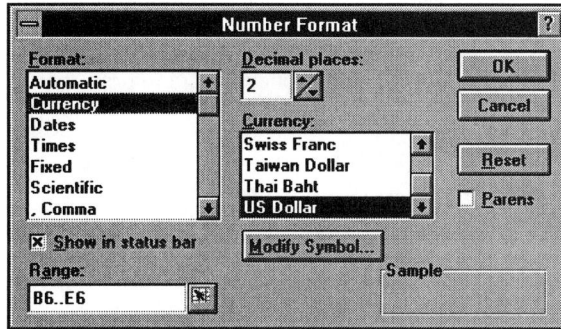

Figure 2 - 20

11. Select cells **B11..E11**.

12. Using the quick menu (right mouse button), apply **Number Format, Currency, 2** Decimal places, **US Dollar** to the selected range.

13. Using whatever method you choose, format cells **E9**, **E18** and **E20**, as: **Currency** with **2** Decimal places, **US Dollar**.

    When you are finished, your worksheet should look like Figure 2 - 21.

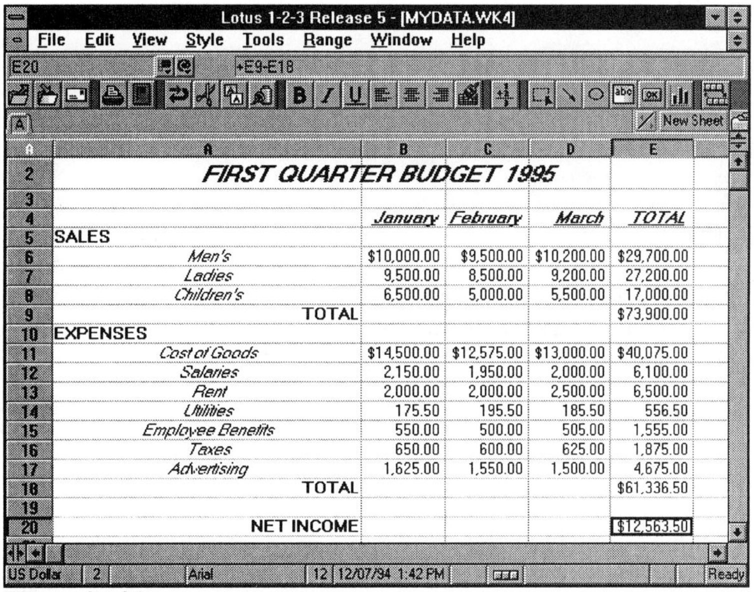

Figure 2 - 21

SAVE YOUR FILE

You are finished with this lesson. Remember to save your file.

Activity 2.8: Saving your file

1. From the menu bar choose **FILE/Save As**.

2. Give your file a new name: **MYDATA2**.

3. Make sure that your file will be saved on the correct drive and in the correct directory.

4. Choose **OK**.

PRINT YOUR WORKSHEET

When you are finished with **MYDATA2**, you probably want to print it out.

Activity 2.9: Printing the worksheet

1. From the menu bar choose **FILE/Print**.

2. Click on **OK**.

   Your printed worksheet should now look like Figure 2 - 22.

```
              (YOUR NAME) CLOTHING STORE
              FIRST QUARTER BUDGET 1995

                         January  February   March    TOTAL
SALES
        Men's           $10,000.00  $9,500.00 $10,200.00 $29,700.00
        Ladies            9,500.00   8,500.00   9,200.00  27,200.00
        Children's        6,500.00   5,000.00   5,500.00  17,000.00
                TOTAL                                     $73,900.00
EXPENSES
        Cost Of Goods   $14,500.00 $12,575.00 $13,000.00 $40,075.00
        Salaries          2,150.00   1,950.00   2,000.00   6,100.00
        Rent              2,000.00   2,000.00   2,500.00   6,500.00
        Utilities           175.50     195.50     185.50     556.50
        Employee Benefits   550.00     500.00     505.00   1,555.00
        Taxes               650.00     600.00     625.00   1,875.00
        Advertising       1,625.00   1,550.00   1,500.00   4,675.00
                TOTAL                                     $61,336.50

            NET INCOME                                   $12,563.50
```

Figure 2 - 22

SUMMARY

In this lesson you learned how to improve the appearance of the data by adding boldfacing, italics, and underlining. You also learned how to increase the font size of the data. Finally, to make all your numbers appear uniform, you learned how to apply number formats and select the number of decimal places these numbers are to contain. The skills you learned in this lesson are summarized in the following table.

KEY TERMS

Alignment	Fonts	Percent Format
Anchor	General Format	Point
Bold	Italics	Range
Comma Format	Label Attributes	Scientific Format
Currency Format	Label-prefix	Typeface
Edit	Named Ranges	Underline
Fixed Format	Normal	
Font Point Size	Number Format	

INDEPENDENT PROJECTS

Independent Project 2.1: Formatting the Worksheet of your Family Investments

In this project, you will enhance the worksheet created in Lesson 1. Your completed worksheet will look like Figure 2 - 23.

A	A	B	C	D	E	F
1		*FAMILY INVESTMENTS*				
2						
3	*TYPE*	1991	1992	1993	1994	
4						
5	*IN BANK*	10,500	14,500	15,900	16,250	
6	*STOCKS*	5,000	4,400	5,225	5,530	
7	*BONDS*	2,500	2,600	2,750	2,950	
8	*IRA'S*	13,500	13,700	14,200	14,700	
9	*MUTUAL FUNDS*	3,000	3,300	3,125	3,260	
10						
11	*TOTAL*	$34,500	$38,500	$41,200	$42,690	
12						
13						
14						

Figure 2 - 23

1. Select **FILE/Open**.

2. The file you want to open is **IA1-1**.

3. Select cells **B3..E3**.

4. **Bold** the years by clicking on the icon.

5. Select cells **A3..A11**.

6. **Bold** and **Italics** the categories by clicking on the icons.

7. Select the range **B5..E9**.

8. Choose **STYLE/Number Format**.

9. The format you want is **Comma** with **0** decimal places.

10. Click on **OK**.

11. Select the range **B11..E11**.

12. Choose **STYLE/Number Format**.

13. The format you want is **Currency** with **0** decimal places.

14. Click on **OK**.

15. Select cell **B1**.

16. Choose **STYLE/Font & Attributes**.

17. Select **Times New Roman, 18 point, Bold, Italics**.

18. Click on **OK**.

19. Select the range **A3..A11**.

20. **Center** the labels by clicking on the icon.

21. **FILE/Save** your file as **IA2-1**.

22. **Print** your worksheet.

23. **FILE/Close** your file.

Independent Project 2.2: Enhancing the Monthly Budget Report

In this project, you will enhance a worksheet created in Lesson 1: The Monthly Budget of the Sales Division of your organization. When you are done, your worksheet should look like Figure 2 - 24.

A	B	C	D	E	F	G
Monthly Budget Report						
Sales Division						
For the month of January, 1995						
				% OVER(UNDER)		
ACCOUNT	*BUDGET*	*ACTUAL*	*DIFFERENC*	*BUDGET*		
Salaries	$40,000	$38,525	$1,475	3.7%		
Travel	12,500	13,450	(950)	-7.6%		
Entertainment	3,250	4,720	(1,470)	-45.2%		
Telephone	1,625	1,460	165	10.2%		
Rent	9,250	9,250	0	0.0%		
Furniture	2,500	725	1,775	71.0%		
Supplies	1,000	1,863	(863)	-86.3%		
Miscellaneous	9,000	8,426	574	6.4%		
Total	$79,125	$78,419	$706	0.9%		

Figure 2 - 24

1. Select **FILE/Open**.

2. The file you want to open is **IA1-2**.

3. Select cells **B1..B3**.

4. Using **STYLE/Fonts & Attributes**, make the **Size 18** points, **Bold,** and **Italics**.

5. Select cells **A5..E6**.

6. Click on the **Bold** and **Italics** Icon.

7. Select cells **A8..A17**.

8. Click on the **Bold** Icon.

9. Select cells **B8..D8**.

10. Use **STYLE/Number Format** to select **Currency 0** decimal places.

11. Select cells **B17..D17**.

12. Use **STYLE/Number Format** to select **Currency 0** decimal places

13. Select cells **B9..D15**.

14. Use **STYLE/Number Format** to select **Comma 0** decimal places

15. Select cells **E8..E17**.

16. Use **STYLE/Number Format** to select **Percent 1** decimal places

17. **FILE/Save** your file as **IA2-2**.

18. **Print** your worksheet.

19. **FILE/Close** your file.

Independent Project 2.3: Enhancing a Salary and Profit Report

In this project, you will enhance a worksheet created to calculate the salaries of your employees, the amounts they are to be billed at, and the profit to the firm. When you are done, your worksheet should look like Figure 2 - 25.

	A	B	C	D	E	F	G	H
1			EMPLOYEE BILLING					
2								
3		*Consulting*	*Salary*	*Total*	*Billing*	*Total*		
4	*Employee*	*Hours*	*Rate*	*Salary*	*Rate*	*Billed*	*Profit*	*% Pro*
5	George Snidowski	32	27.50	880.00	50.00	1,600.00	720.00	81.8
6	Claire Corbow	41	32.50	1,332.50	60.00	2,460.00	1,127.50	84.6
7	Thomas Henderson	29	42.50	1,232.50	75.00	2,175.00	942.50	76.5
8	James Dorning	35	30.00	1,050.00	60.00	2,100.00	1,050.00	100.0
9	Susan Claremont	21	25.00	525.00	58.00	1,218.00	693.00	132.0
10	Eileen Healy	22	45.00	990.00	90.00	1,980.00	990.00	100.0
11								
12								
13								

Figure 2 - 25

1. **Open** the file **IA1-3**.

2. Select the labels in cell **A3..H4**.

3. Add the following attributes: **Bold, Right Align, Italics**.

4. Select the employee names.

5. Make these entries **Bold**.

6. Select all the cells from **C5..G10**.

7. **Format** these values in **Comma** format with **2** decimal places.

8. Select all the values in the **H** column.

9. **Format** these values in **Percent** format with **1** decimal place.

10. Increase the width of the **A** column so all the employee names are visible.

11. Make the label in cell **A1 Center** aligned **Across the Columns, Bold, Italics,** and in an **18** point font.

12. **FILE/Save** your file as **IA2-3**.

13. **Print** your worksheet.

14. **FILE/Close** your file.

Independent Project 2.4: Improving the Appearance of Your Travel and Expense Report

In this project, you will enhance the worksheet created to track your travel expenses when you are on business trips. You have just been informed by your home office that you have a new manager. You are also told that starting immediately, this manager will review and approve all expense reports. Since you want to make a favorable impression, you want to improve the appearance of this expense report. When you are done, your worksheet might resemble Figure 2 - 26.

	A	B	C	D	E	F	G	
1			Travel Report					
2								
3	Destination:	Los Angeles, CA			Week of:	July 23		
4								
5		Sunday	Monday	Tuesday	Wednesday	Thursday	Friday	S
6	Airfare	$899.00						
7	Hotel	$149.50	$149.50	$149.50	$149.50	$149.50	$149.50	
8	Meals	$32.89	$38.98	$43.50	$45.60	$32.45	$42.45	
9	Tips	$7.93	$8.85	$9.53	$9.84	$7.87	$9.37	
10	Auto Rental	$19.95	$19.95	$19.95	$19.95	$19.95	$19.95	
11	Misc.			$14.90				
12	Total	$1,109.27	$217.28	$237.38	$224.89	$209.77	$221.27	
13								
14								

Figure 2 - 26

1. **Open** the file **IA1-4**.

2. Select the days of the week. Make these entries **Bold**.

3. Select the totals. Make these entries **Bold**.

4. Select the categories of expenses. Make these entries **Bold** and **Italics**.

5. Select all the values within the worksheet. Format these entries in **Currency** Format with **2** decimal places.

6. Add any additional formatting you feel is necessary.

7. Save your file as **IA2-4**.

8. **Print** your worksheet.

Copying and Moving

Objectives

In this lesson you will learn how to:

- Delete data in ranges
- Move data to or from ranges
- Copy data from or to ranges

- Print ranges of data
- Insert columns or rows

PROJECT DESCRIPTION

Now that your worksheet is created, you want to change the organization of the data, include more subtotals, and print it out with page numbers. In this lesson, you will organize the data so that the expenses are sequenced from the highest to the lowest, and then print the worksheet.

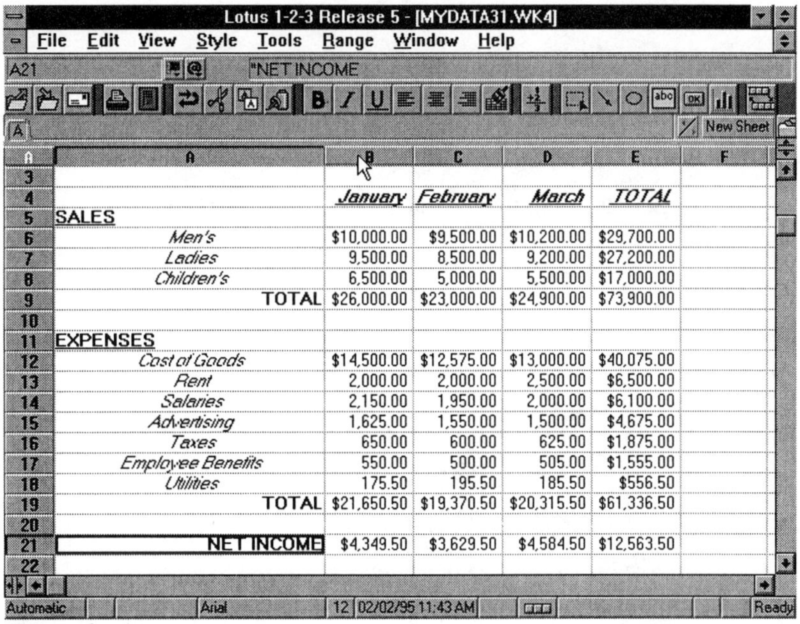

	A	B January	C February	D March	E TOTAL	F
5	SALES					
6	Men's	$10,000.00	$9,500.00	$10,200.00	$29,700.00	
7	Ladies	9,500.00	8,500.00	9,200.00	$27,200.00	
8	Children's	6,500.00	5,000.00	5,500.00	$17,000.00	
9	TOTAL	$26,000.00	$23,000.00	$24,900.00	$73,900.00	
10						
11	EXPENSES					
12	Cost of Goods	$14,500.00	$12,575.00	$13,000.00	$40,075.00	
13	Rent	2,000.00	2,000.00	2,500.00	$6,500.00	
14	Salaries	2,150.00	1,950.00	2,000.00	$6,100.00	
15	Advertising	1,625.00	1,550.00	1,500.00	$4,675.00	
16	Taxes	650.00	600.00	625.00	$1,875.00	
17	Employee Benefits	550.00	500.00	505.00	$1,555.00	
18	Utilities	175.50	195.50	185.50	$556.50	
19	TOTAL	$21,650.50	$19,370.50	$20,315.50	$61,336.50	
20						
21	NET INCOME	$4,349.50	$3,629.50	$4,584.50	$12,563.50	
22						

Figure 3 - 1

REVIEWING RANGES

As you learned in Lesson 2, a *range* is a group of adjacent cells within a worksheet. These cells can be in a column, a row, or groups of columns and rows that form a rectangle or a block. You specify a range by identifying the beginning and ending cells. Ranges can be enclosed in parentheses ( ) and always contain two periods between the beginning and the ending cell. An example of a range is (**C19..F19**).

Selecting Ranges of Data

It is always easier to select the range of cells you wish to work with before you choose the commands you will be performing. You can choose ranges by using either the mouse or the keyboard. If you do not remember how to select a range, look back at Lesson 2.

Deleting Data in a Range

In this lesson, you will learn how to copy data. Therefore, you need to delete some of the formulas you placed into cells in Lesson 2.

To select ranges of data to be deleted:

We will leave the first total in each of the categories, Sales and Expenses. We are going to delete all other totals. To select the data to be deleted:

- Move the mouse pointer to the beginning cell of the range.

- Press and hold down the left mouse button.

  Be sure not to release the left mouse button. If you do release the left mouse button simply start again at the beginning cell.

- While holding down the left mouse button, drag the mouse pointer across or down the worksheet to the ending cell within the range.

- Release the mouse button when the range you want is highlighted.

  Note: A range can be as small as a single cell. An example of a single-cell range is A2..A2.

- Once the range is selected, press the **DELETE** key or

- Once the range is selected, from the menu bar choose **EDIT/Clear**. Click on **OK**.

Activity 3.1: Deleting Ranges

In this activity, we will delete many of the formulas we placed into cells previously. We will later learn to use **Copy** to duplicate a formula once it has been placed into a cell.

1. Open the file **MYDATA2** if it is not already open.

2. Place your mouse pointer in cell **E7**.

3. Press the left mouse button and hold it down. **DO NOT** release the left mouse button.

    If you release the left mouse button, you are indicating that you have reached the end of the range. If you released the left mouse button, simply place your pointer back in the starting cell, E7, and start again.

4. Holding down the left mouse button, drag the pointer down to cell **E8**.

5. When you reach the end of the range, cell **E8,** release the left mouse button. Your range is now selected. See Figure 3 - 2.

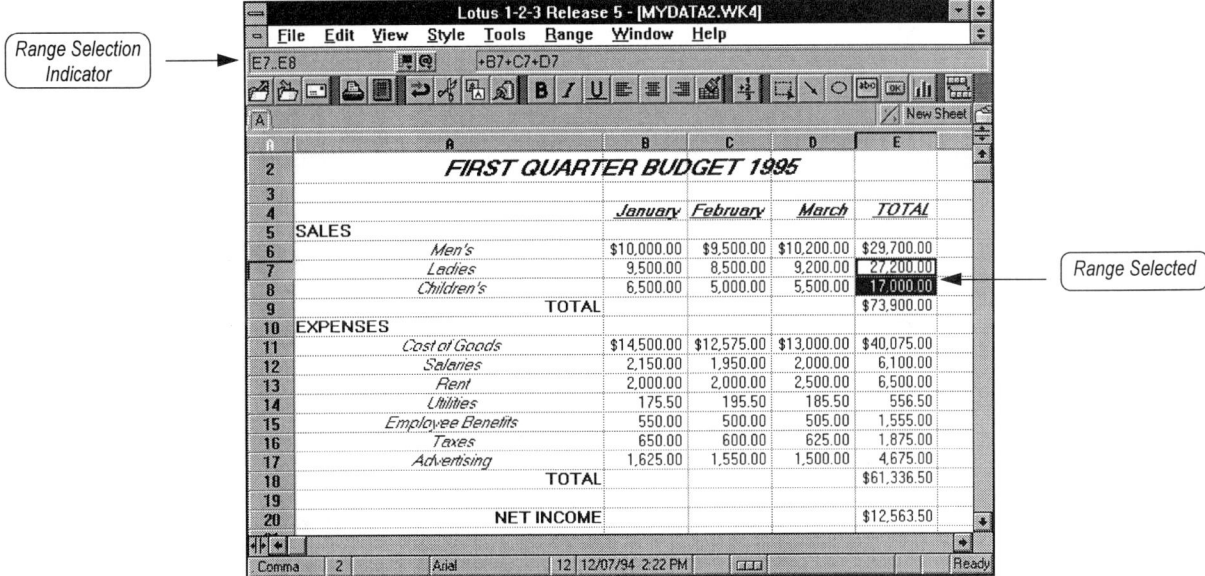

Figure 3 - 2

6. Press the **DELETE** key.

7. Cells **E7..E8** are now empty. Now the total in cell **E9** is only **$29,700**. See Figure 3 - 3.

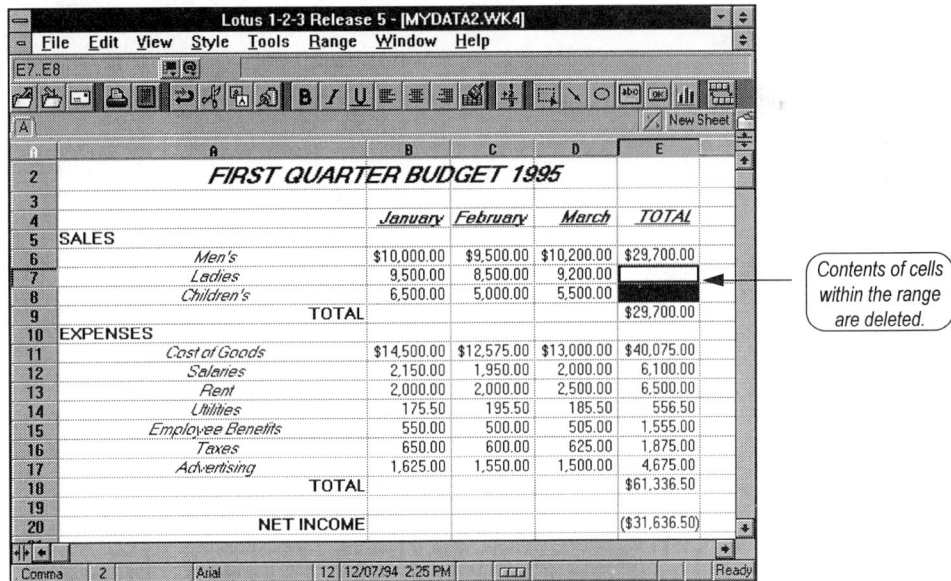

Figure 3 - 3

8. Place your mouse pointer in cell **E12**.

9. Holding down the left mouse button, drag the pointer down to cell **E17**.

10. Press the **DELETE** key.

11. Cells **E12..E17** are now empty. Click on cell **A2** to remove the range selection (Figure 3 - 4).

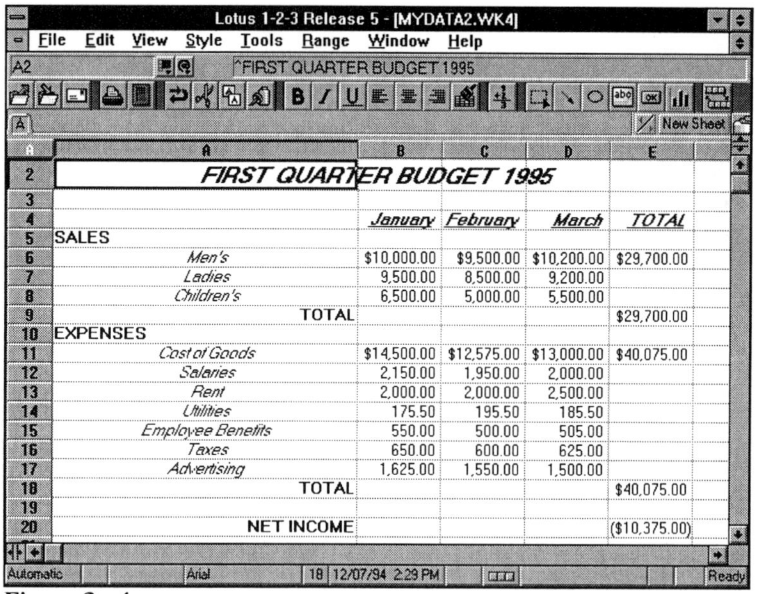

	A		B	C	D	E
2	*FIRST QUARTER BUDGET 1995*					
3						
4			*January*	*February*	*March*	*TOTAL*
5	SALES					
6		*Men's*	$10,000.00	$9,500.00	$10,200.00	$29,700.00
7		*Ladies*	9,500.00	8,500.00	9,200.00	
8		*Children's*	6,500.00	5,000.00	5,500.00	
9		TOTAL				$29,700.00
10	EXPENSES					
11		*Cost of Goods*	$14,500.00	$12,575.00	$13,000.00	$40,075.00
12		*Salaries*	2,150.00	1,950.00	2,000.00	
13		*Rent*	2,000.00	2,000.00	2,500.00	
14		*Utilities*	175.50	195.50	185.50	
15		*Employee Benefits*	550.00	500.00	505.00	
16		*Taxes*	650.00	600.00	625.00	
17		*Advertising*	1,625.00	1,550.00	1,500.00	
18		TOTAL				$40,075.00
19						
20		NET INCOME				($10,375.00)

Figure 3 - 4

12. Again your totals in cell **E18** and in cell **E20** do not represent the quarterly totals.

Copy Data from or to Ranges

The **Copy** process is used to duplicate the contents of one cell or a range of cells to another cell or range of cells. When copying labels or values, the entries are duplicated exactly. When copying formulas, the cell references in the formula that is duplicated will change to reflect the new cell references of the new formula. For example, in cell **E6** there is a formula **+B6+C6+D6**. When that formula is copied to cell **E7**, the resultant formula will be **+B7+C7+D7**. This process is called *relative adjustment.*

!

When copying data, you must use **CAUTION!** If you copy data to a cell or a range of cells that already contains data, *Lotus* will replace the existing data with the data being copied. Thus, this process will delete the data previously in the cell location.

There are a number of ways to copy data in *Lotus*. You can use the menu bar, the SmartIcons, the Quick Menu, or a process of dragging and dropping. We will look at the first three methods.

To copy data using the menu bar:

- Use the mouse to select the data to be copied.
- From the Menu bar choose **EDIT/Copy**.

  The copied data is now stored temporarily in a special area called the ***Clipboard.***

  The ***title bar*** *now says,* ***Select destination and press ENTER or choose Edit Paste.***
- Use the mouse to select the cell or range of cells to receive the copied information. Make sure the cells are blank! If the cells are not blank, their contents will be overwritten.
- From the Menu bar choose **EDIT/Paste**.

  The data stored in the ***Clipboard*** *is now copied to the selected range.*

To copy data using the Quick Menu:

- Use the mouse to select the data to be copied.

- With the mouse pointer somewhere on the selected range, click the right mouse button.

  A Quick Menu appears.

- Choose **Copy**.

  The title bar now says, ***Select destination and press ENTER or choose Edit Paste***

- Use the mouse to select the cell or range of cells to receive the copied information. Make sure the cells are blank! If the cells are not blank, their contents will be overwritten.

- With the mouse pointer somewhere on the selected range, click the right mouse button.

- Choose **PASTE**.

To copy data using the SmartIcons

- Use the mouse to select the data to be copied.

- Click on the **Copy to the Clipboard** 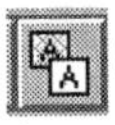 SmartIcon.

  The title bar now says, ***Select destination and press ENTER or choose Edit Paste***.

- Use the mouse to select the cell or range of cells to receive the copied information. Make sure the cells are blank! If the cells are not blank their contents will be overwritten.

- Click on the  SmartIcon, **Paste Clipboard Contents**.

Activity 3.2: Copying Data

In this activity, you are going to duplicate the formulas in cells **E6** and **E11** to the appropriate blank cells in the **E** column. We will learn to copy using all three methods described above.

1. Place your cell pointer in cell **E6**.

2. First, you will copy using the menu bar. From the menu bar choose **EDIT/Copy**.

    The title bar now says, ***Select destination and press ENTER or choose Edit Paste***. *See Figure 3 - 5.*

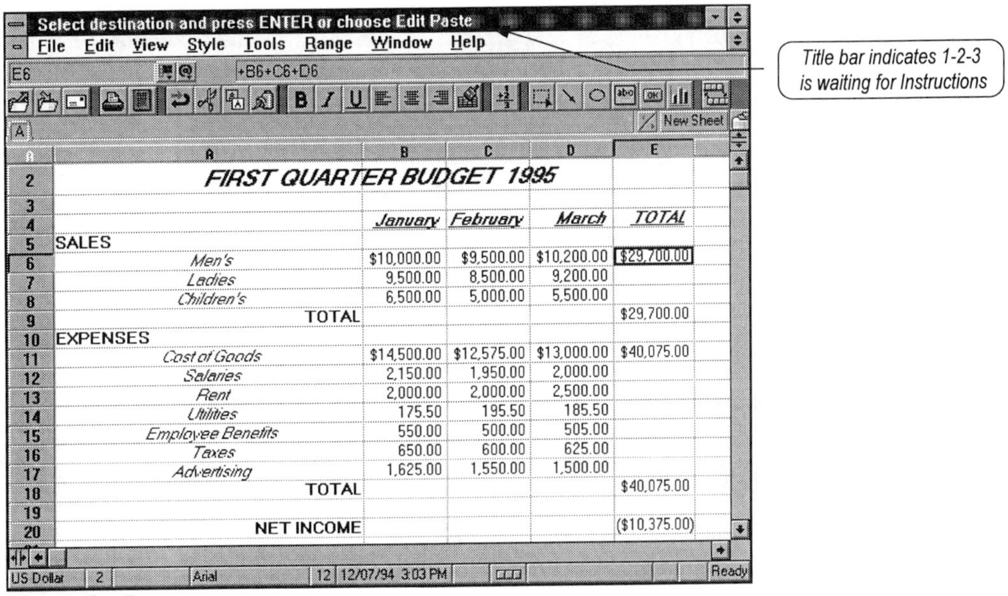

Title bar indicates 1-2-3 is waiting for Instructions

Figure 3 - 5

3. We want to copy the formula from **E6** to the range **E7..E8**.

Problem: *If your cell pointer was not in the correct cell to start, click on a blank cell and press **ENTER**. This will copy the contents of the mistakenly selected cell to a blank cell. Then press the **DELETE** key to erase the posted cell contents. Start the activity again by moving your cell pointer to the correct starting cell, **E6**.*

4. Place your mouse pointer in cell **E7** and select the range **E7..E8**. Your screen should look like Figure 3 - 6.

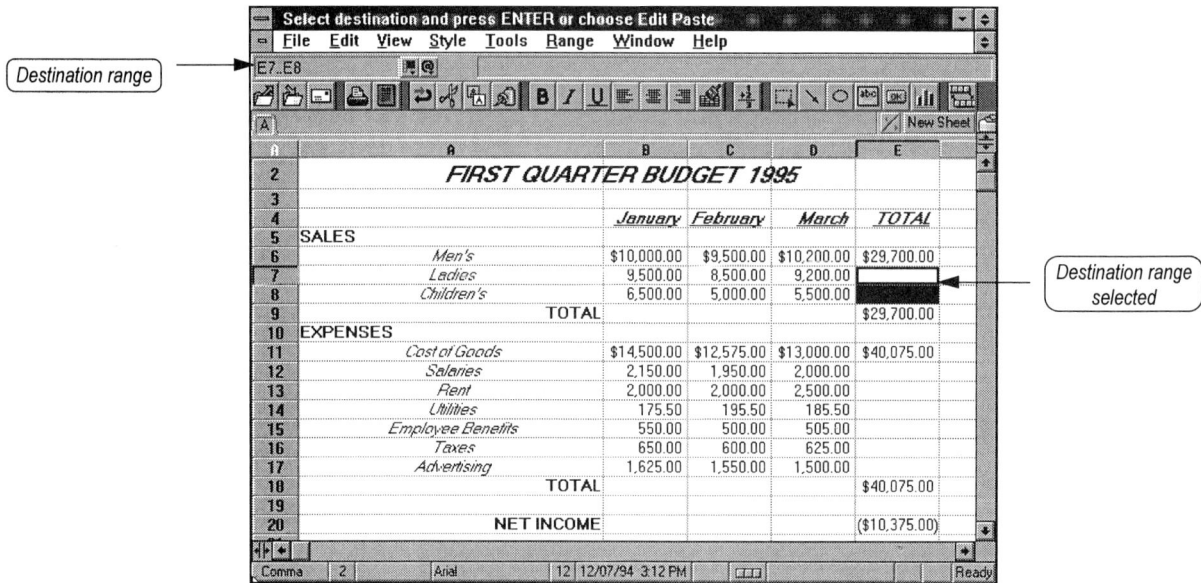

Figure 3 - 6

5. From the menu bar choose **EDIT/Paste**.

6. Click on cell **E7**. You will see the formula **+B7+C7+D7** in the **Contents Box**. Click on cell **E8**, and you will see the formula **+B8+C8+D8** in the **Contents Box**. The total in **B9** should again be **$73,900.00**. See Figure 3 - 7.

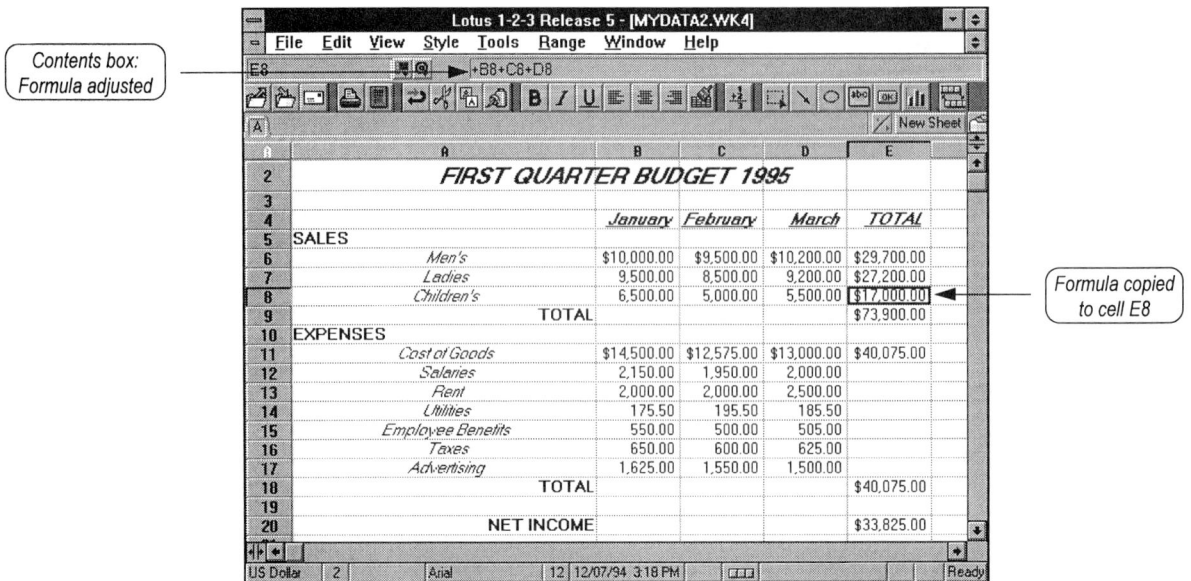

Figure 3 - 7

7. Place your cell pointer in cell **E11**.

8. Choose **EDIT/Copy**.

9. Place your mouse pointer in cell **E12** and select the range **E12..E17**.

10. From the menu bar choose **EDIT/Paste**.

11. Click on cell **E12**. The formula **+B12+C12+D12** appears in the **Contents Box**. In cells **E12** through **E17** *Lotus* performed a relative adjustment. The total in **B18** should again be **$61,336.50**. **Net Income** in cell **E20** should be **$12,563.50**.

12. Using the other methods, you are going to copy the formulas in cell **E9**, **E18**, and **E20** to the left to obtain monthly sales and expense totals and net income. First, you will use the Quick Menu method. Use the mouse to select **E9**.

13. With your mouse pointer resting on the selected cell, **E9**, click the right mouse button.

    A Quick Menu appears. Your screen now looks like Figure 3 - 8.

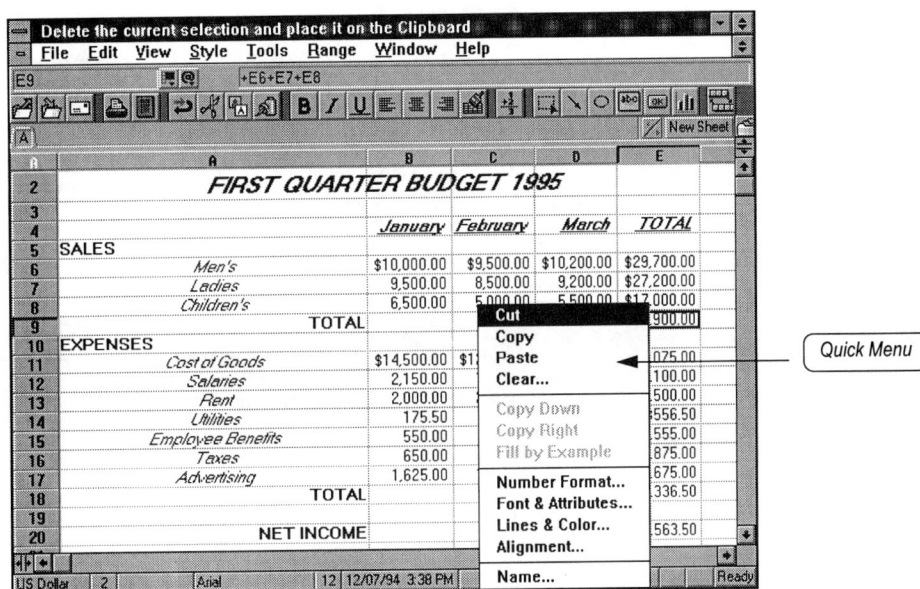

Figure 3 - 8

14. Choose **Copy**.

    The title bar now says ***Select destination and press ENTER or choose Edit Paste.***

15. Use the mouse to select **B9..D9**.

16. With your mouse pointer resting on the selected range, click the right mouse button.

17. From the Quick Menu, choose **PASTE**.

18. Again, Lotus performed a relative adjustment and copied the adjusted formula to the left.

19. Let's use the Quick Menu again. Use the mouse to select **E18**.

20. With your mouse pointer resting on the selected cell, click the right mouse button.

21. From the Quick Menu, choose **COPY**.

22. Use the mouse to select **B18..D18**.

23. With your mouse pointer resting on the selected range, click the right mouse button.

24. Choose **PASTE**.

25. For your final copy, you will use the SmartIcons. Use the mouse to select **E20.**

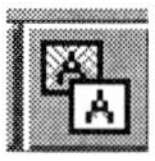

26. Click on the **Copy to the Clipboard** SmartIcon.

    *The title bar now says, **Select destination and press ENTER or choose Edit Paste.***

27. Use the mouse to select **B20..D20**.

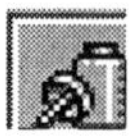

28. Click on the **Paste Clipboard contents** SmartIcon.

    Net Income is now calculated for January through March.

    Your file now looks like Figure 3 - 9.

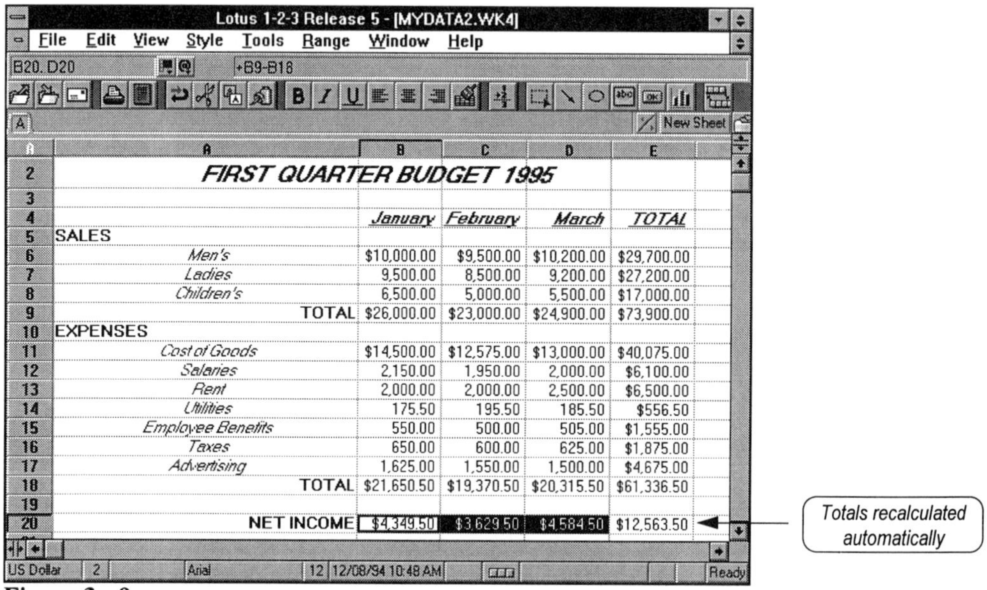

	A	B	C	D	E
2	FIRST QUARTER BUDGET 1995				
3					
4		January	February	March	TOTAL
5	SALES				
6	Men's	$10,000.00	$9,500.00	$10,200.00	$29,700.00
7	Ladies	9,500.00	8,500.00	9,200.00	$27,200.00
8	Children's	6,500.00	5,000.00	5,500.00	$17,000.00
9	TOTAL	$26,000.00	$23,000.00	$24,900.00	$73,900.00
10	EXPENSES				
11	Cost of Goods	$14,500.00	$12,575.00	$13,000.00	$40,075.00
12	Salaries	2,150.00	1,950.00	2,000.00	$6,100.00
13	Rent	2,000.00	2,000.00	2,500.00	$6,500.00
14	Utilities	175.50	195.50	185.50	$556.50
15	Employee Benefits	550.00	500.00	505.00	$1,555.00
16	Taxes	650.00	600.00	625.00	$1,875.00
17	Advertising	1,625.00	1,550.00	1,500.00	$4,675.00
18	TOTAL	$21,650.50	$19,370.50	$20,315.50	$61,336.50
19					
20	NET INCOME	$4,349.50	$3,629.50	$4,584.50	$12,563.50

Figure 3 - 9

29. **Save** your file using **FILE/Save As**. Call your file **MYDATA3**.

INSERTING COLUMNS OR ROWS

Once your worksheet is created, you might want to rearrange the information in it. Before you move data around, however, you must first make sure there is space available. Remember, if you move or copy data to a cell or a range that already contains data, *Lotus* replaces the existing data with the data being moved or copied.

We will now look at how to insert columns and rows to create empty space within your worksheet. Use caution when inserting or deleting columns or rows, for these operations may affect formulas or the values they refer to.

Inserting or Deleting Columns or Rows

To insert columns or rows using the menu bar:

- Select as many columns or rows as you want to insert.
- Choose **EDIT/Insert**.
- The **Insert** dialog box appears. Make sure the range selected is correct and *Lotus* has properly interpreted whether you want to insert columns or rows.

CAUTION: *If you select the column and row headings (1,2,3; A,B,C) rather than the cells in the columns and rows where you want to insert, Lotus will bypass the **Insert** dialog box and perform the insertion as soon as you choose **EDIT/Insert**.*

- Click on **OK**.
- *Lotus* inserts the number of columns or rows you selected placing the new columns to the left of the columns you selected or the new rows above the rows you selected.

To insert columns or rows using SmartIcons:

- Click on the **SmartIcon Selector** on the status bar .
- The set of SmartIcons you want to choose is the **Editing** set.
- Select as many columns or rows as you want to insert.
- Click on the **Insert rows** SmartIcon to insert rows; or
- Click on the **Insert columns** SmartIcon to insert columns.

To delete columns or rows using the menu bar:

- Select as many columns or rows as you want to delete.
- Choose **EDIT/Delete**.
- The **Delete** dialog box appears. Make sure the range selected is correct and *Lotus* has properly interpreted whether you want to delete columns or rows.

  CAUTION: *If you select the column and row headings (1,2,3; A,B,C) rather than the cells in the columns and rows you want to delete, Lotus will bypass the **Delete** dialog box and perform the insertion as soon as you choose **EDIT/Insert**.*

- Click on **OK**.
- *Lotus* deletes the number of columns or rows you selected.

  *If you delete a column or a row containing a range that a formula refers to, the formula results in an **ERR**. Use caution when deleting columns and rows.*

To delete columns or rows using SmartIcons:

- Click on the **SmartIcon Selector** on the Status Bar .
- The set of SmartIcons you want to choose is the **Editing** set.
- Select as many columns or rows as you want to delete.
- Click on the **Delete selected rows** SmartIcon to delete rows; or
- Click on the **Delete selected columns** SmartIcon to delete columns.

Activity 3.3: Inserting Columns and Rows

In this activity, you will insert some rows so you can later rearrange your worksheet.

1. Place your cell pointer in cell **A14**.

   *We want to insert a row above row **14**. Cell A14 was selected, but any cell in row **14** is acceptable. We simply want to tell Lotus to perform its insertion **above** row 14. Remember, however, to always be cautious about selecting the row heading.*

2. Choose **EDIT/Insert**.

   *The **Insert** dialog box will appear. See Figure 3 - 10.*

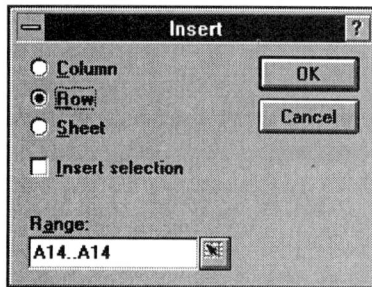

Figure 3 - 10

3. Make sure the **Range** selected is **A14..A14** and the **Row** option button is selected.

4. Click on **OK**.

   *Now row **14** is blank and the remaining data in the worksheet is pushed down one row. Click on cell **B19**. You will notice that the formula has been adjusted to reflect the fact that some data was pushed down one row. It now adds **B11**, **B12**, **B13**, **B15**, **B16**, **B17**, and **B18**. See Figure 3 - 11.*

Figure 3 - 11

5. Place your cell pointer in any cell in row **17**.

6. Choose **EDIT/Insert**.

7. Make sure the **Range** selected includes row **17** and the **Row** option button is selected.

8. Click on **OK**.

9. Place your cell pointer in any cell in row **10**.

10. Click on the **SmartIcon Selector** on the status bar. Click on the **Editing** set.

11. Click on the **Insert rows** SmartIcon.

   A row is inserted at row 10 and again the remaining data is pushed down. You will again notice that your formulas did adjust properly.

12. Now you have almost enough space to reorganize your worksheet. Later you will add the remaining needed space and delete any extra rows.

13. Click on the down arrow of the vertical scroll bar on the right of the work area twice. Net Income can again be seen on your screen. Your file now looks like Figure 3 - 12.

	A	B	C	D	E
		January	*February*	*March*	*TOTAL*
4					
5	SALES				
6	Men's	$10,000.00	$9,500.00	$10,200.00	$29,700.00
7	Ladies	9,500.00	8,500.00	9,200.00	$27,200.00
8	Children's	6,500.00	5,000.00	5,500.00	$17,000.00
9	TOTAL	$26,000.00	$23,000.00	$24,900.00	$73,900.00
10					
11	EXPENSES				
12	Cost of Goods	$14,500.00	$12,575.00	$13,000.00	$40,075.00
13	Salaries	2,150.00	1,950.00	2,000.00	$6,100.00
14	Rent	2,000.00	2,000.00	2,500.00	$6,500.00
15					
16	Utilities	175.50	195.50	185.50	$556.50
17	Employee Benefits	550.00	500.00	505.00	$1,555.00
18					
19	Taxes	650.00	600.00	625.00	$1,875.00
20	Advertising	1,625.00	1,550.00	1,500.00	$4,675.00
21	TOTAL	$21,650.50	$19,370.50	$20,315.50	$61,336.50
22					
23	NET INCOME	$4,349.50	$3,629.50	$4,584.50	$12,563.50

Figure 3 - 12

MOVING DATA FROM OR TO RANGES

The **Move** process is used to rearrange the information within a worksheet. When moving labels or values, the entries are picked up from one location and placed in the new location. When moving formulas, the cell references in the formula remain the same. *Lotus* does not perform a relative adjustment when formulas alone are moved. *Lotus* assumes you want the same formula in a different place. If, however, you move data and a related formula together, *Lotus* will move the data and adjust the formula accordingly.

There are a number of ways to move data in Lotus. You can use the menu bar, the SmartIcons, the Quick Menu, or use a process of dragging and dropping. We will look at the first three methods.

To move data using the menu bar:

- Use the mouse to select the data to be moved.

- From the menu bar choose **EDIT/Cut**.

   *The title bar now says, **Select destination and press ENTER or choose Edit Paste**. Also, the contents of the cell or cells selected is deleted.*

- Use the mouse to select the cell or range of cells to receive the moved information.

- From the menu bar choose **EDIT/Paste**.

To move data using the Quick Menu:

- Use the mouse to select the data to be moved.
- With the mouse pointer resting somewhere on the selected range, click the right mouse button.
- Choose **CUT**.

  *The title bar now says, **Select destination and press ENTER or choose Edit Paste**.*

- Use the mouse to select the cell or range of cells to receive the moved information.
- With the mouse pointer resting somewhere on the selected range, click the right mouse button.
- Choose **PASTE**.

To move data using the SmartIcons:

- Use the mouse to select the data to be moved.
- Click on the **Cut to the Clipboard** SmartIcon .

  *The title bar now says, **Select destination and press ENTER or choose Edit Paste**.*

- Use the mouse to select the cell or range of cells to receive the moved information.
- Click on the **Paste Clipboard contents** Smarticon .

Activity 3.4: Moving Data

After creating your worksheet, you notice that your expenses are not organized in any particular sequence. We would like them to be organized from the highest total expense to the lowest. The sequence should be: Cost of Goods, Rent, Salaries, Advertising, Taxes, Employee Benefits, Utilities.

Note: Although you will use moving, there is an alternative way to reorganize your data from highest to lowest expense, using sorting. We will learn how to sort in Lesson 8.

1. Select the range **A20..E20**.

   *We want to move the label **Advertising**, and the related numbers and formula to row **15**.*

2. From the menu bar choose **EDIT/Cut**.

   *The title bar now says, **Select destination and press ENTER or choose Edit Paste**. Also, the contents of **A20..E20** is deleted. The range you selected is now blank.*

3. Use the mouse to select cell **A15**.

   Since you have cut a range to the Clipboard, you do not have to select a range to receive the data. It is not incorrect to select a range to paste to, but it is easier to simply select the starting point for the paste.

4. From the menu bar choose **EDIT/Paste**. Your worksheet now looks like Figure 3 - 13.

   ***Advertising** and the related data are placed in row **15**.*

5. Select the range **A16..E16**.

   *We want to take the label **Utilities**, the related numbers, and formula and move it all to row **18**.*

6. From the menu bar choose **EDIT/Cut**.

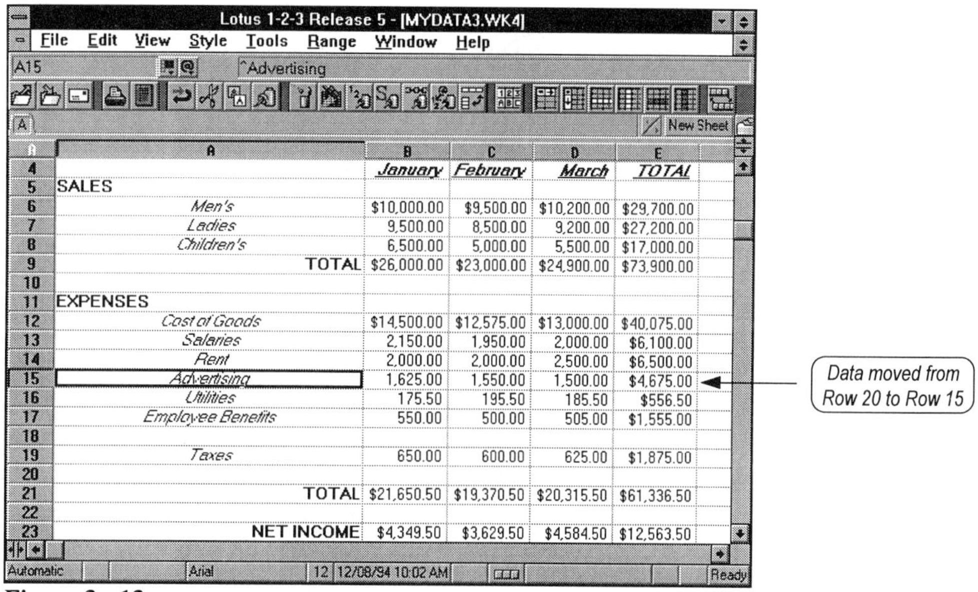

Figure 3 - 13

7. Use the mouse to select cell **A18**.

8. From the menu bar choose **EDIT/Paste**.

*Next, you will move the label **Taxes** and the related data to row **16** using the SmartIcons.*

9. Use the mouse to select **A19..E19**.

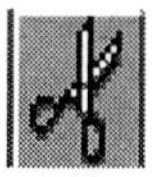

10. Click on the **Cut to the Clipboard** SmartIcon.

11. Use the mouse to select **A16**.

12. Click on the **Paste Clipboard contents** SmartIcon.

Your worksheet now looks like Figure 3 - 14.

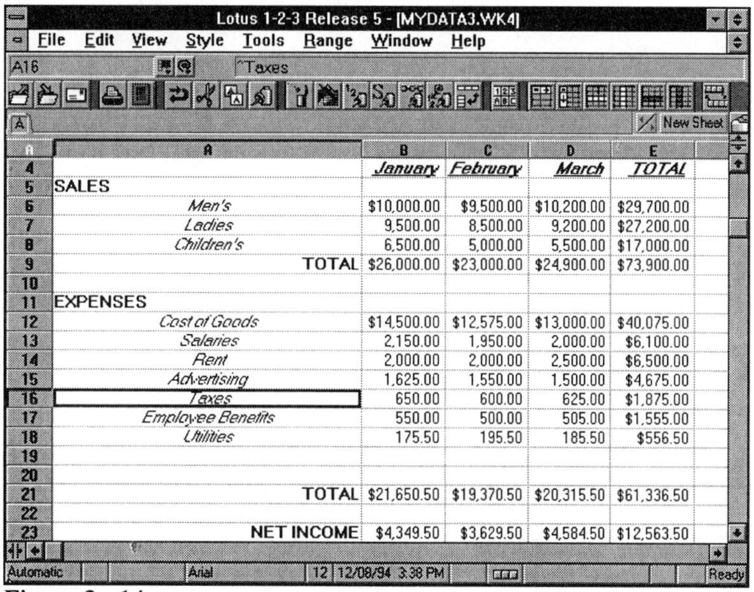

Figure 3 - 14

13. Finally, you need to move **Rent** to row **13** and **Salaries** to row **14**. However, if you move data to a cell or a range of cells that already contains data, *Lotus* will replace the existing data with the data being moved. Therefore, you need to begin by inserting a blank row, between **Salaries** and **Rent**. Select cell **A14**.

14. From the menu bar, choose **EDIT/Insert**.

15. Make sure that the range selected is **A14..A14** and the **Row** option button is selected.

16. Click on **OK**.

   *A blank row is inserted at row 14. Now you can move the **Salary** information in row 13 to row 14.*

17. Use the mouse to select **A13..E13**.

18. Using one of the move methods you have seen, move the data you have selected to row **14**.

19. The last step is to move **Rent** to row **13**. Select **A15..E15**.

20. Using one of the move methods you have seen, move the data you have selected to row **13**.

   Your worksheet now shows all expense information correctly organized, from highest total expense to lowest. It should look like Figure 3 - 15.

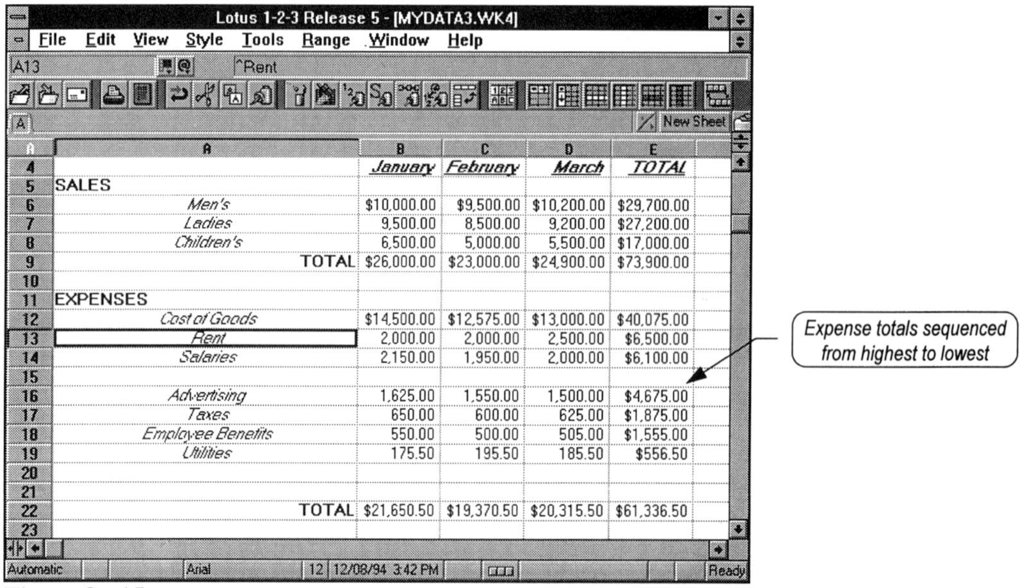

Figure 3 - 15

Activity 3.5: Deleting Columns and Rows

You can see that there is an extra row in our Expenses section, and that there are some extra rows between the expenses and the totals for the expenses. Now you will delete these extra rows.

1. Select cell **A15**.

   *Again, it is not necessary to select all the cells in row 15, it is only necessary to select a cell in the row you want to delete. In your case, you could also have selected **A15..E15** or simply, for example, **C15**.*

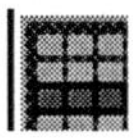

2. Click on the **Delete selected rows** SmartIcon to delete row **15**.

3. Select the cells **A19..A20**.

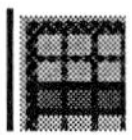

4. Click on the **Delete selected rows** SmartIcon to delete rows **19** and **20**.

5. The label **Totals** and the formulas are now moved up to row **19**. The formulas have adjusted, so they are still correct. Your worksheet now looks like Figure 3 - 16.

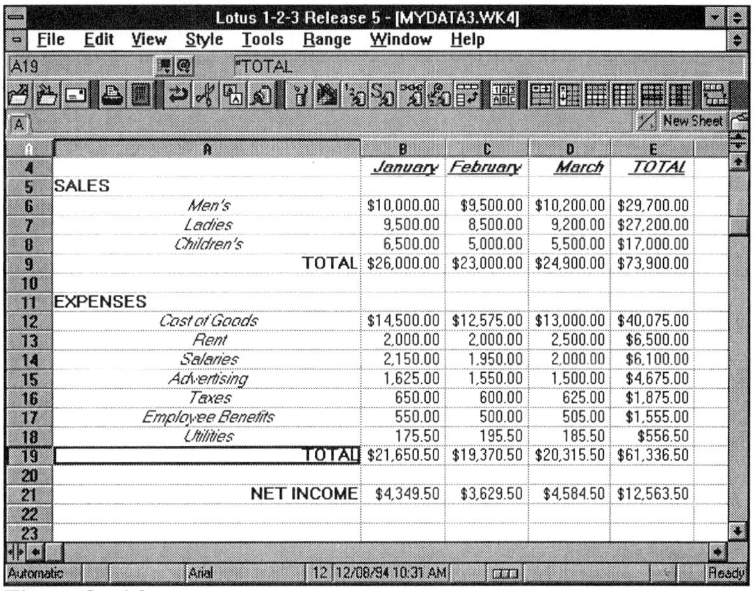

Figure 3 - 16

PRINTING YOUR WORKSHEET

Up to this point, you have printed your worksheet using the defaults in *Lotus*. Now you will look at how to change some of the defaults and add some enhancements to the printed output.

Using Print Preview

The **Print Preview** feature permits you to view on the screen how your printed output will look prior to actually printing. It is very useful for checking the layouts of pages before printing and thus not wasting paper when printing.

To use the menu bar for print preview:

- If you want to preview the entire file, select only **one** cell. If you want to preview a range, use the mouse to select the range.

- From the main menu choose **FILE/Print Preview**.

- The **Print Preview** dialog box appears. Make sure the correct preview option is selected. Your options are:

  o **Current Worksheet:** previews the active area of the worksheet;

  o **All Worksheets:** previews the entire file;

  o **Selected Range:** previews only the range selected.

- Choose **OK**.

  A preview screen appears showing how your output will look.

- To return to your worksheet you can press the **ESCAPE** key or click on the **Close the Print Preview window** SmartIcon.

Activity 3.6: Previewing Your Output

Before printing the worksheet, first preview it to see if you care to make any improvements.

1. Place your cell pointer in a single cell (i.e., **A4**).

2. From the main menu choose **FILE/Print Preview**.

   *A **Print Preview** dialog box appears. Make sure the correct preview option is selected. We want to preview the **Current Worksheet**. See Figure 3 - 17.*

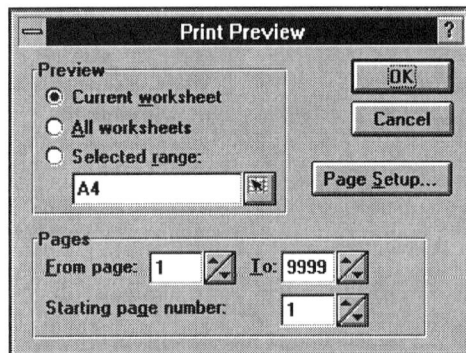

Figure 3 - 17

3. Click on **OK**. You are now previewing your output. See Figure 3 - 18.

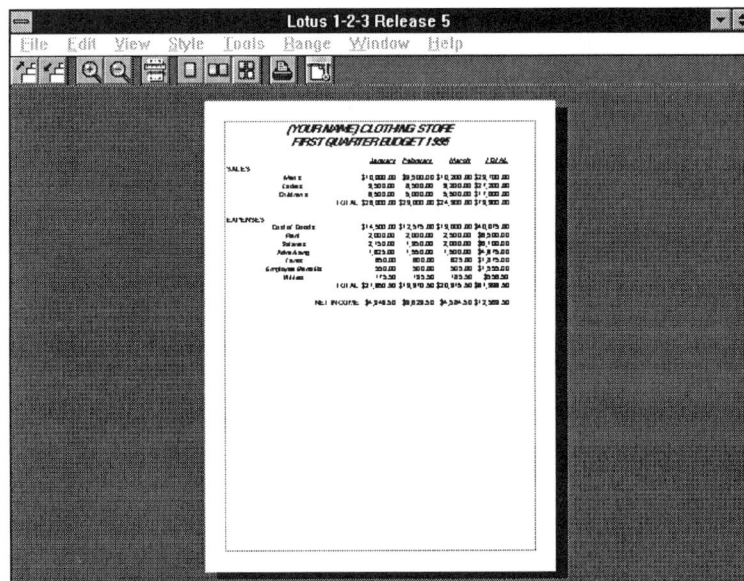

Figure 3 - 18

4. When you are finished looking at your output on the screen, press the **ESCAPE** key or click on the **Close the Print Preview window** SmartIcon.

Adding a Header and Footer to Improve the Appearance of Your Output

A *Header* is a line of text printed above the top margin of each page, and a *Footer* is a line of text printed below the bottom margin of each page. Up to approximately 79 characters can be entered in a header or a footer. However, *Lotus* does not print any text that extends beyond the right margin of the printed page. Headers and footers are used to customize your output and are broken down into three segments: text to appear on the left; text to appear in the center; and text to appear on the right.

To use the menu bar to add headers and footers:

- Choose **FILE/Page Setup**.

- In the **Page Setup** dialog box there are five buttons that can be used to add specific information into the header or footer. You can also type the characters rather than use the buttons. The buttons and corresponding characters are:

Button	Meaning	Characters to be typed
	Current system date	@ (at sign)
	Current time	+ (plus sign)
	Page number	# (pound sign)
	File name	^ (caret)
	Cell contents	\ (backslash) followed by the cell address or the range name

- Initially, the buttons above are in gray. You must first click on one of the three header boxes or one of the three footer boxes to activate the buttons.

- Click on one or more of the buttons to insert text in the header and/or footer.

- Click on **OK**.

Activity 3.7: Adding a Header and Footer

You will add a header and a footer to the worksheet to customize the output. The header will have your name on the left and the date on the right. The footer will have the page number in the center and the filename on the right.

1. Choose **FILE/Page Setup**.

2. In the **Page Setup** dialog box, click on the left **Header** text box. See Figure 3 - 19.

   *You will notice that the **Insert** buttons are now in color. This means they now can be used.*

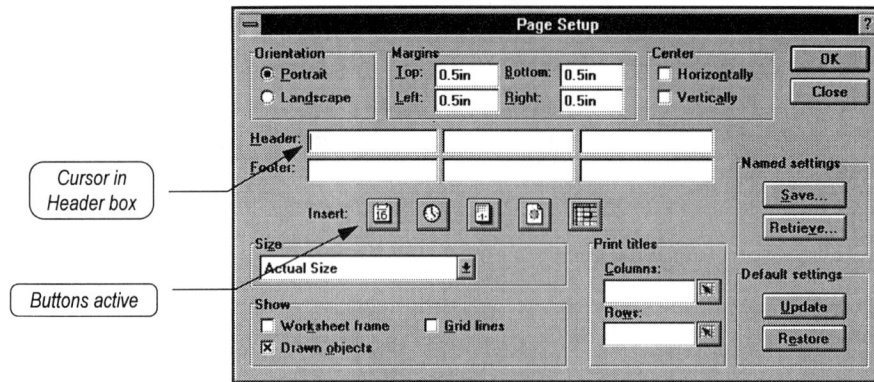

Figure 3 - 19

3. Type your name (first name and last name) as you want it to appear at the top of your printed output.

4. Click on the right **Header** text box.

5. Click on the **Current system date** button.

   Notice that the @ sign is placed in the right Header text box.

6. Click on the center **Footer** text box.

7. Click on the **Page number** button.

   Notice that the # sign is placed in the center footer box. If you want the footer to say "Page 1", you need to type the word Page prior to inserting the # sign.

8. Click on the right **Footer** text box.

9. Click on the **File name** button.

   *Notice that the caret (^) is placed in the box. Your **Page Setup** box now looks like Figure 3 - 20.*

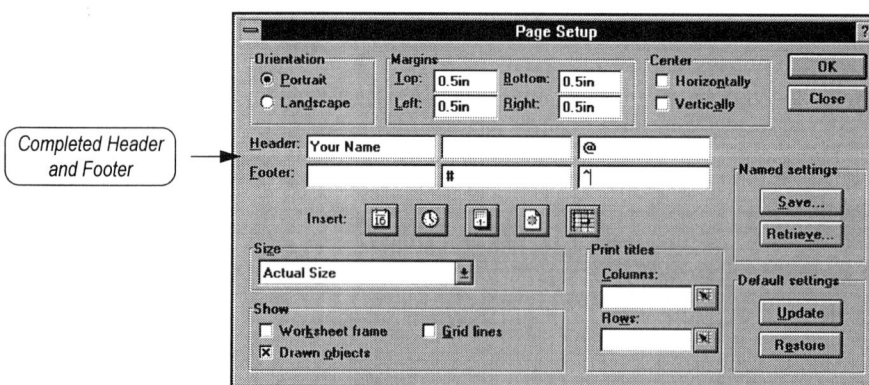

Figure 3 - 20

10. Choose **OK**.

11. From the menu bar choose **FILE/Print**.

12. Click on **OK**.

   Now your worksheet is printed with a Header and a Footer.

Using the Page Setup to Further Change the Appearance of the Printed Output

Up till now, you have been using the defaults set by *Lotus* for printing. We can improve the appearance of the printed output by changing some of the **Page Setup** settings. These settings permit us to change, for example, margins, the amount of data that fits on one page, the orientation (portrait or landscape), and whether a frame or grid lines are included on your output.

If you plan to change the settings and want to continue to use the changed settings in the future, you can save the changed settings. Saved settings can then be used whenever output is printed.

To use the menu bar to change the page setup:

- Choose **FILE/Page Setup**.

- The **Orientation** dialog box elements are option buttons -- choose either **Portrait** or **Landscape**.

  Portrait means the output is printed vertically down the page; Landscape means the output is printed horizontally across the page. You can fit more data across the page when you choose Landscape orientation.

- For **Margins**, you can enter new measurements to leave more spacing at the top, bottom, or on either side of the printed page.

- You can **Center** your output **Horizontally, Vertically,** or **Both**.

  This is helpful if your worksheet is not too large and you simply want it in the middle of the page. You no longer have to adjust the margins to have the output centered.

- For **Size**, there is a drop-down list box that allows you to choose to fit all the data on one page, fit all columns, fit all rows, or manually scale the output.

  This option is helpful if you need to squeeze more data on a page of output.

- **Show** permits you to choose to have a frame appear around the outside of the page of printed output, have grid lines on the page, or show all drawn objects.

  A frame consists of the column letters and row numbers that appear on the worksheet itself. In most cases you will not need a frame, but if you are doing an analysis and changing formulas, the frame might be useful. Grid lines are horizontal and vertical lines that are drawn to make it easier to read the data. Again it is likely that you do not want this on your final output, but it might be helpful if you are performing data analysis.

- **Save** is used to save the settings so you may use them at any time.

- Click on **OK**.

- Use **Print Preview** to check the adjustments before printing.

Activity 3.8: Changing Page Setup Options

You will change the appearance of your output by changing some of the **Page Setup** options.

1. Choose **FILE/Page Setup**.

2. In the **Page Setup** dialog box, in the **Center** area, click on both the **Horizontally** and **Vertically** check boxes.

   This will center your output.

3. In the **Show** area, click on both the **Worksheet frame** and **Grid lines** check boxes.

This will add the column letters and the row numbers to your output as well as horizontal and vertical grid lines.

4. If your printer allows, you can also change the orientation. Check with your instructor to determine if your printer supports **Landscape** orientation. If so, click on **Landscape**. Your **Page Setup** dialog box looks like Figure 3 - 21.

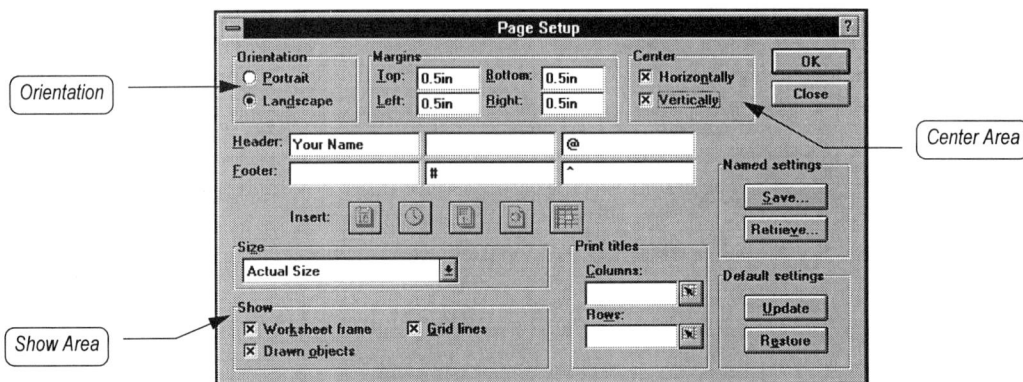

Figure 3 - 21

5. Choose **OK**.

6. Choose **FILE/Print Preview**. Choose **OK**.

7. Click on the **Print the current selection** SmartIcon. Click on **OK**.

   You now have your output with modifications.

SAVE YOUR FILE

You are finished with this lesson. Remember to save your file.

Activity 3.9: Saving Your File

1. From the menu bar choose **FILE/Save As**.

2. Give your file a new name: **MYDATA4**.

3. Choose **OK**.

SUMMARY

In this lesson you learned how to move data around the worksheet, copy labels and formulas, insert and delete columns and rows, and customize your printed output. The skills you have learned are summarized in the Key Terms. Now you can practice these skills in the following Independent Projects.

KEY TERMS

Clipboard	Header	Paste
Copy	Insert Column	Portrait Orientation
Cut	Insert Row	Print Preview
Delete Column	Landscape Orientation	Quick Menu
Delete Row	Move	Ranges
Footer	Orientation	Relative Adjustment
Gridlines	Page Setup	Worksheet Frame

INDEPENDENT PROJECTS

Independent Project 3.1: Moving and Copying Data

In this project, you will practice moving and copying data within the worksheet. Your completed worksheet will look like Figure 3 - 22.

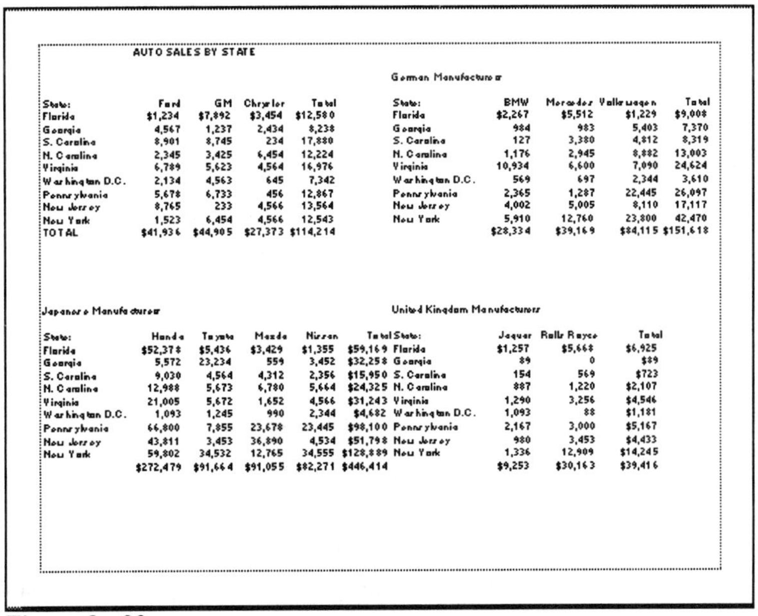

AUTO SALES BY STATE

State:	Ford	GM	Chrysler	Total
Florida	$1,234	$7,892	$3,454	$12,580
Georgia	4,567	1,237	2,434	8,238
S. Carolina	8,901	8,745	234	17,880
N. Carolina	2,345	3,425	6,454	12,224
Virginia	6,789	5,623	4,564	16,976
Washington D.C.	2,134	4,563	645	7,342
Pennsylvania	5,678	6,733	456	12,867
New Jersey	8,765	233	4,566	13,564
New York	1,523	6,454	4,566	12,543
TOTAL	$41,936	$44,905	$27,373	$114,214

German Manufacturer

State:	BMW	Mercedes	Volkswagen	Total
Florida	$2,267	$5,512	$1,229	$9,008
Georgia	984	983	5,403	7,370
S. Carolina	127	3,380	4,812	8,319
N. Carolina	1,176	2,945	8,882	13,003
Virginia	10,934	6,600	7,090	24,624
Washington D.C.	569	697	2,344	3,610
Pennsylvania	2,365	1,287	22,445	26,097
New Jersey	4,002	5,005	8,110	17,117
New York	5,910	12,760	23,800	42,470
	$28,334	$39,169	$84,115	$151,618

Japanese Manufacturer

State:	Honda	Toyota	Mazda	Nissan	Total
Florida	$52,378	$5,436	$3,429	$1,355	$59,169
Georgia	5,572	23,234	559	3,452	$32,258
S. Carolina	9,030	4,564	4,312	2,356	$15,950
N. Carolina	12,988	5,673	6,780	5,664	$24,325
Virginia	21,005	5,672	1,652	4,566	$31,243
Washington D.C.	1,093	1,245	990	2,344	$4,682
Pennsylvania	66,800	7,855	23,678	23,445	$98,100
New Jersey	43,811	3,453	36,890	4,534	$51,798
New York	59,802	34,532	12,765	34,555	$128,889
	$272,479	$91,664	$91,055	$82,271	$446,414

United Kingdom Manufacturers

State:	Jaguar	Rolls Royce	Total
Florida	$1,257	$5,668	$6,925
Georgia	89	0	$89
S. Carolina	154	569	$723
N. Carolina	887	1,220	$2,107
Virginia	1,290	3,256	$4,546
Washington D.C.	1,093	88	$1,181
Pennsylvania	2,167	3,000	$5,167
New Jersey	980	3,453	$4,433
New York	1,336	12,909	$14,245
	$9,253	$30,163	$39,416

Figure 3 - 22

1. Select **FILE/Open**.
2. The file you want to open is **IA3-1**.
3. Select cells **A6..A14** (the state labels).
4. Click on the **Copy** icon to copy the data to the clipboard.
5. Press the **PAGE DOWN** key to move the cursor to cell **A24**.
6. Click on the **Paste** icon. The state labels are now copied to **A24..A32**.
7. Select cells **A24..A32**.
8. Click on the **Copy** icon to copy the data to the clipboard.
9. Press the **PAGE DOWN** key to move the cursor to cell **A44**.
10. Click on the **Paste** icon. The state labels are now copied to **A44..A52**.
11. Select cells **A44..A62**.
12. Follow steps 8 to 10 and copy the state labels to cells **A64..A72**.
13. Press the **HOME** key to place your cursor at the beginning of the worksheet.
14. Select cells **B6..E6**.
15. Click on the **SUM** icon. The total is placed in **E6**.
16. Select cell **E6**.
17. Click on the **Copy** icon to copy the data to the clipboard.

18. Select cells **E7..E14**. Click on the **Paste** Icon. Now the sum formula in **E6** is copied to cell **E7..E14**.

19. Place your cursor in cell **A15** and enter the label **TOTAL**.

20. Select cells **B6..B15**. Click on the **SUM** icon. The total is placed in **B15**.

21. **Copy** the total in cell **B15** to cells **C15..E15**. You can use the icons to perform the copy.

22. Place your cursor in cell **A41**. We are going to move the data in **A41..E73** to the right of the data at the top of the worksheet.

23. Select cells **A41..E73**. Click on the **Cut** icon.

24. Press the **HOME** key to move your cursor back to the beginning of the worksheet.

25. Place your cursor in cell **G3** and click on the **PASTE** icon. Now the data is moved from the bottom of the worksheet up to the top right side of the worksheet.

26. Select the data in cell **G23..J35**.

27. **Move** the data for the United Kingdom Manufacturer so it starts in cell **H21**.

28. Improve the appearance of the data in the worksheet by performing the following:

    The first row of numbers in each set of data should be formatted as **Currency** with **Zero** decimal places;

    The last row of data should be also be formatted as **Currency** with **Zero** decimal places;

    All data between the first and the last row of data should be formatted as **Comma** format with **Zero** decimal place;

    All Auto Manufactures labels at the top of the of the columns should be right aligned;

    The **A** and **G** columns should be wide enough to accommodate the longest labels;

    If the column is not wide enough for the name of the manufacturer, make the column wider.

29. **FILE/Save** your file as **IA3-1DNE**.

30. **Print** your worksheet.

31. **FILE/Close** your file.

Independent Project 3.2: More Practice Moving and Copying Data

In this project, you will move and copy data within a worksheet already created for you. When you are done, your worksheet should look like Figure 3 - 23.

1. Select **FILE/Open**

2. The file you want to open is **IA3-2**.

3. Place your cursor in cell **C23**. Select the range **C23..F33**.

4. Using the **icons**, move the data to the left one column. Select the **Cut** icon, click on cell **B23** and select the **Paste** icon.

5. Place your cursor in cell **C24**. To bring the total from **F7** down to **F24** without copying or moving the data, just place the formula in **C24** of **+F7**. Now the total from **F7** is placed in **C24**.

6. **Copy** the formula in **C24** to cells **C25..C31**. Select the **Copy** icon, click on cell **C25..C31** and select the **Paste** icon.

7. In cell **D24**, insert a formula to subtract the Actual Sales from the Projected Sales (**+C24-B24**).

PRODUCT	Eastern	Western	Northern	Southern
Baseball Bats	$8,056	$2,297	$1,768	$4,807
Olympic Frisbees	6,017	6,647	6,926	1,474
Golf Club Sets	4,663	8,717	8,458	7,536
Athletic Wear	10,325	2,234	1,823	9,236
Kayaks	4,328	4,773	3,572	1,160
Camping Equipment	6,147	2,543	3,420	11,222
Football Pads	7,968	9,584	6,489	6,210
Boxing Gloves	1,569	2,884	3,607	1,310
Totals	$49,073	$39,679	$36,063	$42,955

Projected Vs. Actual Sales

DOLLAR VOLUME SOLD

Product	Projected	Actual	Variance	% Variance
Baseball Bats	$16,000	$16,928	$928	5.8%
Olympic Frisbees	22,000	21,064	(936)	-4.3%
Golf Club Sets	30,000	29,374	(626)	-2.1%
Athletic Wear	25,000	23,618	(1,382)	-5.5%
Kayaks	12,000	13,833	1,833	15.3%
Camping Equipment	25,000	23,332	(1,668)	-6.7%
Football Pads	28,000	30,251	2,251	8.0%
Boxing Gloves	10,000	9,370	(630)	-6.3%
Totals	$168,000	$167,770	($230)	-0.1%

Figure 3 - 23

8. **Copy** the formula in **D24** to cells **D25..D31**.

9. In cell **E24** place a formula to divide the Variance by the Projected sales (**+D24/B24**).

10. **Copy** the formula in **E24** to cells **E25..E31**.

11. **Copy** the formula in **B33** to cells **C33..D33**.

12. **Copy** the formula in **E31** to cell **E33**. (You must copy the formula for the variance because it is meaningless to add variances).

13. **Format** your results as follows:

    B24..D24 should be formatted as **Currency** with **Zero** decimal places;

    B33..D33 should be formatted as **Currency** with **Zero** decimal places;

    B25..D31 should be formatted as **Comma** with **Zero** decimal places;

    E24..E33 should be formatted as **Percent** with **1** decimal place;

14. All labels at the top of the columns, titles in the worksheet, and the product labels should be **Bold**.

15. The heading in cells **A2..A3** should be centered over the range **A2..F3**.

16. The heading in cells **A19** should be centered over the range **A19..F19**.

17. **FILE/Save** your file as **IA3-2DNE**.

18. **Print** your worksheet.

19. **FILE/Close** your file.

Independent Project 3.3: Moving and Copying Data within the Worksheet

In this project, you will move and copy data within the worksheet of your travel agency. You want to track ticket sales data during peak travel times and during off-peak travel times. This will indicate to you how to spend your advertising budget. When you are done, your worksheet should look like Figure 3 - 24.

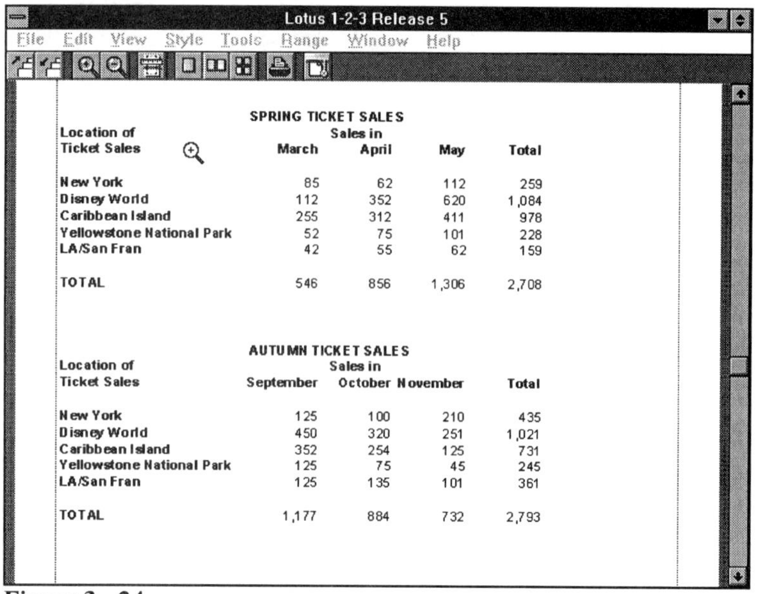

Figure 3 - 24

1. **Open** the file **IA3-3**.

2. Place your cursor in cell **E6**.

3. Place a formula in **E6** to add the values in the row.

4. **Copy** the total in **E6** to cells **E7..E10**.

5. Enter **TOTAL** in cell **A12**.

6. Place a formula in cell **B12** to total **B6..B10**.

7. **Copy** the total in **B12** to cells **C12..E12**.

8. **Right Align** the labels in cells **B4..E4**.

9. Select the range **A3..E12**. **Copy** the data so it starts in cell **A16**.

10. In cell **B15** enter the label **SPRING TICKET SALES**.

11. Change the months to **March, April** and **May**.

12. Enter the ticket sales as follows:

	March	April	May
New York	85	62	112
Disney World	112	352	620
Caribbean	255	312	411
Yellowstone	52	75	101
LA/San Fran	42	55	62

13. Select the range **A3..E12**. **Copy** the data so it starts in cell **A30**.

14. In cell **B29** enter the label **AUTUMN TICKET SALES**.

15. Change the months to **September, October** and **November**.

16. Enter the ticket sales as follows:

	Sept.	Oct.	Nov.
New York	125	100	210
Disney World	450	320	251
Caribbean	352	254	125
Yellowstone	125	75	45
LA/San Fran	125	135	101

17. Place the cursor back in cell **A1**. **Bold** the name of your company. Center the name across the range **A1..E1**.

18. **Bold** the column and row headings within the worksheet.

19. **Format** all values as **Comma** format with **0** decimal places.

20. Make the **A** column wide enough for the longest entry.

21. **FILE/Save** your file as **IA3-3DNE**.

22. **Print** your worksheet.

23. **FILE/Close** your file.

Independent Project 3.4: Tracking Sales Invoices

In this project, you will complete and enhance a worksheet that tracks sales invoices. Sales invoices are assigned sequential numbers. Often, customers will add to their order. When a customer adds to their order, you are to insert a row, number the invoice as the prior number followed by an A, and then add the additional information. You are to complete the worksheet that was started and add the new items ordered. When you are done, your worksheet might resemble Figure 3 - 25.

	A	B	C	D	E	F	G
3	Invoice Nu	Name	Amount of Sale	Tax (6.75%)	Shipping	Total Due	
4	00115	Peter Lynch	842.40	56.86	5.00	904.26	
5	00116	Nancy Smith	597.78	40.35	5.00	643.13	
6	00116A	Nancy Smith	458.56	30.95	5.00	494.51	
7	00117	Jacklyn Jones	779.33	52.60	5.00	836.93	
8	00118	Barry Turko	997.41	67.32	5.00	1,069.73	
9	00118A	Barry Turko	415.50	28.05	5.00	448.55	
10	00118B	Barry Turko	125.52	8.47	4.00	137.99	
11	00119	Samuel Patter	647.03	43.67	5.00	695.71	
12	00120	Jerry Gerald	181.65	12.26	3.00	196.91	
13	00121	Kurry Hirray	22.37	1.51	3.00	26.88	
14	00122	Nurnak Rumold	758.20	51.18	5.00	814.38	
15	00123	Stan Williams	293.73	19.83	3.00	316.56	
16	00123A	Stan Williams	110.25	7.44	4.00	121.69	
17	00124	Jennifer Lewis	75.48	5.10	3.00	83.58	
18	00125	Sharon Jeeves	975.94	65.88	5.00	1,046.82	
19	00125A	Sharon Jeeves	725.66	48.98	10.00	784.64	
20	00126	Willie White	152.04	10.26	3.00	165.31	

Figure 3 - 25

1. **Open** the file **IA3-4**.

2. Add the following data to the worksheet:

Invoice	Name	Amount	Shipping
00116A	Nancy Smith	458.56	5.00
00118A	Barry Turko	415.50	5.00
00118B	Barry Turko	125.52	4.00
00123A	Stan Williams	110.25	4.00
00125A	Sharon Jeeves	725.66	10.00

3. Calculate the tax based on the rate of 6.75% of the sales amount.

4. **Copy** the formula down the **D** column.

5. Calculate the total amount due from each customer.

6. **Copy** the formula down the **F** column.

7. **Format** the data in the **D** column as **Comma** notation with **2** decimal places.

8. **Save** your file as **IA3-4DNE**.

9. **Print** your worksheet.

4 Using Functions and Formulas

Objectives

In this lesson you will learn how to:

- Understand formulas
- Understand more complex formulas
- Understand functions

- Understand rules of hierarchy in formulas
- Use functions in a worksheet

PROJECT DESCRIPTION

You have organized your portfolio of Investments. Information included in the worksheet is the name of the investment, where it was purchased, the cost, and its current market value per share. Using this data, you want to calculate the total market value, the gain or loss on each investment, the percentage each stock has increased or decreased and the average market price of the stocks.

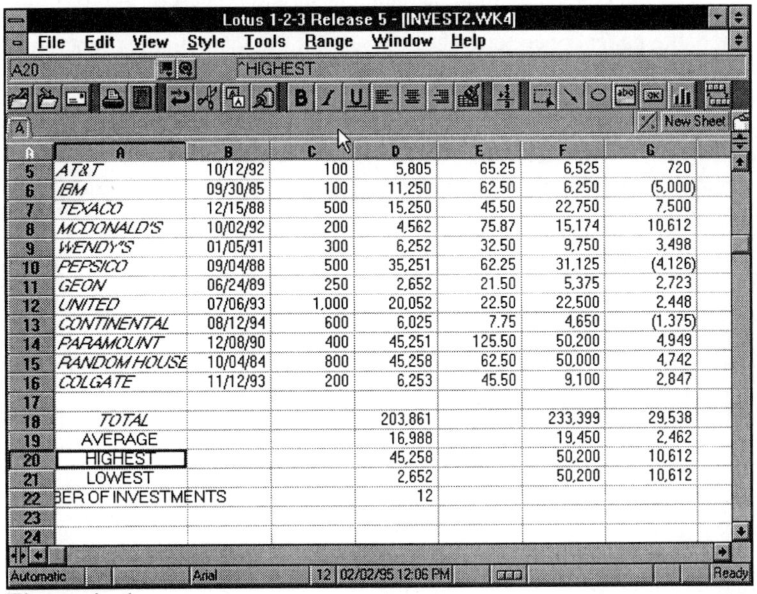

Lotus 1-2-3 Release 5 - [INVEST2.WK4]

File Edit View Style Tools Range Window Help

A20 ^HIGHEST

	A	B	C	D	E	F	G
5	AT&T	10/12/92	100	5,805	65.25	6,525	720
6	IBM	09/30/85	100	11,250	62.50	6,250	(5,000)
7	TEXACO	12/15/88	500	15,250	45.50	22,750	7,500
8	MCDONALD'S	10/02/92	200	4,562	75.87	15,174	10,612
9	WENDY'S	01/05/91	300	6,252	32.50	9,750	3,498
10	PEPSICO	09/04/88	500	35,251	62.25	31,125	(4,126)
11	GEON	06/24/89	250	2,652	21.50	5,375	2,723
12	UNITED	07/06/93	1,000	20,052	22.50	22,500	2,448
13	CONTINENTAL	08/12/94	600	6,025	7.75	4,650	(1,375)
14	PARAMOUNT	12/08/90	400	45,251	125.50	50,200	4,949
15	RANDOM HOUSE	10/04/84	800	45,258	62.50	50,000	4,742
16	COLGATE	11/12/93	200	6,253	45.50	9,100	2,847
17							
18	TOTAL			203,861		233,399	29,538
19	AVERAGE			16,988		19,450	2,462
20	HIGHEST			45,258		50,200	10,612
21	LOWEST			2,652		50,200	10,612
22	BER OF INVESTMENTS			12			
23							
24							

Automatic   Arial   12 02/02/95 12:06 PM   Ready

Figure 4 - 1

PERFORMING CALCULATIONS IN THE WORKSHEET

As you have already discovered, proper formulas are the basis of all calculations in *Lotus*. When you calculate values in a worksheet using a formula, your data is dynamic. If the referenced values included in a formula change, so does the result of the formula.

WHAT ARE FORMULAS?

A formula is an entry in a cell that calculates data. Up to this point, the calculations we have performed are simple. Now, we are going to perform more complex computations using the data in our worksheet. Formulas can include values, cell addresses, mathematical operand, range names, @functions, and even other formulas. We are going to explore more sophisticated formulas and how they are used within worksheets.

LEVEL OF HIERARCHY IN FORMULAS

Most formulas in a worksheet are numeric formulas. Numeric formulas use + for addition, - for subtraction, * for multiplication, / for division, and ^ for exponentiation. When entering formulas, it is important to remember a rule of mathematics: multiplication and division take precedence over addition and subtraction. Therefore, the formula **+C2-C3*C4** is different from **+(C2-C3)*C4**. The first formula **+C2-C3*C4** first multiplies **C3** and **C4** and then subtracts from the total **C2**. The second formula first subtracts **C3** from **C2** and then multiplies by **C4**. If you find it difficult to remember the precedence, you can always use parentheses around the tasks you want completed first. If you want the addition to take place before the multiplication, use parentheses around the addition.

A review of how to enter a formula using pointing:

- Select the cell to contain the formula.

- Type the plus (+) sign.

- Click on the first cell containing the data that should be part of the formula.

- Type a mathematical operator. The symbols for the mathematical operators are:

Operator	Used For:
+	Addition
-	Subtraction
*	Multiplication
/	Division
^	Exponentiation

- Repeat the last two steps until the formula is complete. **DO NOT** type a mathematical operator or an equal sign after the last cell address.

- Press **ENTER** or click on the **Confirm** Button.

Activity 4.1: Entering More Complex Formulas

1. Use **FILE/Open** to select the file **INVEST**.

2. Use pointing to place a formula in cell **F5** that will multiply the number of shares (**C5**) by the market value per share (**E5**). The formula should be **+C5*E5**.

   If you do not remember how to use pointing, look back at the Entering Formulas section of Lesson 1.

3. Use pointing to place a formula in cell **G5** that will subtract the Cost (**D5**) from the Dec 31 Total Market Value (**F5**). The formula should be **+F5-D5**.

   If the Market Value is higher, you want the result to be positive, which means there is an overall increase. If the Market Value is lower than the cost, you want the result to be negative, showing that there is an overall decrease.

4. Use pointing to place a formula in cell **H5** that will divide the Increase (Decrease) (**G5**) by the Cost (**D5**). The formula should be **+G5/D5**.

   Hint: Use the horizontal scroll bar to enable column H to be viewed.

5. Use pointing to place a formula in cell **I5** that will add the Cost and the Dec 31 Total Market Value and then divide by 2. The formula should be **+(D5+F5)/2**.

   You need to enclose the cell addresses (D5 and F5) in parenthesis so Lotus knows to do the addition before the division. Rules of mathematics would perform the division before the addition.

6. Use **EDIT/Copy** or use the **Copy to the Clipboard** SmartIcon to copy all the formulas you just created to rows **6** through **16**.

   If you do not remember how to use the Copy function, look back at Lesson 3.

7. **Format** the values in the **F**, **G**, and **I** columns as **, Comma, 0** decimal places. Format the values in the **H** column as **Percent, 2** decimal places. Your document should look like Figure 4 - 2.

   Note: Use the horizontal scroll bar to view various horizontal sections of the worksheet.

	Number of Shares	Cost (plus fees)	Dec 31, 95 Market Value Per Share	Dec 31, 95 Total Mkt Value	Increase (Decrease) Overall	Percentage Increase (Decrease)	Average Market Value
5	100	5,805	65.25	6,525	720	12.40%	6,165
6	100	11,250	62.50	6,250	(5,000)	-44.44%	8,750
7	500	15,250	45.50	22,750	7,500	49.18%	19,000
8	200	4,562	75.87	15,174	10,612	232.62%	9,868
9	300	6,252	32.50	9,750	3,498	55.95%	8,001
10	500	35,251	62.25	31,125	(4,126)	-11.70%	33,188
11	250	2,652	21.50	5,375	2,723	102.68%	4,014
12	1,000	20,052	22.50	22,500	2,448	12.21%	21,276
13	600	6,025	7.75	4,650	(1,375)	-22.82%	5,338
14	400	45,251	125.50	50,200	4,949	10.94%	47,726
15	800	45,258	62.50	50,000	4,742	10.48%	47,629
16	200	6,253	45.50	9,100	2,847	45.53%	7,677

Figure 4 - 2

8. **SAVE** your file as **INVEST1**.

9. **CLOSE** your file.

UNDERSTANDING FUNCTIONS

Lotus contains many built-in functions. These functions, **@functions**, are built-in formulas that perform specialized calculations automatically. The purpose of these @functions is to make using worksheets easier. Some @functions perform simple calculations such as adding a range of cells or averaging a range of cells. Other @functions perform more complex calculations such as the Net Present Value of a Series of Cash Flows. In this lesson, we will concentrate on how to use simple @functions in our worksheet.

Using Simple @Functions in Your Worksheet

The five simple statistical functions we will learn are:

@SUM	Adds a list of values
@AVG	Averages a list of values
@MAX	Finds the highest value in a range
@MIN	Finds the lowest value in a range
@COUNT	Counts the **nonblank** cells in a range

The calendar function we will learn is:

@TODAY	Places today's date in a cell

@SUM

The **@SUM** function is used to add a range or a named range of cells. The format of the function is **@SUM(RANGE)**. If you want to add a range of cells starting at **C5** and ending at **C25**, the formula would look like: **@SUM(C5..C25)**. (The word **SUM** and the cell addresses *do not* have to be in upper case.) As you can easily see, using the **@sum** function can save a significant amount of time. Rather than typing the plus sign and all the cell locations, you simply have to type @sum and the range you want to add.

@AVG

The **@AVG** function is used to average a range or a named range of cells. The format of the function is **@AVG(RANGE)**. If you want to average a range of cells starting at **C5** and ending at **C25**, the formula would look like: **@AVG(C5..C25)**. Again you can see how easy it is to compute an average. It is not necessary to add every cell and divide by the number of entries. *Lotus* performs those computations for you.

@MAX

The **@MAX** function is used to determine the highest value in a range or a named range of cells. The format of the function is **@MAX(RANGE)**. If you need to determine the largest entry in a range of cells starting at **C5** and ending at **C25**, the formula would look like: **@MAX(C5..C25)**. If you have a large worksheet and it is necessary to determine the highest value in a column or a row, the **@MAX** function does that for you.

@MIN

The **@MIN** function is used to determine the lowest value in a range or a named range of cells. The format of the function is **@MIN(RANGE)**. If you need to determine the smallest entry in a range of cells starting at **C5** and ending at **C25**, the formula would look like: **@MIN(C5..C25)**.

@COUNT

The **@COUNT** function counts the **nonblank** cells in a range or a named range of cells. Often, it is necessary to determine the number of entries there are within a column or a row. The **@COUNT** function can determine how many non-blank entries there are within a column, row, or range of cells. The format of the function is **@COUNT(RANGE)**. If you need to determine the number of nonblank cells in a range of cells starting at **C5** and ending at **C25**, the formula would look like: **@COUNT(C5..C25)**.

@TODAY

The **@TODAY** function calculates the date number that corresponds to the current date on the computer's clock. This function counts the number of days since January 1, 1900, and places that number into the cell. Then, you can format the number in one of many date formats to have the number appear as today's date. The date is recalculated whenever your date is recalculated.

To type in an @function:

- Select the cell to contain the formula.

- Type the @ symbol

- Type the name of the function

- Type the left parenthesis

- Select the range of cells

- Type the right parenthesis

To select an @function using the @function selector:

- Select the cell to contain the formula.

- Click on the **@function selector** [@].

- If the @function you want appears on the @function menu, select it. (See the next section if the @function you want does not appear initially.)

  After the function is selected, it appears in the cell with a placeholder in the form of the word **list** *enclosed in parenthesis.*

- Use the mouse to select the range or type the range address to be used with the @function.

  When the range is selected it will replace the placeholders in the @function.

- Click on the **Confirm** button or press the **ENTER** key.

To add an @function to the @function selector menu:

- Select the cell to contain the formula.

- Click on the **@function selector**.

- Select **List All**.

- If you know the category of the **@function** you want, select the category from the **Category** drop-down list box.

- Select the **@function** from the **@functions** list box.

- Select **OK**.

- Now you can access the @function from the **@function selector**.

- Follow the steps for selecting an @function using the **@function selector** (see above).

Activity 4.2: Entering @Functions

1. Use **FILE/Open** to select the file **INVEST1** if the file is not already open

2. Place your cell pointer in cell **A19**. Enter labels as indicated:

Cell	Label	Alignment
A19	**Average**	**Center**
A20	**Highest**	**Center**
A21	**Lowest**	**Center**
A22	**Number of Investments**	**Center**

PROBLEM SOLVER*: If you want to center align these labels using the **Center data** SmartIcon but it is not displayed as one of your SmartIcons, click on the **SmartIcons Selector** and click on **Default sheet**. Now the **Center data** SmartIcon appears.*

3. Make sure you can see all the values in column **D** and down at least to row **18**. Place your cell pointer in cell **D18**. In cell **D18** you want to **SUM** the cost of all your investments. To do this, type: **@SUM(**

4. Use the mouse to select the range **D5..D16**. Close the parenthesis.

5. Press **ENTER**.

6. **Copy** the formula in cell **D18** to cells **F18** and **G18**.

7. Place your cell pointer in cell **D19**. In cell **D19** you want to **AVERAGE** the cost of all your investments. To do this, click on the **@function selector**.

*Your screen now resembles Figure 4 - 3, although your **@function selector** menu may contain different or additional choices.*

@ function selector list

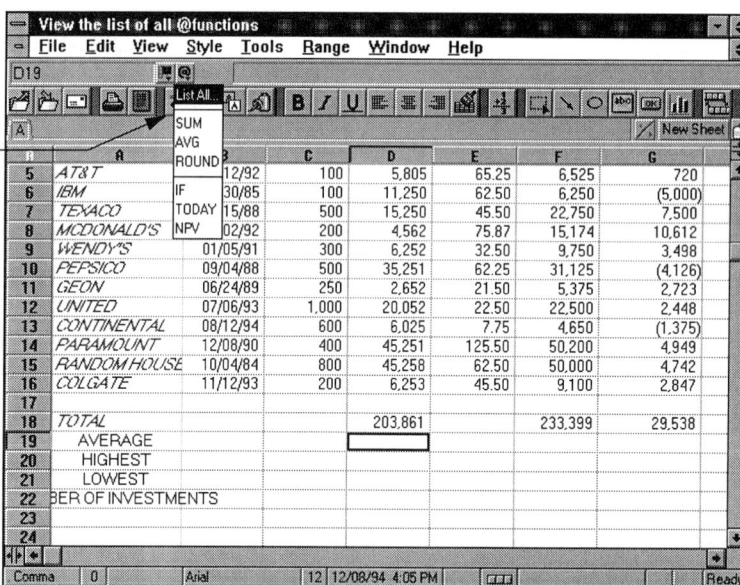

Figure 4 - 3

8. Click on **AVG**.

9. Use the mouse to select the range **D5..D16**.

10. Press **ENTER**.

11. **Copy** the formula in cell **D19** to cells **F19** and **G19**.

12. Place your cell pointer in cell **D20**. In cell **D20** you want to find the **HIGHEST** cost of all your investments. To do this, click on the **@function selector**.

13. Click on **List All**.

    Your screen should show a dialog box like the one in Figure 4 - 4.

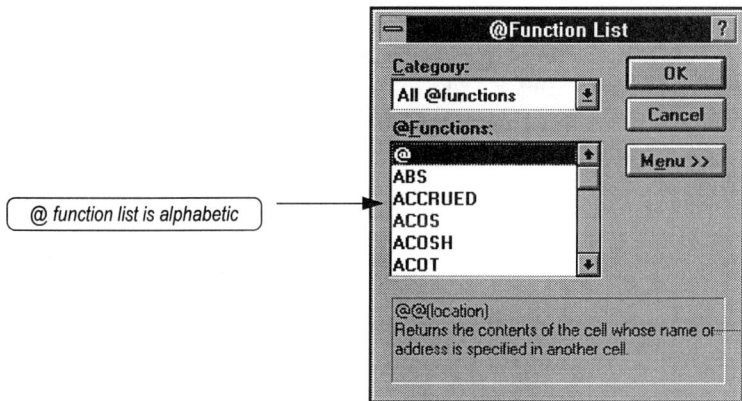

Figure 4 - 4

14. Scroll down the alphabetic list of @functions until you find **MAX**. Select **MAX** and click on **OK**.

15. Use the mouse to select the range **D5..D16**.

16. Press **ENTER**.

17. **Copy** the formula in cell **D20** to cells **F20** and **G20**.

18. Place the **@MIN** formula for the same range in cell **D21** using one of the above methods and copy the resultant formula to cell **F21** and **G21**.

19. Place the **@COUNT** formula in cell **D22** using one of the above methods.

20. **Format** all of the formulas in rows 18 to 22 for **, Comma** notation with **0** decimal places. Click on cell **A5** to remove the selection.

    The results of your work should be the same as Figure 4 - 5.

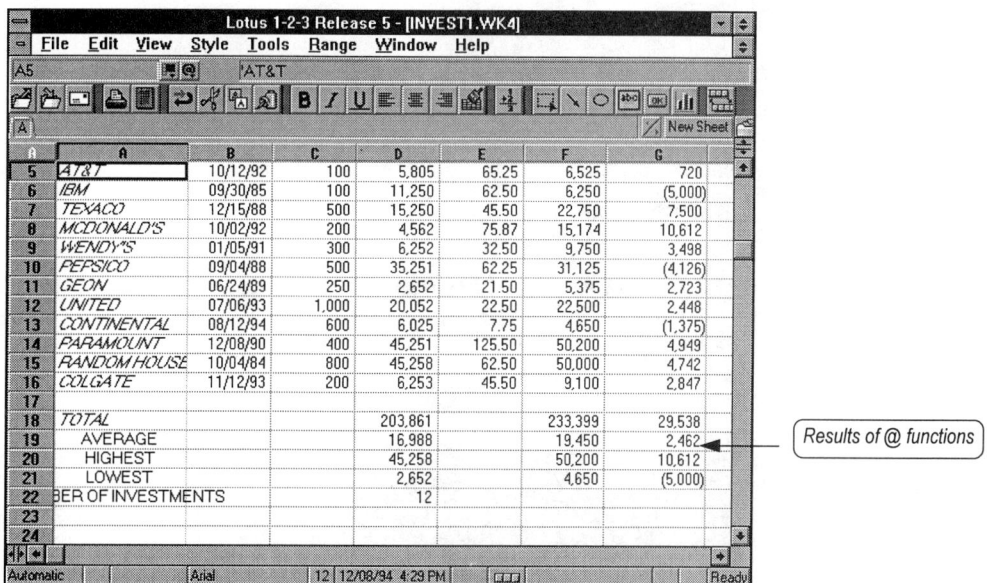

Figure 4 - 5

21. Before we **Save** the file, we want to place today's date in the top left corner. Place the cell pointer in cell **A3**.

22. Type **@TODAY**. Press **ENTER**.

23. Format cell **A3** using one of the date formats. To do this, select **STYLE/Number Format** from the Menu Bar. At the **Number Format** dialog box, click on **Dates** in the **Format** list box. Select one of the formats in the **Dates** list box. The one you select is up to you. If you do not like your choice, select another. Now today's date is in the top left corner of the worksheet.

24. **Save** your file as **INVEST2**.

25. **Close** your file.

DISPLAYING AND PRINTING FORMULAS

After completing a worksheet with complex formulas, many people like to print the worksheet and the formulas to document their work. This also serves as a tool to debug you worksheet if there are problems or errors within the worksheet. Debugging is the process of locating and correcting errors.

In *Lotus*, you can use **Text** format to display the formula within a cell rather than the results of the formula. When you change from displaying the value to displaying the text, *Lotus* will display the formula within a cell left aligned. If a formula is too long to fit within the cell, the formula is truncated unless the cell to the right is blank. If the cell to the right is empty, the formula will overflow to the right and display in full.

In this next activity we are going to document the formulas within the worksheet we completed above by displaying the formulas. We can then add any additional notes to the worksheet and print it out.

To Display and Print the Formulas within a Worksheet:

- Select the range of cells you want to format as text.

- From the menu select **STYLE/Number Format**.

- The Format you want is **Text**.

- Click on **OK**.

Activity 4-3: Displaying and Printing the Worksheet formulas

1. Use **FILE/Open** to select the file **INVEST2** if the file is not already open.

2. Select the cells **D18..G22**.

3. Select **STYLE/Number Format**. See Figure 4 - 6.

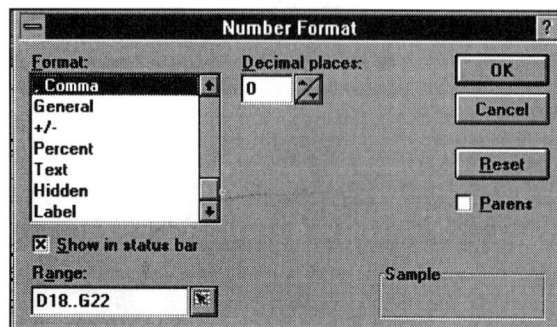

Figure 4 - 6

4. Scroll down the format list box until **Text** appears. Click on **Text**.

5. Click on **OK**.

   *Unfortunately, the data in cells **F18..F21** is truncated because the column is not wide enough. However, if the F column is made wider, we will have complete documentation of the formulas placed at the bottom of the worksheet.*

6. Make the **F** column wider by grabbing the right side of the column heading.

7. Make the column as wide as is necessary to see the entire formula. See Figure 4 - 7.

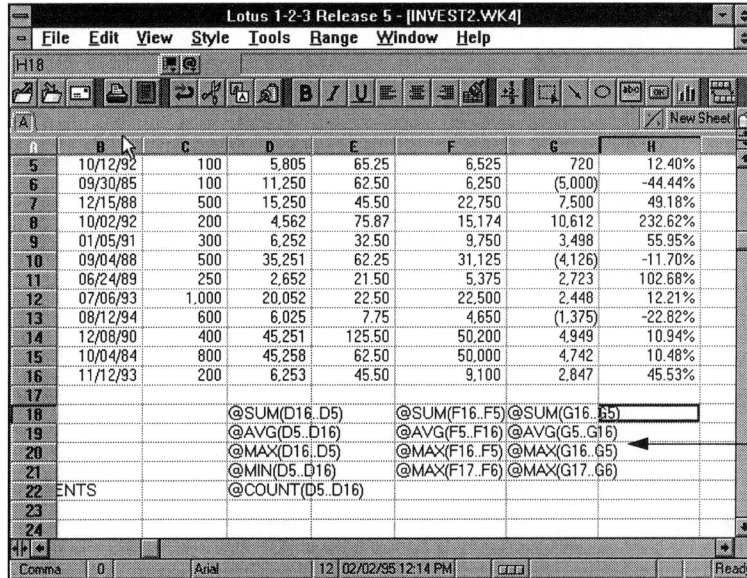

Figure 4 - 7

8. Print the worksheet by selecting **File/Print** or clicking on the **Print** Icon.

9. When the formulas are printed as text they will look like Figure 4 - 8.

10. **Save** your file as **INVEST3**.

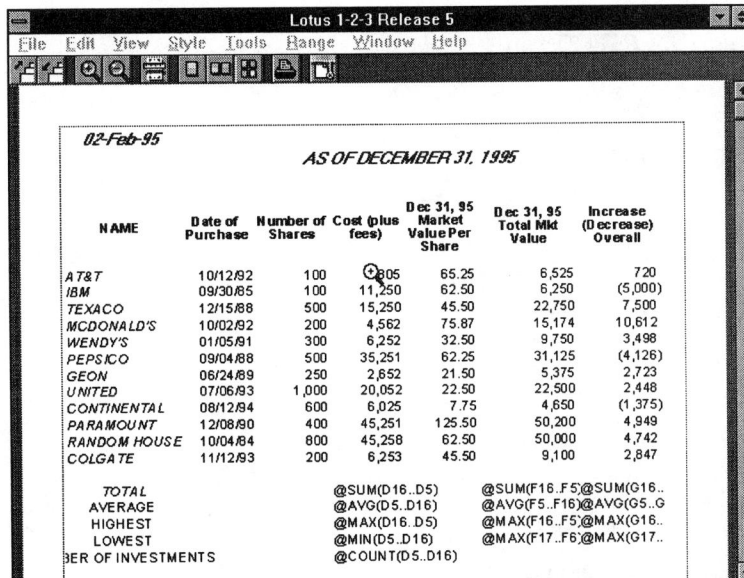

Figure 4 - 8

SUMMARY

In this lesson you learned how to use a few Lotus' built-in functions. The purpose of these @ functions is to make using worksheets easier. Also, by using the @ function selector, you just have to point at the function and click. No typing is required. The skills you learned in this lesson are summarized in the Key Terms. You may practice these skills by working through the Independent Projects.

KEY TERMS

@ Functions	@SUM	Mathmatical Operator
@AVG	@TODAY	Ranges
@COUNT	Complex Formulas	Text Format
@Function Selector	Formula	
@MAX	Levels of Heirarchy	

INDEPENDENT PROJECTS

Independent Project 4.1: Using Functions and Formulas Within Your Worksheet

In this exercise, you will practice entering formulas and built-in functions into your worksheet. Your completed worksheet will look like Figure 4 - 9.

	A	B	C	D	E	F	G	H
5								
6	Categories	02/01/95	02/02/95	02/03/95	02/04/95	02/05/95	Total	
7	Breakfast		7.89	8.99	6.50	4.50	27.88	
8	Dinner		15.50	20.00	22.75	12.00	70.25	
9	Tips		4.21	5.22	5.27	2.97	17.66	
10	Air Fare	358.00					358.00	
11	Car Rental	49.00	49.00	49.00	49.00	49.00	245.00	
12	Hotel	119.00	119.00	119.00	119.00	119.00	595.00	
13	Miscellaneous	5.00	3.50	8.00	2.75	15.00	34.25	
14	Daily Total	$531.00	$199.10	$210.21	$205.27	$202.47	$1,348.04	
15								
16								
17								
18		Minimum	Maximum	Average				
19	Expense	Spent	Spent	Spent				
20	Breakfast	4.50	8.99	6.97				
21	Dinner	12.00	22.75	17.56				
22	Total	$16.50	$31.74	$24.53				
23								

Figure 4 - 9

1. Select **FILE/Open**
2. The file you want to open is **IA4-1**.
3. Place your cursor in cell **B20**. You want to enter a formula to calculate the minimum amount spent on breakfast for your entire trip.
4. Click on the **@function** selector.
5. Click on **List All**.
6. Scroll down until you find **MIN**. Click on it and select **OK**.
7. Select the range **B7..F7**.
8. Press **ENTER**.
9. With your cursor in **B20**, click on the **Copy** icon to copy the data to the clipboard.
10. Place your cursor in cell **B21**.

11. Click on the **Paste** icon. The minimum spent on dinner is now calculated in cell **B21**.

12. Place your cursor in cell **C20**. You want to enter a formula to calculate the maximum amount spent on breakfast for your entire trip.

13. Click on the **@function** selector.

14. Click on **List All**.

15. Scroll down until you find **MAX**. Click on it and select **OK**.

16. Select the range **B7..F7**.

17. Press **ENTER**.

18. With your cursor in **C20**, click on the **Copy** icon to copy the data to the clipboard.

19. Place your cursor in cell **C21**.

20. Click on the **Paste** icon. The maximum spent on dinner is now calculated in cell **C21**.

21. Place your cursor in cell **D20**. You want to enter a formula to calculate the Average amount spent on breakfast for your entire trip.

22. Click on the **@function** selector.

23. Click on **AVG**.

24. Select the range **B7..F7**.

25. Press **ENTER**.

26. With your cursor in **D20**, click on the **Copy** icon to copy the data to the clipboard.

27. Place your cursor in cell **D21**.

28. Click on the **Paste** icon. The average spent on dinner is now calculated in cell **D21**.

29. Place your cursor in cell **B22**. Enter a formula to add cells **B20+B21**.

30. Copy the formula in **B22** to cells **C22..D22**.

31. **FILE/Save** your file as **IA4-1DNE**.

32. **Print** your worksheet.

33. **FILE/Close** your file.

Independent Project 4.2: Entering Formulas and Functions

In this exercise, you will practice entering formulas and functions in your worksheet. This worksheet tracks weather information for a period of time. When you are done, your worksheet should look like Figure 4 - 10.

	A	B	C	D	E	F	G	H	I
1									
2									
3				Weather Information					
4									
5			Temperature (Fahrenheit)			Degree	Snowfall	Centi-	
6	Day	Low	High	Diff.	Average	Days*(inches)		grade	
7									
8	M	15	35	20	25.0	40.0	0.75	1.67	
9	T	26	43	17	34.5	30.5	5.00	6.11	
10	W	28	42	14	35.0	30.0	1.50	5.56	
11	Th	10	38	28	24.0	41.0	0.00	3.33	
12	F	-2	10	12	4.0	61.0	0.25	-12.22	
13									
14					Total Snowfall:		7.50		
15		Average temperature:			25				
16									
17									
18	* Degree days are the number of degrees by which the day's								
19	average temperature is below 65 degrees, the temperature at								
20	which home heating is assumed to begin.								

Figure 4 - 10

1. Select **FILE/Open**.

2. The file you want to open is **IA4-2**.

3. Place your cursor in cell **D8**.

4. In cell **D8**, enter a formula to calculate the difference between the high and the low temperature for the day: **+C8-B8**.

5. Use the icons to copy the formula in **D8** to **D9..D12**.

6. Place your cursor in cell **E8**. You want to calculate the average temperature each day.

7. Click on the **@function** selector.

8. Click on **AVG**.

9. Select the range **B8..C8**.

10. Press **ENTER**.

11. Use the icons to copy the formula in **E8** to **E9..E12**.

12. *Degree days* are the number of degrees by which the day's average temperature is below 65 degrees. This is the point at which it is assumed home heating will begin. Degree days are calculated by subtracting the average temperature from 65 degrees. **(+65-E8)**. Enter the formula in cell **F8**.

13. **Copy** the formula in **F8** to **F9..F12**.

14. Place your cursor in cell **G14**. Use the **@function selector** to total the snowfall in cells **G8..G12**.

15. Place your cursor in cell **E15**. Use the **@function selector** to obtain an average temperature for the week.

16. To convert a Fahrenheit temperature to a centigrade temperature, the formula is: (Fahrenheit temperature - 32)*5/9. You want to convert the Fahrenheit High temperature for the day to centigrade. Place your cursor in cell **H8**. The formula will be: **(+C8-32)*5/9**.

17. **Copy** the formula in **H8** to **H9..H12**.

18. **FILE/Save** your file as **IA4-2DNE**.

19. **Print** your worksheet.

20. **FILE/Close** your file.

Independent Project 4.3: More Practice Entering Formulas and Functions

In this exercise, you practice entering built-in functions and formulas in a worksheet that tracks product sales in your various branch locations. When you are done, your worksheet should look like Figure 4 - 11.

1. **Open** the file **IA4-3**.

2. Place your cursor in cell **B13**.

3. Place a formula in **B13** to add the January Sales for all your branch locations.

4. **Copy** the total in **B13** to cells **C13..D13**.

5. Place a formula in **B14** to average the January Sales for all your branch locations.

6. **Copy** the total in **B14** to cells **C14..D14**.

7. Place a formula in **B15** to calculate the lowest January Sales for all your branch locations.

8. **Copy** the total in **B15** to cells **C15..D15**.

9. Place a formula in **B16** to calculate the highest January Sales for all your branch locations.

	A	B	C	D	E
1					
2	FIRST QUARTER SALES				
3					
4	Branch	January	February	March	
5	White Plains, NY	$164,361	$324,156	$123,456	
6	New York City, NY	567,345	765,435	764,621	
7	Washington, D.C.	345,123	476,587	432,435	
8	Boston, MA	897,453	723,432	632,143	
9	Richmond, VA	983,214	765,456	832,435	
10	Philadelphia, PA	154,325	123,234	175,276	
11	Pittsburgh, PA	234,516	256,473	321,456	
12					
13	Total Sales:	$3,346,337	$3,434,773	$3,281,822	
14	Average:	$478,048	$490,682	$468,832	
15	Minimum:	$154,325	$123,234	$123,456	
16	Maximum:	$983,214	$765,456	$832,435	
17					
18	1st Quarter Total Sales:	$10,062,932			
19	1st Quarter NY Sales:	$2,709,374			
20	1st Quarter PA Sales:	$1,265,280			

Figure 4 - 11

10. **Copy** the total in **B16** to cells **C16..D16**.

11. In cell **B18**, enter a formula to total your sales for all branches for the months of January through March.

12. In cell **B19**, enter a formula to total your sales in the branch locations only within **New York State**.

13. In cell **B20**, enter a formula to total your sales in the branch locations only within **Pennsylvania**.

14. **Format** all your solutions in **Currency** format with **0** decimal places.

15. **FILE/Save** your file as **IA4-3DNE**.

16. **Print** your worksheet.

17. **FILE/Close** your file.

Independent Project 4.4: Creating a Travel and Expense Report

In this exercise, you will complete a worksheet that calculates employee salaries for the week. Some employees are paid on a weekly basis, while others are paid on an hourly basis. If the employee is paid hourly, you need to calculate the gross salary. FICA is calculated as 7.65% of the employee's gross salary. Since all these employees are single with zero exemptions, their State withholding is 7% of their gross salary and their federal withholding is calculated as 14.5% of their gross salary. When you are done, your worksheet might resemble Figure 4 - 12.

	A	B	C	D	E	F	G	H
2	For the week ending:	01/08/94				Single Employees		
3				Gross				Net
4	Employee	Hours	Wage	Pay	FICA	State	Federal	Pay
5	Albert, Joel	80	$6.50	$520.00	$39.78	$36.40	$75.40	$368.42
6	Boyenga, Gladys	80	$5.00	$400.00	$30.60	$28.00	$58.00	$283.40
7	Cruz, Elinor	exempt		$636.00	$48.65	$44.52	$92.22	$450.61
8	Dodd, Doris	78	$3.80	$296.40	$22.67	$20.75	$42.98	$210.00
9	Eisenberg, Sun-Wong	80	$5.50	$440.00	$33.66	$30.80	$63.80	$311.74
10	Farrell, Dudley	exempt		$1,650.00	$126.23	$115.50	$239.25	$1,169.03
11	Glass, Cynthia	exempt		$1,850.00	$141.53	$129.50	$268.25	$1,310.73
12	Harrison, Wilbert	80	$4.50	$360.00	$27.54	$25.20	$52.20	$255.06
13	King, John	76	$5.50	$418.00	$31.98	$29.26	$60.61	$296.15
14	Major, John	exempt		$1,200.00	$91.80	$84.00	$174.00	$850.20
15	Nelson, Charles	exempt		$580.00	$44.37	$40.60	$84.10	$410.93
16	Paige, Carol	exempt		$750.00	$57.38	$52.50	$108.75	$531.38
17	Raymond, Frank	80	$4.50	$360.00	$27.54	$25.20	$52.20	$255.06
18	Stoddard, James	80	$6.50	$520.00	$39.78	$36.40	$75.40	$368.42
19	Thompson, Frederic	75	$7.00	$525.00	$40.16	$36.75	$76.13	$371.96
20	Wagner, George	exempt		$1,800.00	$137.70	$126.00	$261.00	$1,275.30
21	Zandonetta, Bjorn	exempt		$2,000.00	$153.00	$140.00	$290.00	$1,417.00

Figure 4 - 12

1. **Open** the file **IA4-4**.

2. If the employee is an hourly employee, calculate their Gross Pay.

3. Calculate the FICA based on the rate of 7.65% of the Gross Pay for all employees.

4. **Copy** the FICA formula down the **E** column.

5. Calculate the State Withholding based on the rate of 7% of the Gross Pay for all employees.

6. **Copy** the formula down the **F** column.

7. Calculate the Federal Withholding based on the rate of 14.5% of the Gross Pay for all employees.

8. **Copy** the formula down the **G** column.

9. Make the **G** column wider to accommodate all the results.

10. Calculate the Net Pay to each employee by taking the Gross Pay and subtracting FICA, Federal, and State withholdings.

11. **Copy** the formula down the **H** column.

12. Make the **H** column wider to accommodate all the results.

13. **Save** your file as **IA4-4DNE**.

14. **Print** your worksheet.

Absolute and Relative Cell Addressing

Objectives

In this lesson you will learn how to:

- Understand an absolute cell address
- Determine when to use absolute and relative cell addresses

- Understand a relative cell address
- Use the Copy command to copy formulas using absolute and relative cell addresses.

PROJECT DESCRIPTION

In your new job assignment, you have been given worksheet templates created by other employees. You have been asked to fill in these worksheets with current financial information. In doing so, you realize that there are times when you want to enter a formula, and copy the results but have a cell location within the formula remain constant. You pick up your Lotus reference manual and discover there are many types of cell addresses when entering formulas. Now you are going to experiment using these cell addresses.

	A	B	C	D	E	F	
2							
3							
4	EXPECTED ANNUAL GROWTH RATES						
5	SALES		1.04				
6	SALES R&A		2.00%	OF SALES			
7	LABOR		25.00%	OF NET SALES			
8	MATERIALS		17.00%	OF NET SALES			
9	OVERHEAD		150.00%	OF LABOR			
10	SGA		12.00%	OF NET SALES			
11							
12			1994	1995	1996	1997	
13	GROSS SALES		550,000.00	572,000.00	594,880.00	618,675.20	64
14	LESS R&A		11,000.00	11,440.00	11,897.60	12,373.50	1
15	NET SALES		539,000.00	560,560.00	582,982.40	606,301.70	63
16	LESS LABOR		134,750.00	140,140.00	145,745.60	151,575.42	15
17	MATERIALS		91,630.00	95,295.20	99,107.01	103,071.29	10
18	OVERHEAD		202,125.00	210,210.00	218,618.40	227,363.14	23
19	GROSS PROFIT		110,495.00	114,914.80	119,511.39	124,291.85	12
20							
21							

Figure 5 - 1

CELL ADDRESSES

There are eight ways of addressing the contents of a cell in a formula. They are **Absolute, Relative,** and **six** types of **Mixed** cell addresses. So far, we have used only one of these methods — the **relative cell address**. In this chapter we will explore the use of the **Absolute** cell address and briefly introduce the concept of **Mixed** cell addresses. We will not explore **Mixed** cell addresses in too much detail as this concept is beyond the scope of this book.

RELATIVE CELL ADDRESSES

Up to now, we have seen that when a formula or an @function is copied from one cell to another, the resultant formula adjusts accordingly. *Lotus looks at the relationship.* When you create a formula, *Lotus* does not read the cells that are included in the formula but rather the relationship that is exhibited. For example, the formula **+A5+B9** is placed in cell **B7**. *Lotus* looks at the following relationship:

Add the contents of the cell that is **one column** to the **left** and **two rows above** the current cell to the contents of the cell that is **two rows below** the current cell position. Figure 5 - 2 shows how a formula will adjust when it is copied from one cell in the worksheet to another cell in the worksheet.

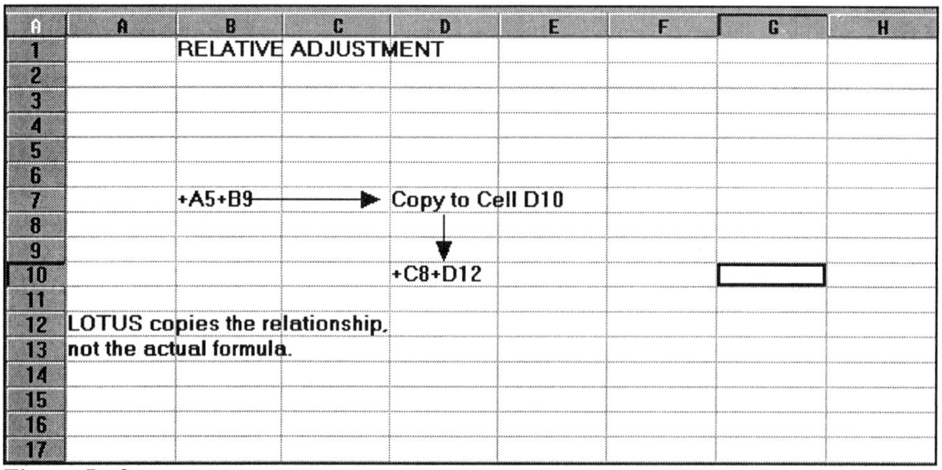

Figure 5 - 2

ABSOLUTE ADDRESSES

There are times when you do *not* want a cell address or cell addresses within a formula to adjust when the formula is copied from one cell to another. Formulas that always refer to the same columns or rows no matter where they are copied or moved to contain what are called **absolute addresses**. **Absolute** cell references contain dollar signs before the column and the row location (i.e., **$A$19**). When a cell is addressed as **absolute** within a formula, it will not adjust when it is copied to another cell location. This is illustrated in Figure 5 - 3.

MIXED ADDRESSES

Mixed addresses are part relative and part absolute. In their simplest form they are half relative and half absolute. Two types of mixed addresses are column relative and row absolute (**B$19**) and column absolute and row relative (**$B19**). There are times when using mixed addresses can save you a significant amount of time when copying formulas. Figure 5 - 4 and Figure 5 - 5 show how a formula is adjusted with mixed addresses.

#	A	B	C	D	E	F	G	H
1		ABSOLUTE CELL ADDRESS						
2								
3								
4								
5								
6								
7		+$A$5+B9	→	Copy to Cell D10				
8								
9				↓				
10				+$A$5+D12				
11								
12	The portion of the formula							
13	that is ABSOLUTE is not							
14	adjusted.							
15								
16								

Figure 5 - 3

#	A	B	C	D	E	F	G	H
1		MIXED CELL ADDRESS						
2		Column Relative and Row Absolute						
3								
4								
5								
6								
7		+A$5+B9	→	Copy to Cell D10				
8								
9				↓				
10				+C$5+D12				
11								
12	The column does a relative							
13	adjustment, the row is absolute.							
14								
15								
16								
17								

Figure 5 - 4

#	A	B	C	D	E	F	G	H
1		MIXED CELL ADDRESS						
2		Column Absolute and Row Relative						
3								
4								
5								
6								
7		+$A5+B9	→	Copy to Cell D10				
8								
9				↓				
10				+$A8+D12				
11								
12	The column does not adjust,							
13	the row does a relative							
14	adjustment.							
15								
16								
17								

Figure 5 - 5

To enter formulas using absolute and relative cell addresses:

- Select the cell to contain the formula.

- Type the plus (+) sign.

- Click on the first cell containing the data that should be part of the formula. If you want the cell address to be an absolute address perform the next step.

- Press the **F4** key. The **F4** key will change the cell reference from relative to absolute.

- Type a mathematical operator.

- Repeat the last three steps until the formula is complete.

Activity 5.1: Entering Formulas Using Absolute and Relative Cell Addresses

1. Use **FILE/Open** to select the file **ABSREL**.

2. Place your cell pointer in cell **D13**. You will use pointing to place a formula in cell **D13** that will multiply the prior year's sales (**C13**) by the expected annual increase per year (**C5**). You will then **copy** the formula across to the other years. When you copy the formula, you want the prior year's sales to adjust (be relative) but you want the cell containing the growth rate to remain the same (be absolute). The formula should be **C13*$C$5**.

3. To enter the formula, first type the + (plus) sign.

4. Point to and click on cell **C13**.

5. Type the * (asterisk) to tell *Lotus* to multiply.

6. Click on cell **C5**. Before pressing **ENTER**, press the **F4** key **once**. Cell **C5** now becomes **$C$5 (an absolute cell address)**. See Figure 5 - 6.

✓ **Problem Solver**: *If you press F4 more than once, you will have a different kind of cell reference for C5. Continued pressing of F4 scrolls you through a variety of addresses. Keep pressing F4 until you see $C$5.*

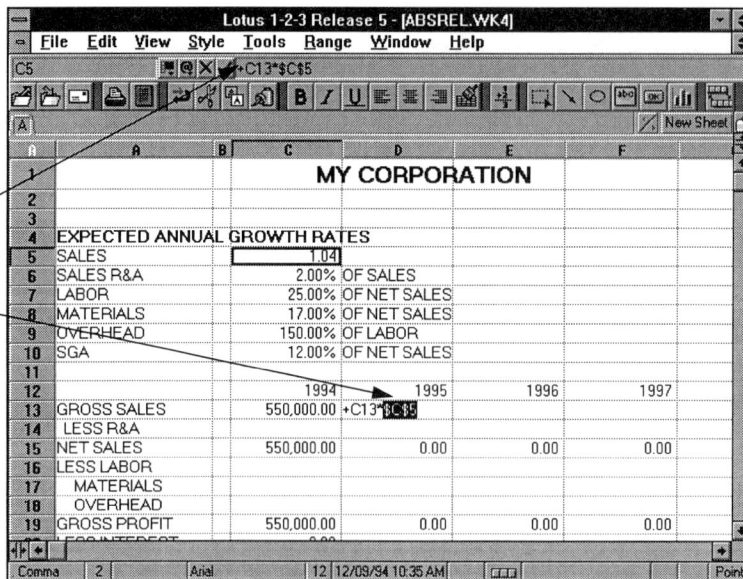

Cell C5 becomes absolute ($C$5) by pressing the F4 key once!

Figure 5 - 6

7. Press **ENTER**.

8. Copy the formula to cells **E13** through **G13**.

Problem Solver: *If you select too large a range to the right (i.e., out to column H),* **do not** *release the mouse button. Simply drag to the left until the proper range is selected.*

9. Select cell **F13**. Notice that while the gross sales figure cell reference has adjusted from the formula in **D13** (which is +**C13*$C$5**), the sales figure cell reference has remained the same (it is **absolute**).

10. Place your cell pointer in cell **C14**. You will use pointing to place a formula in cell **C14** that will multiply the current year's sales (**C13**) by the expected Sales Returns and Allowances Percentage (**C6**). You will then **copy** the formula across to the other years. When you copy the formula, you want the sales to adjust (be relative) but you want the cell containing the percentage rate of returns to remain the same (be absolute). The formula should be **C13*$C$6**.

11. To enter the formula, first type the + (plus) sign.

12. Point to and click on cell **C13**.

13. Type the * (asterisk) to tell *Lotus* to multiply.

14. Click on cell **C6**. Press the **F4** key **once**. Cell **C6** now becomes **$C$6**, (an absolute cell address). Press **ENTER**.

15. Copy the formula to cell **D14** through **G14**.

16. Place a formula in cell **C16** that multiplies the **Net Sales** (relative) by the **Labor** percentage in cell **C7** (absolute).

17. Place a formula in cell **C17** that multiplies the **Net Sales** (relative) by the **Materials** percentage in cell **C8** (absolute).

18. Place a formula in cell **C18** that calculates overhead by multiplying the **Labor** figure in cell **C16** (relative) by the percentage in cell **C9** (absolute).

19. Copy the formulas to the other years. Click on cell **A1** to remove any selection. Your results should now look like Figure 5 - 7.

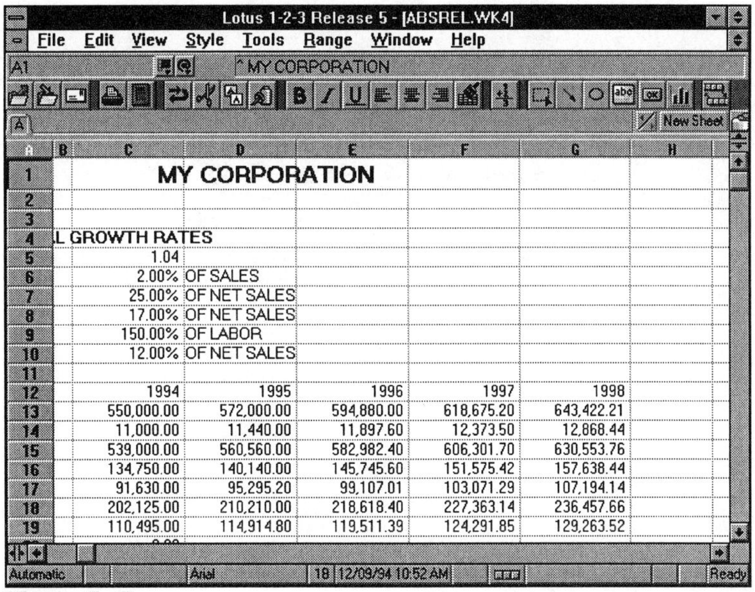

Figure 5 - 7

20. **Save** your file as **ABSREL1**.

21. **Close** your file.

MIXED ADDRESSES

Mixed addresses are part relative and part absolute. In their simplest form they are half relative and half absolute. There are two types of half relative/half absolute mixed addresses: column relative and row absolute (**B$19**) and column absolute and row relative (**$B19**). As you will notice, when creating matrix tables, using mixed addresses can save you a significant amount of time when copying formulas. Sometimes, it is necessary to have a column remain constant, and sometimes it is necessary to have a row remain constant. In the next activity, we will look at how mixed addresses are used in worksheets.

Entering formulas using mixed cell addresses:

- Select the cell to contain the formula.

- Type the plus (+) sign.

- Click on the first cell containing the data that should be part of the formula.

- If you want the cell address to be a mixed address, continued pressing of the **F4** key will change the cell reference from relative to absolute, to the various types of mixed addresses. Scroll through the various **F4** key options until you obtain the correct type of address.

- Type a mathematical operator.

- Repeat the last two steps until the formula is complete.

Activity 5.2: Entering Formulas Using Mixed Cell Addresses

1. Use **FILE/Open** to select the file **MATRIX**.

    In this file, you will notice that the Sales Volumes are all in row 5. You will also notice that the costs are all in column A. It is important to notice this fact because it will affect the copying we will be doing. When we put in our first formula, we want to make sure that, when it is copied, the volume references will remain row 5 and the cost references will remain column A. If we were to use relative cell addresses, if we entered a formula referencing the volume in cell B5 into B6, and then copied the formula from B6 to B7, the cell reference for volume (B5) would change to B6. This obviously is not what we want. We want to place mixed addresses into the formula in cell B6 so the sales volume reference will remain at row 5 when the formula is copied down, and, in addition, so that the cost reference will remain at column A when the formula is copied across.

2. If it is not already there, place your cell pointer in cell **B6**. You will use pointing to place a formula in cell **B6** that will multiply the sales (**B5**) by the cost (**A6**). Then, you will copy the formula across to the other sales volumes and down to the other costs. When you copy the formula across, you want the sales columns to adjust but the cost column to remain constant. When you copy the formula down, you want the cost rows to adjust but the sales row to remain constant. Therefore, the formula should be **B$5*$A6**.

    As to the first cell address in the formula, B$5, by placing the dollar sign in front of row 5 and the not in front of the B column, the row remains constant, but the column will adjust. As to the second cell address in the formula, $A6, by placing the dollar sign in front of column A and the not in front of row 6, the column remains constant, but the row will adjust.

3. To enter the formula, first type the + (plus) sign.

4. Point to and click on cell **B5**.

5. Press the **F4** key **six times**, until the cell address looks like **B$5**.

6. Type the * (asterisk) to tell *Lotus* to multiply.

7. Click on cell **A6**. Before pressing **ENTER**, press the **F4** key seven times. The cell address now looks like **$A6**. See Figure 5 - 8.

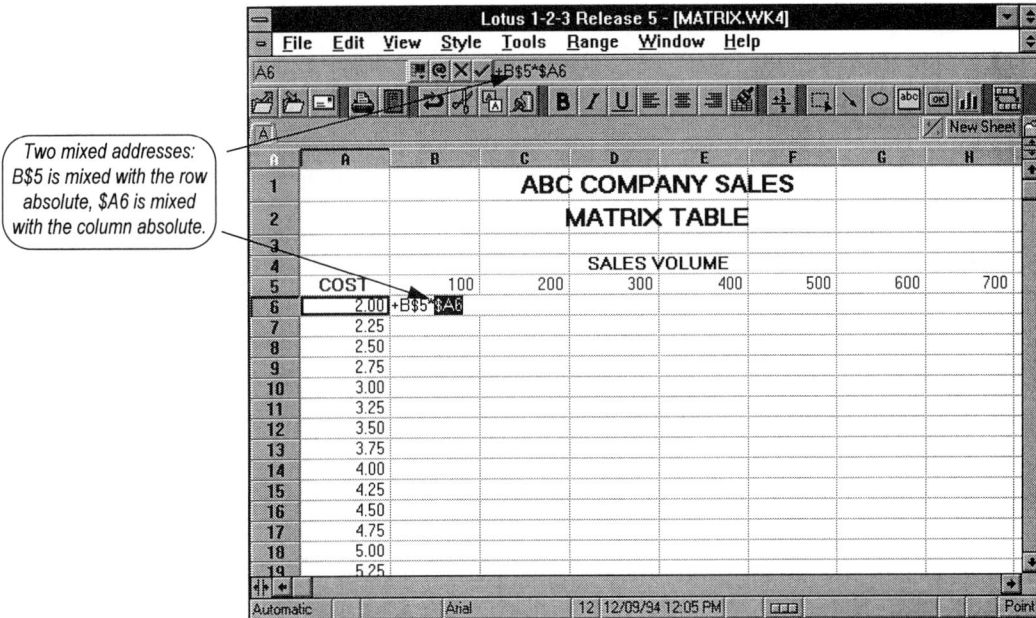

Figure 5 - 8

8. Press **ENTER**.

9. Copy the formula in **B6** to cells **B6** through **H20**.

   *Notice that the range you have selected for copying includes the cell you are copying from. You can always copy a formula on top of itself. If you did not include this cell, you could not copy to the entire range at once. By copying a formula on top of itself, you only have to perform one **paste** operation.*

10. Scroll down so that you can see all the figures you have worked on. Click on cell **A2** to remove the selection. Your results should now look like Figure 5 - 9.

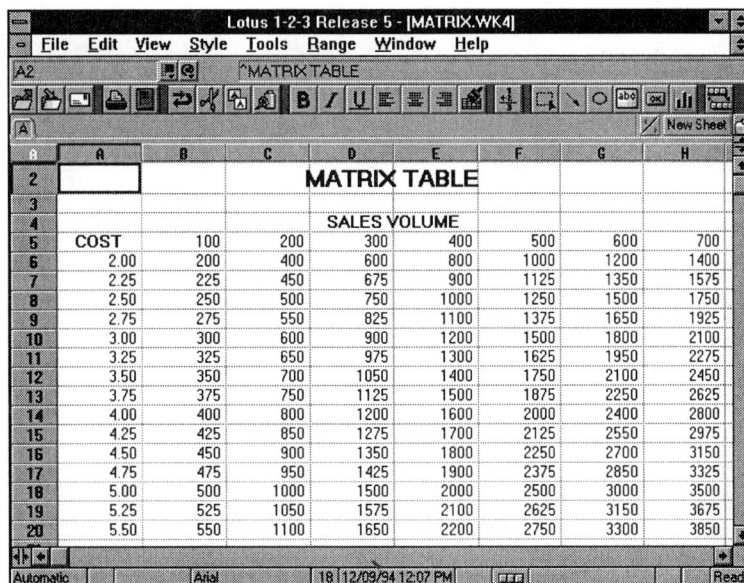

Figure 5 - 9

11. **Format** the results of your formulas as **, Comma** with **2** decimal places. Click on **A2** to remove the selection.

Your final matrix should look like Figure 5 - 10.

	A	B	C	D	E	F	G	H
2				MATRIX TABLE				
3								
4				SALES VOLUME				
5	COST	100	200	300	400	500	600	700
6	2.00	200.00	400.00	600.00	800.00	1,000.00	1,200.00	1,400.00
7	2.25	225.00	450.00	675.00	900.00	1,125.00	1,350.00	1,575.00
8	2.50	250.00	500.00	750.00	1,000.00	1,250.00	1,500.00	1,750.00
9	2.75	275.00	550.00	825.00	1,100.00	1,375.00	1,650.00	1,925.00
10	3.00	300.00	600.00	900.00	1,200.00	1,500.00	1,800.00	2,100.00
11	3.25	325.00	650.00	975.00	1,300.00	1,625.00	1,950.00	2,275.00
12	3.50	350.00	700.00	1,050.00	1,400.00	1,750.00	2,100.00	2,450.00
13	3.75	375.00	750.00	1,125.00	1,500.00	1,875.00	2,250.00	2,625.00
14	4.00	400.00	800.00	1,200.00	1,600.00	2,000.00	2,400.00	2,800.00
15	4.25	425.00	850.00	1,275.00	1,700.00	2,125.00	2,550.00	2,975.00
16	4.50	450.00	900.00	1,350.00	1,800.00	2,250.00	2,700.00	3,150.00
17	4.75	475.00	950.00	1,425.00	1,900.00	2,375.00	2,850.00	3,325.00
18	5.00	500.00	1,000.00	1,500.00	2,000.00	2,500.00	3,000.00	3,500.00
19	5.25	525.00	1,050.00	1,575.00	2,100.00	2,625.00	3,150.00	3,675.00
20	5.50	550.00	1,100.00	1,650.00	2,200.00	2,750.00	3,300.00	3,850.00

Figure 5 - 10

12. **Save** your file as **MATRIX1**.

13. **Print** your sales matrix.

14. **Close** your file.

SUMMARY

In this lesson you learned the difference between absolute, relative, and mixed cell addresses. You also learned when to use each of these cell address types. As you become more experienced in using worksheets you will become more proficient at using the different types of cell addresses in formulas.

KEY TERMS

Absolute Cell Address	**F4**	Relative Cell Address
Cell Address	Mixed Cell Address	

INDEPENDENT PROJECTS

Independent Project 5.1: Using Absolute and Relative Cell Addressing

In this exercise, you will practice entering formulas using absolute and relative cell addresses. The file with which you will be working contains T-shirt sales for the month of March for a group of salespeople. You are going to calculate the total sales, what percentage of shirts were sold each week, and the amount of the commission paid to each salesperson. Your completed worksheet will look like Figure 5 - 11.

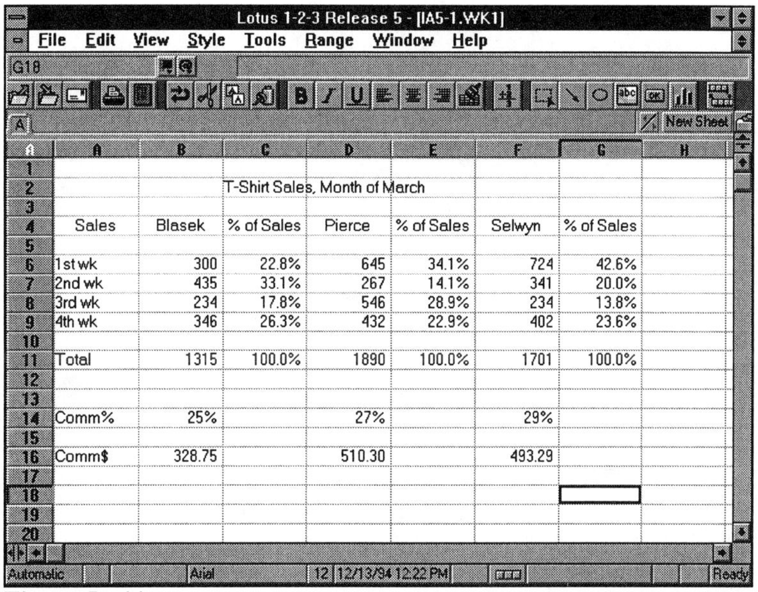

	A	B	C	D	E	F	G	H
1								
2			T-Shirt Sales, Month of March					
3								
4	Sales	Blasek	% of Sales	Pierce	% of Sales	Selwyn	% of Sales	
5								
6	1st wk	300	22.8%	645	34.1%	724	42.6%	
7	2nd wk	435	33.1%	267	14.1%	341	20.0%	
8	3rd wk	234	17.8%	546	28.9%	234	13.8%	
9	4th wk	346	26.3%	432	22.9%	402	23.6%	
10								
11	Total	1315	100.0%	1890	100.0%	1701	100.0%	
12								
13								
14	Comm%	25%		27%		29%		
15								
16	Comm$	328.75		510.30		493.29		
17								
18								
19								
20								

Figure 5 - 11

1. Select **FILE/Open**
2. The file you want to open is **IA5-1**.
3. Place your cursor in cell **B11**. You want to enter a formula to total the sales of this sales person for the four weeks in March.
4. Click on the **@function** selector.
5. Click on **SUM**.
6. Select the range, **B6..B9**.
7. Press **ENTER**.
8. **Copy** the formula in **B11** to **D11**and **F11**.
9. With your cursor in **B11**, click on the **Copy** icon to copy the data to the clipboard.
10. Place your cursor in cell **D11**.
11. Click on the **Paste** icon. The formula was copied to **D11**.
12. Repeat these steps to copy the formula from **B11** to **F11**.
13. Place your cursor in cell **C6**. You want to enter a formula to calculate the first week sales of Ms. Blasek in relation to the Total Sales for the month. Before you create the formula, think ahead. After you create this formula you want to copy it down the **C** column. When you copy the formula, you want the data for the weeks to change (relative adjustment), but you want the total to always remain in cell **B11** (absolute cell reference).
14. The formula should be: **+B6/$B$11**. Type the formula.
15. **Copy** the formula in **C6** to **C7..C9** and **C11**.
16. Place your cursor in cell **E6**. You want to enter a formula to calculate the first week sales of Mr. Pierce in relation to the Total Sales for the month.
17. The formula should be: **+D6/$D$11**. Type the formula.
18. **Copy** the formula in **E6** to **E7..E9** and **E11**.

19. Repeat this process for the values in the **F** column. Place the formula in **G6** and **Copy** the results to **G7..G9** and **G11**.

20. Using **STYLE/Number Format**, format all the values in the **C, E,** and **G** columns as **Percent** with **1** decimal place.

21. Place your cursor in cell **B16**. The commission is calculated by multiplying the Commission Percentage by the Total Employee Sales.

22. The formula should be: **+B11*B14**. Type the formula.

23. Copy the formula in **B16** to **D16** and **F16**.

24. Format the results in row 16 using **Fixed** format with **2** decimal places.

25. **FILE/Save** your file as **IA5-1DNE**.

26. **Print** your worksheet.

27. **FILE/Close** your file.

Independent Project 5.2: Entering Formulas and Functions

In this exercise, you will practice entering formulas using both absolute and relative cell references in your worksheet. The worksheet file we will be using will allow us to calculate projected sales based on an assumed growth rate and an assumed inflation rate. When you are done, your worksheet should look like Figure 5 - 12.

	A	B	C	D	E	F
1						
2		Nationwide Sporting Goods				
3		Projected 1996 National Sales				
4	ASSUME:					
5	Growth Rate =	8.0%		DOLLAR VOLUME SOLD		
6	% Inflation =	2.6%				
7				1996	1996	
8	PRODUCT		1995	(in 1996 $)	(in 1995 $)	
9	Baseball Bats		$16,928	$18,282	$17,819	
10	Olympic Frisbees		$21,064	$22,749	$22,173	
11	Golf Club Sets		$29,374	$31,724	$30,920	
12	Athletic Wear		$23,618	$25,507	$24,861	
13	Kayaks		$13,833	$14,940	$14,561	
14	Tennis Raquets		$19,818	$21,403	$20,861	
15	Camping Equipment		$23,332	$25,199	$24,560	
16	Football Pads		$30,251	$32,671	$31,843	
17	Boxing Gloves		$9,370	$10,120	$9,863	
18						
19	Totals		$187,588	$202,595	$197,461	
20						

Figure 5 - 12

1. Select **FILE/Open**

2. The file you want to open is **IA5-2**.

3. Place your cursor in cell **D9**.

4. In cell **D9**, you want to enter a formula to calculate projected 1996 sales in 1996 dollars. The general format for the formula is: **1995 Sales*(1+Growth Rate)**.

5. In cell **D9** type the formula: **+C9*(1+$B$5)**. The product sales are a relative cell reference because when they recopied, the location of the product sales will change. The growth rate is an absolute cell reference because the growth rate will remain in cell **B5**.

6. **Copy** the formula from **D9** to **D10..D17**.

7. In cell **E9**, you want to enter a formula to calculate projected 1996 sales in 1995 dollars. The general format for the formula is: **1996 Projected Sales/(1+ Inflation Rate)**.

8. In cell **D9** type the formula: **+D9/(1+$B$6)**. The product sales are a relative cell reference because when they are copied, the location of the product sales will change. The inflation rate is an absolute cell reference because the inflation rate will remain in cell **B6**.

9. **Copy** the formula from **E9** to **E10..E17**.

10. **Format** the results calculated in the **D** and **E** columns as **Currency** with **0** decimal places.

11. Place a formula in **D19** and **E19** to sum the columns.

12. **Format** the totals calculated as **Currency** with **0** decimal places.

13. **FILE/Save** your file as **IA5-2DNE**.

14. **Print** your worksheet.

15. **FILE/Close** your file.

Independent Project 5.3: Practice Entering Formulas Using Absolute, Relative, and Mixed Cell References

In this exercise, you practice entering formulas in a worksheet using absolute, relative and mixed cell references. This worksheet will calculate the total sales price by multiplying the price by the quantity assuming different prices, quantities, and discounts. When you are done, your worksheet should look like Figure 5 - 13.

Nationwide Sports Quantity Discount Schedule

A.

price	quantity	total
$3.95	100	395.00
$3.95	200	790.00
$3.95	300	1,185.00

B.

price	quantity	total
$3.95	100	395.00
	200	790.00
	300	1,185.00

C.

				quantity		
market	price	100	200	300	400	500
Chicago	$3.95	395.00	790.00	1,185.00	1,580.00	1,975.00
Los Angeles	$3.95	395.00	790.00	1,185.00	1,580.00	1,975.00
New York	$3.95	395.00	790.00	1,185.00	1,580.00	1,975.00

D. Chicago

				quantity		
item	price	100	200	300	400	500
Baseballs	$3.95	395.00	790.00	1,185.00	1,580.00	1,975.00
Basketballs	$4.95	495.00	990.00	1,485.00	1,980.00	2,475.00
Golf Balls	$0.75	75.00	150.00	225.00	300.00	375.00

Figure 5 - 13

1. **Open** the file **IA5-3**.

2. Place your cursor in cell **C9**.

3. Place a formula in **C9** to multiply the price in **A9** by the quantity in **B9**. The cell locations of both the price and the quantity will adjust as the total is copied down the column. Therefore, the cell addresses of both the price and the quantity should be relative.

4. **Copy** the total in **C9** to cells **C10..C11**.

5. Place a formula in **G9** to multiply the price (which will remain in cell **E9**) by the quantity (which will adjust as the total is copied down the column).

6. **Copy** the total in **G9** to cells **G10..G11**.

7. Place a formula in **C18** to multiply the price by the quantity. Before you enter the formula, remember that you want to enter the formula only once and then copy the results to all other cells. Do not pay attention to the cell values of the price or quantity. You want to enter a formula to multiply the first price by the first quantity: as the formula is copied, both the price and quantity will adjust. To determine the type of cell references you need, make a list of the cell locations of all the prices and a list of the cell references of all the prices. You will notice that all the prices are in the **B** column and all the quantities are in row **16**. Therefore, we need two mixed addresses. The formula is: **+C$16*$B18**.

8. **Copy** the total in **C18** to cells **C18..G20**. (You should always copy a formula onto itself. This saves you from performing the copy multiple times).

9. Place a formula in **C27** to multiply the price by the quantity. Use the same process we used in step 7 to determine the type of cell references necessary.

10. **Copy** the total in **C27** to cells **C27..G29**.

11. Place a formula in **C36** to calculate the price multiplied by the quantity assuming the customer is to receive a quantity discount. The general format for the formula is: **Price*Quantity*(1-Discount)**. Determine the type of cell references the price and quantity need to be by following the same procedure as in step 7. Remember that the cell location of the discount does not change. Therefore, the discount will be an absolute reference.

12. **Copy** the total in **C36** to cells **C36..G38**.

13. **Format** all your solutions in **Comma** format with **2** decimal places.

14. **FILE/Save** your file as **IA5-3DNE**.

15. **Print** your worksheet.

16. **FILE/Close** your file.

Independent Project 5.4: Common Size Income Statements

In this exercise, you will complete a worksheet that is a "Common Size Income Statement". Common Size Income Statements show the costs and expenses for a period in relation to the sales for that period. The purpose of common size statements is to take the numbers away from the statement and only show relationships. These statements are important when performing financial statement analysis. When you are done, your worksheet might resemble Figure 5 - 14.

	A	B	C	D	E	F
1	ECAP CORPORATION					
2						
3	Item:	1995	% 1995	1994	% 1994	
4						
5	Net Sales	300,000	100%	270,000	100%	
6						
7	Cost of Goods Sold	180,000	60%	175,000	65%	
8	Gross Profit	120,000	40%	95,000	35%	
9						
10	General & Administration	50,000	17%	44,000	16%	
11	Selling Expenses	40,000	13%	32,000	12%	
12						
13	Operating Income	30,000	10%	19,000	7%	
14	Interest Expense	5,000	2%	3,500	1%	
15						
16	Income before Taxes	25,000	8%	15,500	6%	
17	Taxes	3,700	1%	2,950	1%	
18						
19	Net Income (Loss)	21,300	7%	12,550	5%	

Figure 5 - 14

1. **Open** the file **IA5-4**.

2. Place your cursor in cell **C5**. Enter a formula to calculate the Net Sales in relation to itself. Before entering the formula, remember when you copy the formula, the numerator of the formula will be the cost or expense category, the denominator will always be the Net Sales.

3. **Copy** the formula down the **C** column.

4. Place your cursor in cell **E5**. Enter another formula to calculate the Net Sales in relation to itself.

5. **Copy** the formula down the **E** column.

6. Format the values in the **B** and **D** columns in **Comma** format with **0** decimal places.

7. Format the values in the **C** and **E** columns in **Percent** format with **0** decimal places.

8. **Save** your file as **IA5-4DNE**.

9. **Print** your worksheet.

Lesson 6

Multiple Worksheets

Objectives

In this lesson you will learn how to:

- Create multiple worksheets in a file
- Use Group mode to format multiple worksheets
- Use the **Insert** command to insert a new worksheet after the current worksheet
- Create formulas that refer to cells in multiple sheets.
- Use the **Copy** command to copy formulas between worksheets

PROJECT DESCRIPTION

In your new position in the accounting department, you have been asked to track income and expenses for all twelve months and to total the results for the year. It would not be a problem to track the monthly results in twelve separate files, but totaling the annual results could be cumbersome. Therefore you refer to your *Lotus* manual and discover you can have up to 256 sheets within each worksheet file. Now you decide to explore how to insert sheets and how to add data between the sheets.

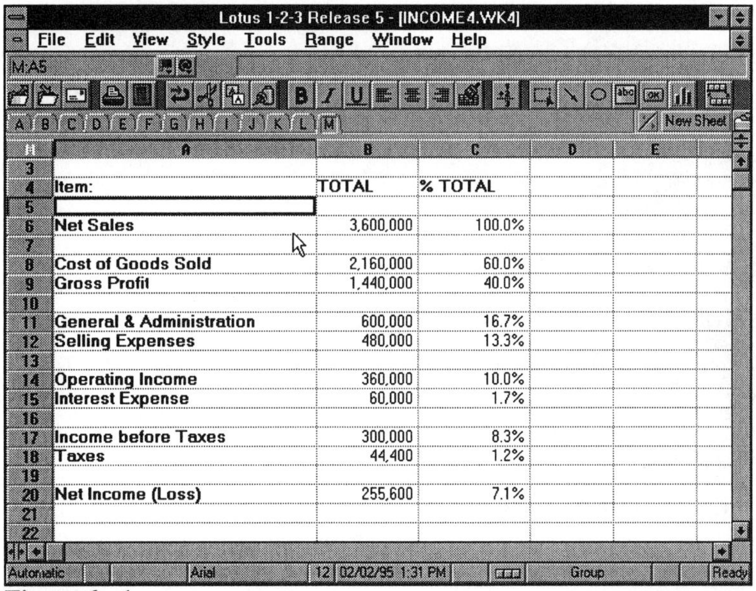

Lotus 1-2-3 Release 5 - [INCOME4.WK4]
File Edit View Style Tools Range Window Help
M:A5
New Sheet
Item:
TOTAL
% TOTAL
Net Sales 3,600,000 100.0%
Cost of Goods Sold 2,160,000 60.0%
Gross Profit 1,440,000 40.0%
General & Administration 600,000 16.7%
Selling Expenses 480,000 13.3%
Operating Income 360,000 10.0%
Interest Expense 60,000 1.7%
Income before Taxes 300,000 8.3%
Taxes 44,400 1.2%
Net Income (Loss) 255,600 7.1%
Automatic
Arial
12 02/02/95 1:31 PM
Group
Ready

Figure 6 - 1

When your spreadsheets become larger, it is often easier to break your file down into multiple segments and place the multiple segments into different worksheets in the same file. You can use multiple worksheets in accounting to perform consolidations or to track monthly financial information and total the results in a final worksheet. Overall, multiple worksheets will allow you to organize information in your file more efficiently and effectively.

MULTIPLE WORKSHEETS

You can insert worksheets before or after the current worksheet. A total of 255 worksheets can be inserted, but this total depends upon the amount of memory available on your system and the number of worksheets in other active files. When you begin a new file, *Lotus* provides you with a single worksheet, which it lables **A**. When you add new sheets, *Lotus* assigns the labels **B**, **C**, **D**, etc. to each consecutive new sheet.

To insert one worksheet at a time:

Using the **New Sheet** button is the quickest way to insert one sheet at a time. Each time you click on the **New Sheet** button, one worksheet is inserted **after** the current worksheet.
- Click on the **New Sheet** button `New Sheet`

To insert a specified number of worksheets:

The **New Sheet** button inserts only one sheet at a time. If you want to insert more than two or three sheets, there is a more efficient method of inserting sheets. This method is also the only method available if inserting sheets **before** the current sheet.

- Choose **EDIT/Insert**.

- The **Insert** dialog box appears.

- Click on **Sheet**.

- Select **Before** or **After**.

  This will determine if you want the sheet(s) inserted before or after the current sheet.

- In the **Quantity** spin box, either click on the up or down arrow to select the quantity desired, or click in the **Quantity** text box and type in the number of worksheets you want to insert.

- Click on **OK**.

Activity 6.1: Inserting Multiple Worksheets

1. Use **FILE/Open** to select the file **INCOME**.

   *This worksheet contains the Income Statement for **ECAP CORPORATION** for the month of January. We are going to expand this worksheet so it contains the Income Statements for January through December, and place a summary Income Statement at the end totaling all items at the end of the year.*

2. Choose **EDIT/Insert**. The **Insert** dialog box will appear (Figure 6 - 2).

3. Click on **Sheet**.

   *The **Before** and **After** option buttons, and the **Quantity** spin box, appear in the **Insert** dialog box.*

4. Verify that **After** is selected, so that we will place the number of sheets we choose **after** the January worksheet.

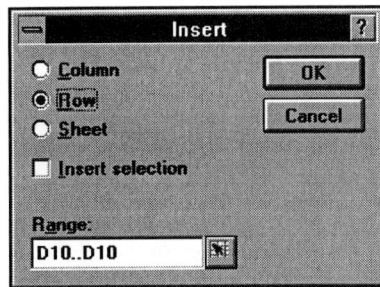

Figure 6 - 2

5. In the **Quantity** box, click on the up arrow until you scroll to the number **12**. This tells *Lotus* we want 12 worksheets inserted **after** the current sheet.

6. Click on **OK**.

   Although it appears that all your data has disappeared, it has not. In order to understand where your data is, let's look at various parts of your screen. See Figure 6 - 3.

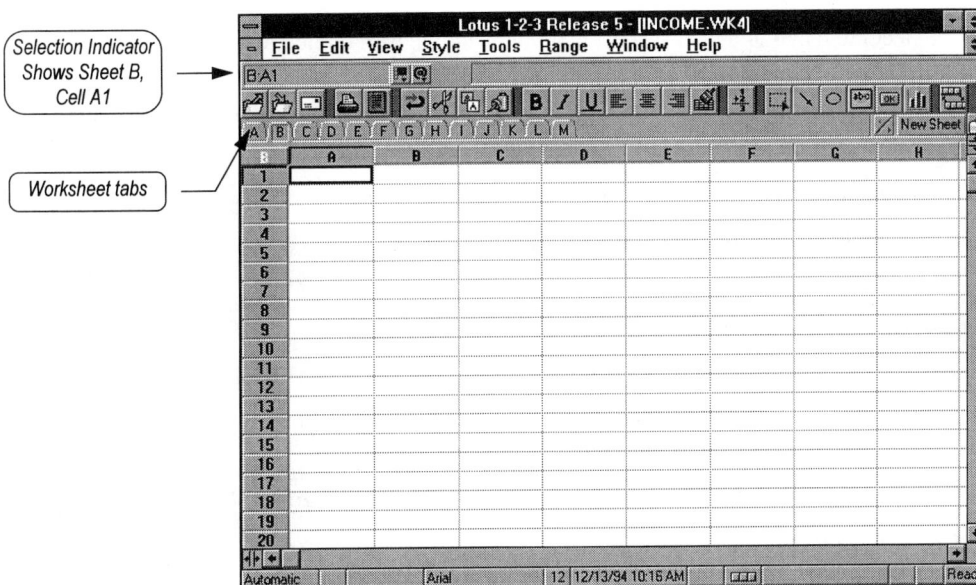

Figure 6 - 3

*Your Selection Indicator now reads **B:A1** rather than just **A1**. That is because you are no longer in a file with a single worksheet labeled **A**, but rather you are presently in the **B** worksheet of a file containing multiple worksheets. Your cell pointer is in cell **A1**; thus, the address **B:A1** means that your cell pointer is in cell **A1** (following the:) of the **B** worksheet (preceding the :). Another way to determine which is the current worksheet is to look at the Worksheet Letter, to the left of the column labels. Therefore, the reason it appears that your data has disappeared is because you are looking at worksheet **B**, which is presently empty, rather than worksheet **A**, which contains your data. Lotus places you in the next worksheet after the current worksheet when you insert sheets **after** the current sheet.*

Finally, you will notice the Worksheet Tabs just below the SmartIcons. You can use these tabs to move from sheet to sheet. Although you can rename these tabs, the Selection Indicator and Worksheet Letter always reflect the letter originally assigned to that sheet.

7. To move back to sheet **A** click on the **A** Worksheet Tab.

8. **Save** your file as **INCOME1**. DO NOT CLOSE your file.

COPYING DATA BETWEEN SHEETS

Once the basic information is created in the first worksheet and the additional worksheets are inserted, we can use the **Copy** and the **Paste** commands to take information from the first sheet and duplicate it in other or all sheets. The **Copy** and **Paste** commands work the same way over multiple worksheets as they do within one worksheet.

To copy data between sheets:

*   Select the range to **Copy**.

*   Click on the **Copy to the Clipboard** [SmartIcon] SmartIcon.

    *The title bar now says, **Select destination and press ENTER or choose Edit Paste**.*

*   Use the mouse to select the cell or range of cells to receive the copied information:

    *   Move the mouse pointer to one corner of the range in the same worksheet, just as you would in an ordinary copy and paste operation within a single worksheet.

    *   Select the range in the worksheet that you want the data copied to.

*   To copy the information to the same range in more than one consecutive worksheet, hold down the **SHIFT** key and click on the last worksheet tab to be included in whatever range of worksheets you would like to copy the data to.

    Your complete range now appears in the selection indicator.

*   Click on the **Paste Clipboard Contents** [SmartIcon] SmartIcon .

Activity 6.2: Copying Data to Multiple Worksheets

1. Use **FILE/Open** to select the file **INCOME1** if it is not already **OPEN**.

2. You want to place your cell pointer in sheet **A** cell **A1**. Click on the **A** Worksheet Tab if you are not already in worksheet **A**, and press the **HOME** key.

3. Select the range to **Copy**. In this case, you want to select the range **A1..C20**. Use the mouse to select the range.

    *Once your range has been selected, the **Selection Indicator** should read A:A1..A:C20.*

4. Click on the **Copy to the Clipboard** SmartIcon or select **EDIT/Copy**.

    *The title bar now says, **Select destination and press ENTER or choose Edit Paste**.*

5. The destination is going to be the same range in all the other worksheets **B** through **M**. You will use the mouse to select the range of cells to receive the copied information. Click on Worksheet Tab **B**.

6. Make sure the cell pointer is in cell **A1** of worksheet **B**.

    Your Selection Indicator should read B:A1.

    *Since we want all the data we selected from sheet A copied into all the other sheets, we do not have to select the entire paste range in the later sheets. We **only** have to select the starting cell.*

7. To extend the range to all other worksheets, hold down the **SHIFT** key and click on the last Worksheet Tab **M**.

    *Your range of **B:A1..M:A1** now appears in the selection indicator (Figure 6 - 4).*

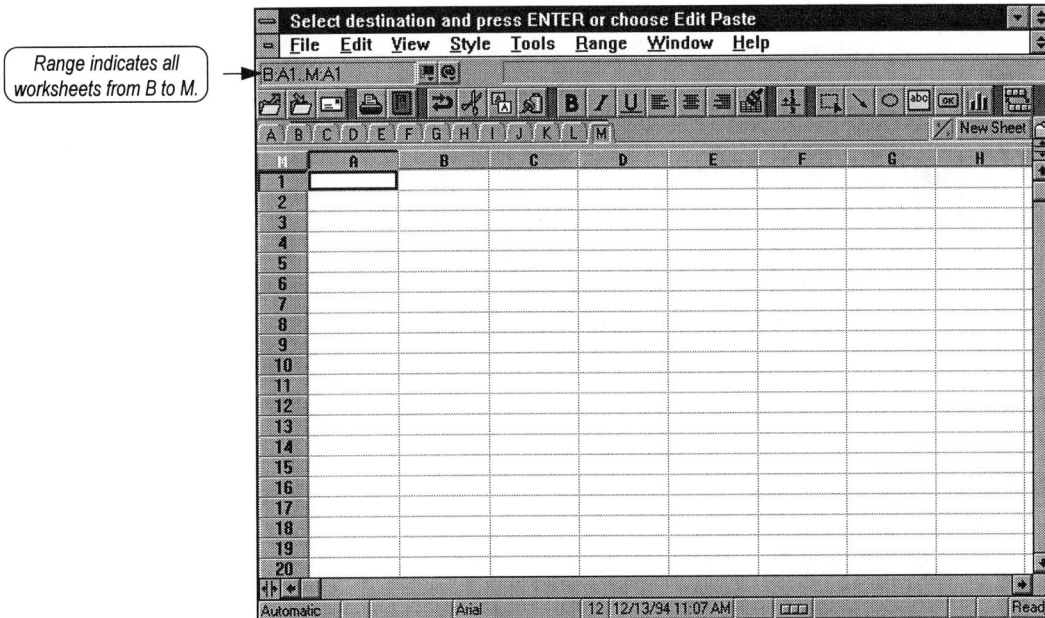

Figure 6 - 4

8. Click on the **Paste Clipboard Contents** SmartIcon or choose **EDIT/Paste**.

   All 13 sheets now contain the same data. All labels and formulas have been copied Next, we simply have to change the months and the financial information, and do some formatting of the data. Click on any of the Worksheet Tabs and you will see the same data.

9. **Save** your file as **INCOME2**.

USING GROUP MODE TO FORMAT MULTIPLE WORKSHEETS

Whenever you copy data from the first worksheet to worksheets inserted later, column widths are not carried from the first sheet to the subsequent sheets. Also, and in our case, if the data in the first sheet was not formatted, the data in the subsequent sheets is also not formatted. Now we will look at how to group the data in the multiple worksheets to improve the appearance of all of the data together.

To group multiple worksheets:

- Place your cell pointer in cell **A1** of worksheet **A**.

- Choose **STYLE/Worksheet Defaults**.

- In the **Other** area of the **Worksheet Defaults** dialog box, click on the **Group Mode** check box

- Click on **OK**.

- The Status Indicator of the of the status bar now displays **Group**.

- Until you turn off *Group* mode, whatever you do on worksheet **A** will also affect all other worksheets. Also, any formatting or changes in column widths that affected worksheet **A** now are reflected in all other worksheets.

Activity 6.3: Grouping Multiple Worksheets

1. Use **FILE/Open** to select the file **INCOME2** if it is not already open.

2. If it is not already there, place your cell pointer in sheet **A** cell **A1**.

3.   Choose **STYLE/Worksheet Defaults**. See Figure 6 - 5.

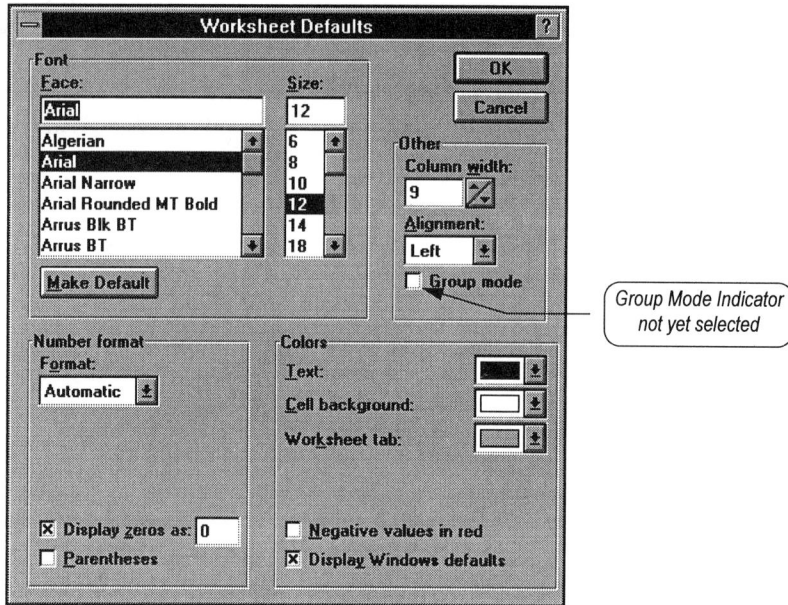

Figure 6 - 5

4.   In the **Other** area of the dialog box, click on the **Group Mode** check box.

5.   Click on **OK**.

*The Status Indicator of the status bar now displays **Group** (Figure 6 - 6).*

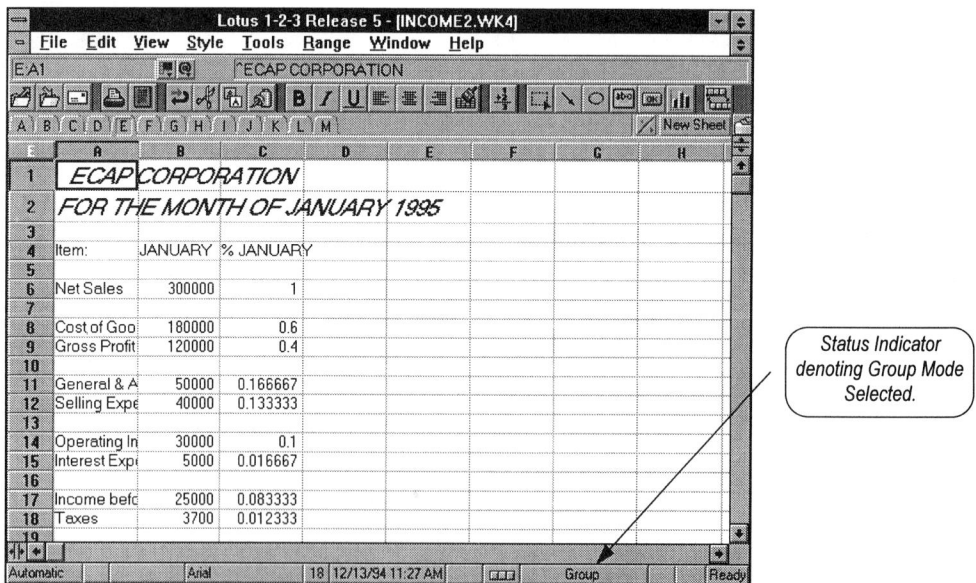

Figure 6 - 6

6.   Click on any Worksheet Tab other than **A**. You will notice that now the widths of the **A** through **C** columns have been expanded just as they were in worksheet **A**.

7.   Return to worksheet **A** by clicking on Worksheet Tab **A**.

8. Select all the labels in the **A** column and click on the **Bold** icon.

9. Click on any Worksheet Tab other than **A**. You will notice that now all the labels in the **A** column of other worksheets are also now bold.

   *Any formatting done in any of the worksheets will affect all other worksheets when **Group** mode is turned on.*

10. In any worksheet, make the labels in **B4** and **C4** bold. Again all other worksheets are affected.

11. **Format** the data in the range **B6..B20** as, **Comma** with **0** decimal places.

12. **Format** the data in the range **C6..C20** as **Percent** with **1** decimal place.

   Notice the formatting follows through for all worksheets (Figure 6 - 7).

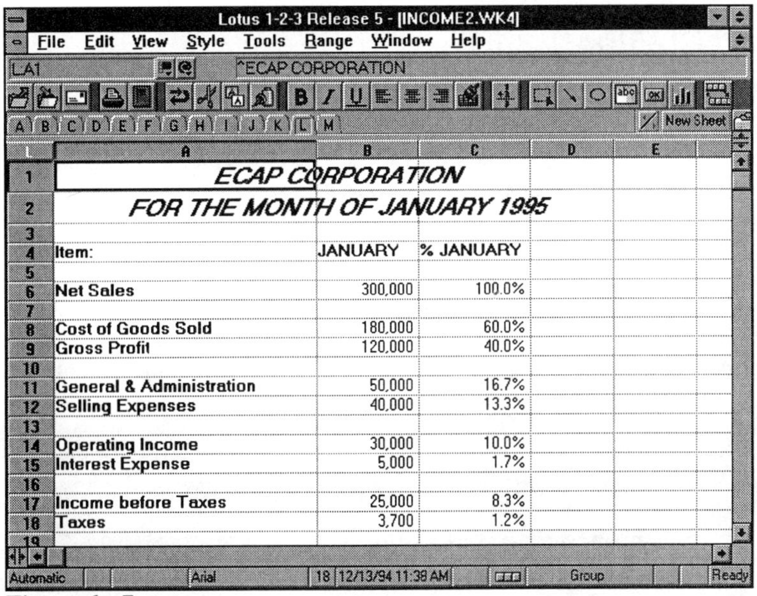

Figure 6 - 7

13. Choose **STYLE/Worksheet Defaults**.

14. In the **Other** area of the dialog box, click on **Group Mode** again to turn off Group mode.

15. Click on **OK**.

   *The Status Indicator of the status bar no longer displays **Group**.*

16. Starting with worksheet **B**, you want to change the second line of the title and the labels for columns **B** and **C** to reflect the correct month (**February** for worksheet **B**, **March** for worksheet **C**, etc.). For sheet **M**, change the second line of the title to read **TOTAL FOR THE YEAR 1995**, and the labels for columns **B** and **C** to read **TOTAL** and **% TOTAL** respectively. Do not worry if some of your column **B** and **C** labels are a little too long to fit within the columns.

17. **Save** your file as **INCOME3**.

CREATING FORMULAS THAT REFER TO CELLS IN MULTIPLE SHEETS

The next step in our process is to create a formula in the last worksheet that will total all of the values in all prior worksheets. We want to create a formula that is a three-dimensional formula. In our case, we can use the **@sum** function to add all the values between sheet **A** and sheet **L**.

To create three-dimensional formulas using @sum:

- Select the cell to contain the formula.

- Select the **@function selector** on the Edit Line.

- Click on **SUM**.

- Click on the Worksheet Tab of the first worksheet to be included, and then click on the first cell to be included in the formula.

- Hold down the **SHIFT** key and click on the Worksheet Tab of the last worksheet to be included in the formula.

- Press **ENTER**.

Activity 6.4: Creating Three-dimensional Formulas Using @sum

1. Use **FILE/Open** to select the file **INCOME3** if it is not already open.

2. Select sheet **M**. Then, select all the data from **B6..B20**. Press the **DELETE** key to erase all prior data.

   We want to create a formula starting in B6 that will total all the data for ECAP for the year. When the data in column B is erased, ERR appears in the column C. Do not be alarmed!

3. Click on cell **M:B6**.

4. Click on the **@function selector** on the Edit Line.

5. Click on **SUM**.

6. Click on the Worksheet Tab for the first worksheet to be included in the formula, sheet **A**, and then click on the first cell to be included in the formula, **A:B6**.

7. Hold down the **SHIFT** key and click on the Worksheet Tab for the last worksheet to be included in the formula, sheet **L**. Your screen should look like Figure 6 - 8.

Lotus 1-2-3 Release 5 - [INCOME3.WK4]		
File Edit View Style Tools Range Window Help		
L:B6 @SUM(A:B6..L:B6)		

	A	B	C	D	E
1	*ECAP CORPORATION*				
2	*FOR THE MONTH OF DECEMBER 1995*				
3					
4	Item:	DECEMBER	% DECEMBER		
5					
6	Net Sales	300,000	100.0%		
7					
8	Cost of Goods Sold	180,000	60.0%		
9	Gross Profit	120,000	40.0%		
10					
11	General & Administration	50,000	16.7%		
12	Selling Expenses	40,000	13.3%		
13					
14	Operating Income	30,000	10.0%		
15	Interest Expense	5,000	1.7%		
16					
17	Income before Taxes	25,000	8.3%		
18	Taxes	3,700	1.2%		
19					

| Comma | 0 | Arial | 12 | 12/13/94 12:00 PM | | | Point |

Figure 6 - 8

8. Press **ENTER**.

   Your total should be 3,600,000. If your total is incorrect, just follow the steps above again carefully. Don't forget to hold down the SHIFT key when selecting the range.

9. Use the **Copy** command to duplicate the formula to cells **B8**, **B9**, **B11**, **B12**, **B14**, **B15**, **B17**, **B18**, and **B20**.

10. Now you can change any of the data in any worksheet and your summary sheet (**M**) will reflect the new totals. Your summary sheet should look like Figure 6 - 9.

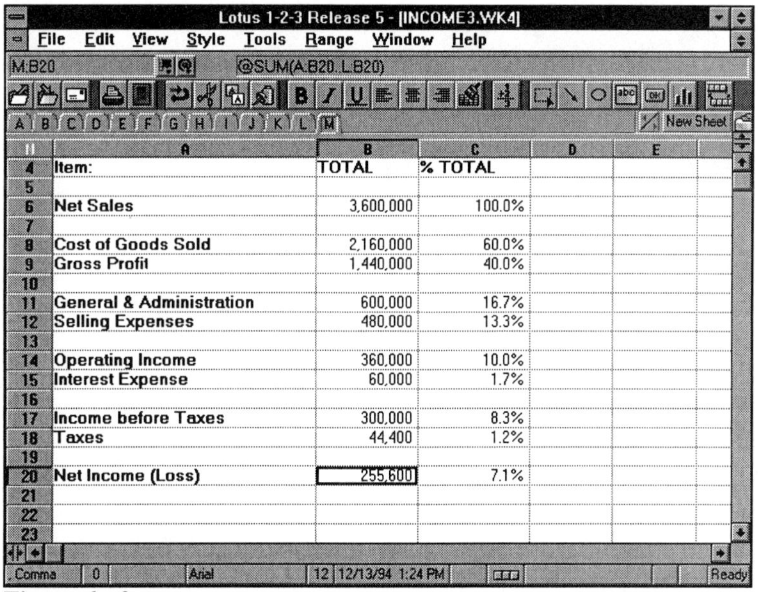

Figure 6 - 9

11. Click on each Worksheet Tab individually and where necessary the **B** and **C** column widths so that the total label in column **B** and the % total label in column **C** fit properly within the column. Refer to Lesson 1 if you need to review changing column width.

12. **Save** your file as **INCOME4**.

SUMMARY

In this lesson you explored how to add sheets to an existing worksheet. Release 5 permits up to 256 sheets within one worksheet file. Release 5 also permits copying from one sheet to another, and the ability to format only one sheet and have all other sheets follow suit by using GROUP mode. Now you can practice the skills you have learned by working through the independent projects.

KEY TERMS

Delete	Insert	Three Dimensional
Edit	Newsheet Button	Formulas
Group Mode		Worksheet Defaults

INDEPENDENT PROJECTS

Independent Project 6.1: Creating Multiple Sheets

In this exercise, you will practice creating multiple sheets in your worksheet. The file with which you will be working contains quarterly salary and billing information for a consulting firm. You are going to create four additional sheets behind the current sheet so you can track all information for the following three quarters and a summary sheet for the year. Sheet **E** of your completed worksheet will look like Figure 6 - 10.

	A	B	C	D	E
1		EMPLOYEE BILLING			
2	For the Year Ended December 31, 1995				
3					
4					
5		*Total*	*Total*		
6	*Employee*	*Salary*	*Billed*	*Profit*	
7	George Snidowski	10,880.00	19,500.00	8,620.00	
8	Claire Corbow	11,335.50	18,525.00	7,189.50	
9	Thomas Henderson	12,325.50	18,000.00	5,674.50	
10	James Dorning	11,050.00	17,500.00	6,450.00	
11	Susan Claremont	9,525.00	15,252.00	5,727.00	
12	Eileen Healy	7,990.00	11,500.00	3,510.00	
13					
14					
15					
16					
17					

Figure 6 - 10

1. Select **FILE/Open**.

2. The file you want to open is **IA6-1**.

3. You first want to enter four sheets behind the current sheet. Select **EDIT/Insert**. Click on **Sheet** and **After**. The number of sheets you need is **4**.

4. Click on **OK**.

5. Click on Worksheet Tab **A**.

6. Place your cursor back in cell **A1**. Before formatting and copying the data, we want to turn on **Group Mode**. When **Group Mode** is turned on, whatever is done in sheet **A** will also be done for all other sheets.

7. To turn on **Group Mode**, choose **STYLE/Worksheet Defaults**. In the **Other** area, click on **Group Mode**.

8. Click on **OK**.

9. Now, the data from the first sheet can be copied to the other four sheets. Select the range **A1..D12**.

10. Click on the **Copy** icon

11. Click on Worksheet Tab **B**. The range you will copy to starts at sheet **B** and continues to sheet **E**. Place your cursor in sheet **B** cell **A1**. To specify the range to copy through, hold down the **SHIFT** key and click on Worksheet Tab **E**.

12. Press **ENTER**.

13. Place your cursor back in sheet **B** by clicking on Worksheet Tab **B**. Select the range **B7..C12**. Erase the data in the range by pressing the **DELETE** key.

14. Click on Worksheet Tab **C**. Erase the data in the range from **B7..C12**.

15. Repeat this process for sheet **D** through **E**.

16. Change the heading in row **2** to be the appropriate quarter:

    Sheet B for the Quarter Ended June 30, 1995

    Sheet C for the Quarter Ended September 30, 1995

    Sheet D for the Quarter Ended December 31, 1995

    Sheet E for the Year Ended December 31, 1995

17. Click on Worksheet Tab **E**. Place your cursor in cell **B7**. You want to create a formula that will total the yearly salary for each employee. To do this, you will add the cells in the four prior sheets. Select the **@function** selector on the Edit Line.

18. Click on **SUM**. Click on Worksheet Tab **A** and click on the first cell, **B7**. Hold down the **SHIFT** key and click on Worksheet Tab **D**. Press **ENTER**.

19. **COPY** the formula from **B7** to **C12**.

20. **FILE/Save** your file as **IA6-1DNE**.

21. **Print** your worksheet.

22. **FILE/Close** your file.

Independent Project 6.2: Creating More 3D Files in 1-2-3 for Windows

In this exercise, you will create additional sheets within your worksheet. The worksheet file we will be using contains quarterly sales information for your stores in different locations. Your worksheet file also contains calculations of average sales, lowest sales, and highest sales. When you are done, your summary sheet should look like Figure 6 - 11.

	A	B	C
1			
2	FOR THE YEAR ENDED 1996		
3			
4	Branch	TOTAL	
5	White Plains, NY	$611,973	
6	New York City, NY	$2,097,401	
7	Washington, D.C.	$1,254,145	
8	Boston, MA	$2,253,028	
9	Richmond, VA	$2,581,105	
10	Philadelphia, PA	$452,835	
11	Pittsburgh, PA	$812,445	
12			
13	Total Sales:	$10,062,932	
14	Average:	$1,437,562	
15	Minimum:	$452,835	
16	Maximum:	$2,581,105	
17			
18	1st Quarter Total Sales:	$10,062,932	
19	1st Quarter NY Sales:	$2,709,374	
20	1st Quarter PA Sales:	$1,265,280	

Figure 6 - 11

1. Select **FILE/Open**.

2. The file you want to open is **IA6-2**.

3. Enter four sheets behind the current sheet by selecting **EDIT/Insert**. Click on **Sheet** and **After**. The number of sheets you need is **4**.

4. Click on **OK**.

5. Click on Worksheet Tab **A**.

6. Place your cursor back in cell **A1**. Turn on **Group Mode** by choosing **STYLE/Worksheet Defaults**. In the **Other** area, click on **Group Mode**.

7. Click on **OK**.

8. Copy the data from the first sheet to the other four sheets. Select the range **A1..D20**.

9. Click on the **Copy** icon.

10. Click on Worksheet Tab **B**. The range you will copy to starts at sheet **B** and continues to sheet **E**. Place your cursor in sheet **B** cell **A1**. To specify the range to copy through, hold down the **SHIFT** key and click on Worksheet Tab **E**.

11. Press **ENTER**.

12. Place your cursor back in sheet **B**. Select the range **B5..D11**. Erase the data in the range by pressing the **DELETE** key. (Do not be alarmed when you see 0 and ERR on your screen. Formulas are located in those cells. When the data is filled in, the formulas will recalculate.)

13. Click on Worksheet Tab **C**. Erase the data in the range **B7..C12**.

14. Repeat this process for sheet **D** through **E**.

15. Change the heading in row **2** and the months to apply to the appropriate quarter:

    Sheet B Second Quarter Sales   **April, May, June**

    Sheet C Third Quarter Sales   **July, August, September**

    Sheet D Fourth Quarter Sales   **October, November, December**

    Sheet E For the Year Ended 1996

16. Click on Worksheet Tab **E**. Place your cursor in cell **B4**. Enter the label, **TOTAL**.

17. In cell **B5**, create a formula that will total the yearly sales information for each branch location. To do this, you will add all the cells in the four prior sheets. Select the **@function** selector on the Edit Line.

18. Click on **SUM**. Click on Worksheet Tab **A** and select the range **B5..D5**. Hold down the **SHIFT** key and click on Worksheet Tab **D**. Press **ENTER**.

19. **Copy** the formula from **B5** to **B11**.

20. Erase any data in the **C** and **D** columns of sheet **E**.

21. **FILE/Save** your file as **IA6-2DNE**.

22. **Print** your worksheet.

23. **FILE/Close** your file.

Independent Project 6.3: Creating More 3D Worksheets

In this exercise, you will create a 3D payroll worksheet. This worksheet contains information about employees wages and withholdings for a week in May. In this activity, you will create a worksheet containing all the salary information for the month of May. When you are done, your summary worksheet will look like Figure 6 - 12.

1. **Open** the file **IA6-3**.

2. Enter two sheets behind the current sheet by selecting **EDIT/Insert**.

3. Click on Worksheet Tab **A**.

4. Place your cursor back in cell **A1**. Turn on **Group Mode** by choosing **STYLE/Worksheet Defaults**.

5. Copy the data from the first sheet to the other two sheets. Select the range **A1..H26**.

6. Click on the **Copy** icon.

7. Click on Worksheet Tab **B**. Place your cursor in sheet **B** cell **A1**. To specify the range to copy through, hold down the **SHIFT** key and click on Worksheet Tab **C**.

8. Press **ENTER**.

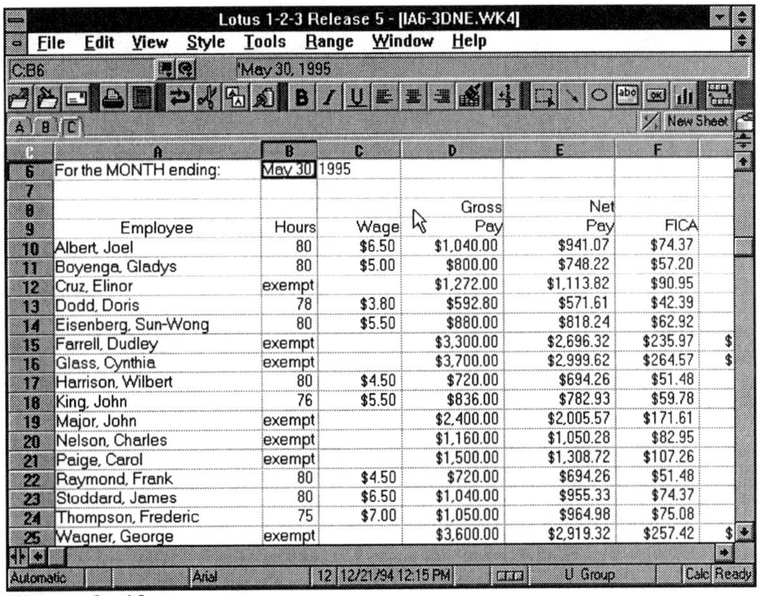

	A	B	C	D	E	F
6	For the MONTH ending:	May 30	1995			
7						
8				Gross	Net	
9	Employee	Hours	Wage	Pay	Pay	FICA
10	Albert, Joel	80	$6.50	$1,040.00	$941.07	$74.37
11	Boyenga, Gladys	80	$5.00	$800.00	$748.22	$57.20
12	Cruz, Elinor	exempt		$1,272.00	$1,113.82	$90.95
13	Dodd, Doris	78	$3.80	$592.80	$571.61	$42.39
14	Eisenberg, Sun-Wong	80	$5.50	$880.00	$818.24	$62.92
15	Farrell, Dudley	exempt		$3,300.00	$2,696.32	$235.97
16	Glass, Cynthia	exempt		$3,700.00	$2,999.62	$264.57
17	Harrison, Wilbert	80	$4.50	$720.00	$694.26	$51.48
18	King, John	76	$5.50	$836.00	$782.93	$59.78
19	Major, John	exempt		$2,400.00	$2,005.57	$171.61
20	Nelson, Charles	exempt		$1,160.00	$1,050.28	$82.95
21	Paige, Carol	exempt		$1,500.00	$1,308.72	$107.26
22	Raymond, Frank	80	$4.50	$720.00	$694.26	$51.48
23	Stoddard, James	80	$6.50	$1,040.00	$955.33	$74.37
24	Thompson, Frederic	75	$7.00	$1,050.00	$964.98	$75.08
25	Wagner, George	exempt		$3,600.00	$2,919.32	$257.42

Figure 6 - 12

9. Place your cursor back in sheet **B**. All employees worked 80 hours. Change any other number in column **B** to **80**.
10. Click on Worksheet Tab **C**. Erase the data in the range **D10..H26**.
11. In sheet **C**, change the Label in **A6** to For the Month Ended. Change the date to May 30.
12. Change the date in sheet **B** to May 30.
13. Click on Worksheet Tab **C**. Place your cursor in cell **D10**. In cell **D10,** create a formula that will total the monthly salary information for each employee. Select the **@function** selector on the Edit Line.
14. Click on **SUM**. Click on Worksheet Tab **A** and select cell **B10**. Hold down the **SHIFT** key and click on Worksheet Tab **B**. Press **ENTER**.
15. **COPY** the formula from **D10** to **H26**.
16. **FILE/Save** your file as **IA6-3DNE**.
17. **Print** your worksheet.
18. **FILE/Close** your file.

Independent Project 6.4: Creating a 3D Travel and Expense Report

In this exercise, you will create a 3D Travel and Expense Report from the data in a worksheet created in Activities 1 and 2. The purpose of this worksheet is to keep track of all your travels and the amounts spent for the year in each of the expense categories.

1. **Open** the file **IA2-4**.
2. Enter five sheets behind the current sheet by selecting **EDIT/Insert**.
3. Turn on **Group Mode**.
4. Copy the data from the first sheet to the other five sheets.
5. Place your cursor back in sheet **B**. Fill in data for your trip to Las Vegas.
6. Click on Worksheet Tab **C**. Fill in data for your trip to London.

7. Continue this for sheets **D** and **E**.

8. In sheet **F**, total the data from the prior five sheets.

9. **COPY** the formula to all cells in sheet **F**.

10. **FILE/Save** your file as **IA6-4DNE**.

11. **Print** your worksheet.

12. **FILE/Close** your file.

Lesson 7 Creating Charts

Objectives

In this lesson you will learn how to:

- Identify the types of charts in *Lotus*
- Select and change the chart type
- Identify the components of a chart
- Enhance a chart

- Name a chart
- Create an automatic chart
- Print a chart

PROJECT DESCRIPTION

In your new position within the company, you were asked to create charts representing the financial operating results for the year. The worksheets have been created but the president needs to have charts created so she can present the good news to the Board of Directors. The president has requested that you create a variety of charts clearly explaining how well the corporation has performed. You refer back to your *Lotus* manual to determine how to create the requested charts.

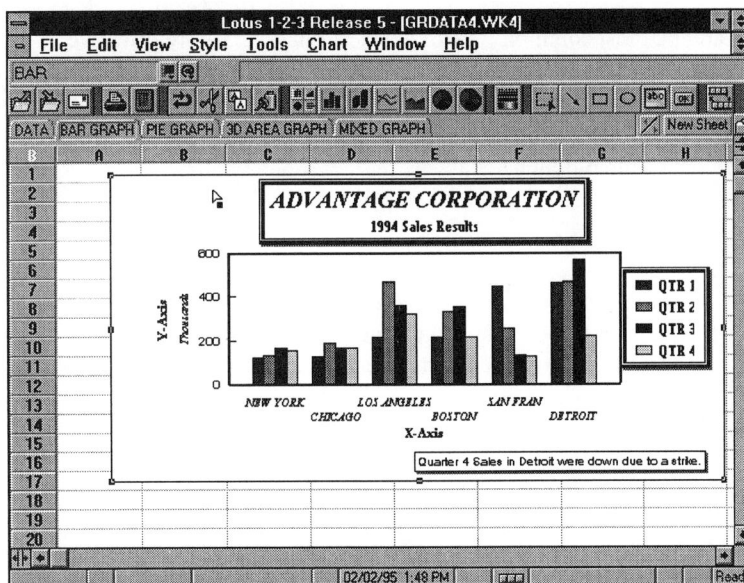

Figure 7 - 1

WHAT ARE CHARTS

Charts or **charts** are pictorial representations of data in your worksheet. Charts can show relationships that numbers in the worksheet may not convey clearly. This may become even more appropriate as the amount of data in the worksheet increases. *Lotus 1-2-3* allows you to develop, display, and print charts using the data in your worksheet. Charts or charts are also dynamic. If the data in the worksheet changes, so will the chart. Since when you chart you refer to cell locations, as the values in the cells change, so does the picture. Charts are a very important method of conveying information in worksheets.

TYPES OF CHARTS

You can create many types of charts in *Lotus*. The type of chart you choose to create will depend on the information you want to portray. Sometimes, you want to show how one piece of data relates to others. Often a pie chart will serve your needs in this case. If you want to show the magnitude of one piece of data in relation to others, a line chart or a bar chart can be used. There are eight types of charts you can create in *Lotus*. They are:

- Bar charts
- Line charts
- Area charts
- Mixed charts
- XY charts
- Pie charts
- High-Low-Close-Open charts
- Radar charts

Bar Charts

Bar charts are the most common type of business chart. Bars are effective if you do not have a great amount of data for which you wish to show relationships. Each bar in the chart represents a piece of data. The height of the bars show the magnitude of the relationships. Standard bar charts emphasize the individual values and their relationships to other values in the worksheet. Bar charts can be flat or three-dimensional.

Line and Area Charts

Line charts show the changes in a set of data over a period of time. Line and area charts usually show a time progression from left to right. These charts work well when you have a large number of data elements. Area charts show trends in data over a period of time by emphasizing the area located under the curve created by each data series. Line and area charts can be flat or three-dimensional.

Mixed Charts

Mixed charts combine parts from both a line chart, a bar chart, or an area chart. This type of chart lets you plot more than one data series in multiple forms on the same chart. Using this form of chart, you can also, for example, plot two very different types of data forms: numbers versus percentage. This is the perfect format to show both numbers and trends in a chart.

XY Charts

XY charts are similar to line charts except that the data points are plotted against both the X and the Y axes. XY charts are also called **scattergrams**. XY charts usually show relationships between two sets of data by plotting points. If there is a relationship between the data, the scattergram resembles a line, if there is not a relationship, the scattergram shows a random plotting of data points.

Pie Charts

Pie charts compare segments of a range to the entire range or parts to the whole. Each data item is represented by a wedge of the pie. The size of a slice corresponds to the percentage of the data range it represents. You can explode segments to separate them out from the rest of the data for emphasis, and you can make your pie chart look three-dimensional.

HLCO Charts

HLCO charts are used almost exclusively in the stock market to track fluctuations over a period of time. These charts show both ranges and data points. Due to the limited use of these charts, they will not be covered in this lesson.

Radar Charts

Radar charts are line or area charts wrapped around a central point. Each axis represents a set of data points. Radar charts are useful to show symmetry between data items or uniformity in data. Due to the limited use of these charts, they too will not be covered in this lesson.

COMPONENTS OF CHARTS

Before you can create charts, you need to be able to identify the components of a chart. Figure 7 - 2 shows a bar chart with the components labeled.

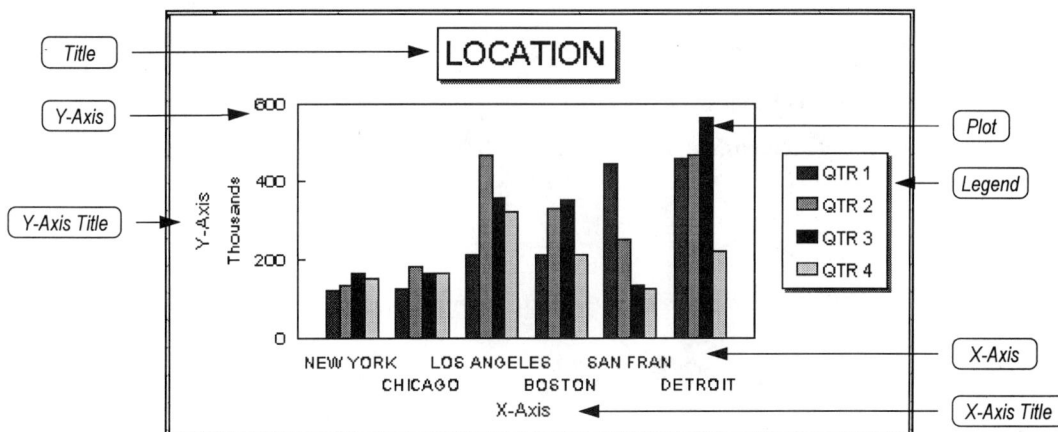

Figure 7 - 2

All charts (except for the pie chart) have a horizontal axis called the **X-axis** and a vertical axis called the **Y-axis**. The values identified on the X-axis are called the **X-axis labels**. In Figure 7 - 2, the **X-axis labels** are the geochartical regions. The **Y-axis** or the vertical axis is the measure of the items in the data ranges selected. The **Y-axis** shows the magnitude of the data being measured.

Lotus plots the data selected as **data series**. Each data series or range of data is assigned its own color or hash mark. You can plot up to **23 data series** or ranges of data, represented by the letters **A** through **W**. In the chart in Figure 7 - 2, the **first data series** (or **A**) is the results from the **First Qtr**. The **second data series** (or **B**) is the results from the **Second Qtr**. The section of the chart containing the charted data is called the **plot**. The **legend** of the chart identifies colors or hash lines used in the chart's data series.

STEPS TO CREATE AN AUTOMATIC CHART

To create an automatic chart, you need only select the complete range in the worksheet you want to chart and then click on the 📊 **Draw a chart using the selected range** SmartIcon, or choose **TOOLS/Chart** from the Menu Bar.

There are some important rules to keep in mind when you create an automatic chart. *Lotus* uses some very specific rules when creating automatic charts. First, when you select the range, *Lotus* finds the first cell containing a value that is not a date in the range. Then, *Lotus* counts the number of columns and rows that contain values. If there are more rows than columns, *Lotus* plots the data series by **columns**. The first column of values in the selected range becomes the first data range or series, the second column of values in the selected range becomes the second data range or series, etc. If there are more columns than rows or an equal number of columns and rows, *Lotus* plots the data series by **rows**. The first row of values in the selected range becomes the first data range or series, the second row of values in the selected range becomes the second data range or series, etc.

Creating an Automatic Chart

To create an automatic chart to plot the data in your worksheet:

- Select the range in the worksheet you want to chart.
- Click on the 📊 **Draw a Chart using the selected range** SmartIcon or choose **TOOLS/Chart** from the Menu Bar.
- Select the area in the worksheet where you want your chart to appear.
- Release the left mouse button when the chart is the desired size.

Activity 7.1: Creating Automatic Charts

1. Use **FILE/Open** to choose the file **GRDATA**.

   This worksheet contains the Sales Results for ADVANTAGE CORPORATION for 1994. You are going to chart the data in the worksheet and place the charts you create in separate worksheets behind the data.

2. Select the range **A5..E11**.

3. Click on the **Draw a chart using the selected range** SmartIcon or select **TOOLS/Chart** from the Menu Bar.

   Now, when pointing to cells, your mouse pointer changes to a small bar chart with crosshairs attached.

4. To place the chart in a new sheet, click on the **New Sheet**.

   Your mouse pointer changes back to an arrow when you move up toward the SmartIcons. The current worksheet is now B; your cell pointer is in B:A1.

5. By holding down the left mouse button and dragging, you will select the area in the worksheet where you want your chart to appear. You are going to select the area **A1..G16**. This will ensure that the chart is large enough to be seen clearly.

Selecting the area for the chart to be located is slightly different than selecting ranges for, for example, copying and moving data. Your crosshairs will guide you in this instance. Simply place the crosshairs as close as possible to the top, left edge of cell A1, then click and hold down the left mouse button. A box will appear as you move your mouse, indicating the selected area.

6. When you have reached the lower right edge of cell **G16**, release the mouse button. Your chart will appear.

    If your area is not exactly A1..G16, do not worry. Just make sure the area is large enough to contain a chart, but no so large that it covers multiple screens.

    You will notice that when Lotus created this automatic chart, since there were more rows containing values (six) than columns containing values (four) selected, Lotus plotted the data series by **columns***. The first column in the selected range (the locations) became the X-axis labels, and the second column in the selected range (QTR 1 sales results) became the first data range or series. The first cell in the selected range became the title (**LOCATION**) and the remaining cells in the first row became the legend lables (**QTR1** to **QTR4**).*

    Your charting results will look like Figure 7 - 3.

    Lotus creates an automatic bar chart. Next, you will create a few more automatic charts.

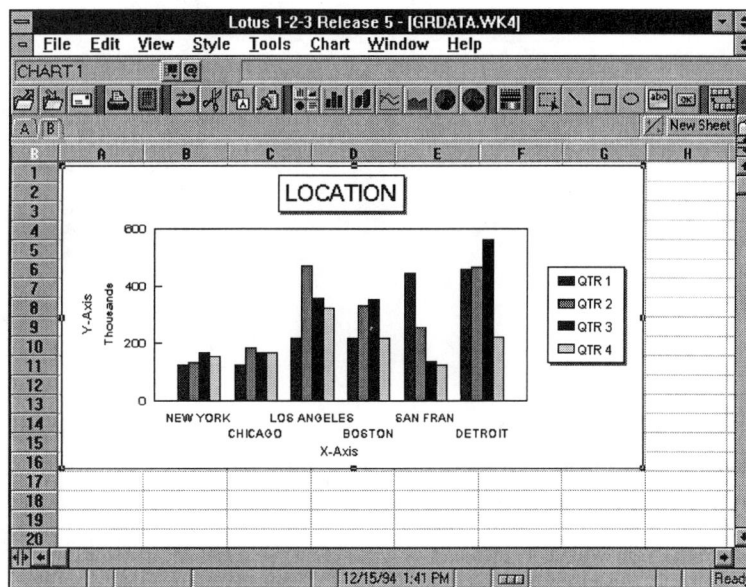

Figure 7 - 3

7. Make sure sheet **B** is the current sheet, and click on the **New Sheet** button **three times**.

    You now should have Worksheet Tabs C through E added.

8. Click on the **A** Worksheet Tab to return to sheet **A**.

9. Select the range **A:A5..A:B11**. You will use this data to again create an automatic chart. Later you will change the appearance of this chart to a 3D pie chart.

10. Click on the **Draw a chart using the selected range** SmartIcon, or select **TOOLS/Chart** from the Menu Bar.

11. Click on Worksheet Tab **C**.

12. By holding down the left mouse button, select the area in the worksheet where you want your chart to appear. Select the approximate range **A1..G16**.

✓ **Problem Solver**: *If a **Chart Assistant** dialog box appears, that simply means you clicked on Worksheet Tab **C** and then clicked on the **Draw a chart using the selected range** SmartIcon. Simply click on **CANCEL**, and repeat the exercise again from step **8**.*

13. Release the left mouse button and your chart will appear.

    Again an automatic bar chart is created. You will later change this chart to a 3D pie chart.

    Your charting results will look like Figure 7 - 4.

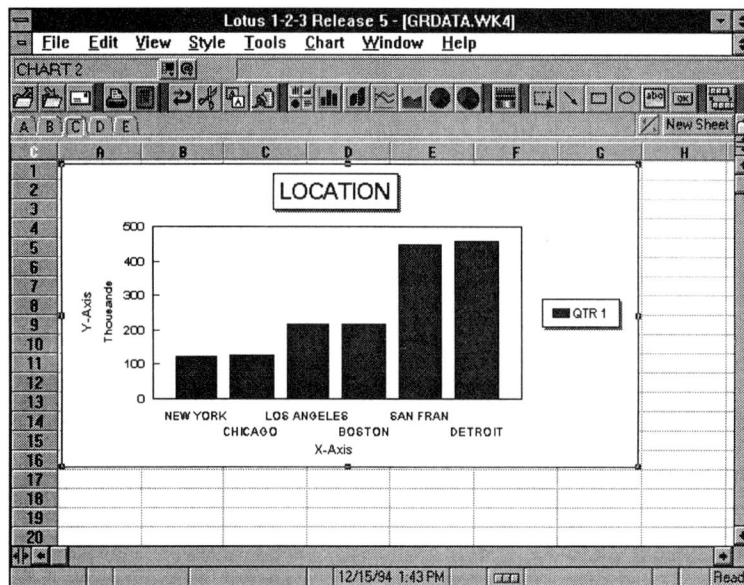

Figure 7 - 4

14. Return to sheet **A**.

15. Select the range **A:A5..A:E7**.

16. Click on the **Draw a chart using the selected range** SmartIcon or select **TOOLS/Chart** from the Menu Bar.

17. Click on Worksheet Tab **D**.

18. By holding down the left mouse button, select the area in the worksheet where you want your chart to appear. Select the approximate range **A1..G16**.

19. Release the left mouse button and your chart will appear.

    Again an automatic bar chart is created. Later, you will change this chart to a 3D area chart.

    *You will notice that this chart was created differently than the first two charts. When Lotus created this automatic chart, since there were more columns of values than rows of values selected, it plotted the data series by **rows**. As with the first two charts, the first cell in the selected range became the chart title. However, unlike the first two charts, the remainder of the first **row** in the selected range became the X-axis labels, and the second row of values in the selected range (for **NEW YORK**) became the first data range or series. The first column in the selected range, following the chart title, became the legend labels.*

    Your charting results will look like Figure 7 - 5.

20. Return to sheet **A**.

21. Select the range **A:A21..A:E25**.

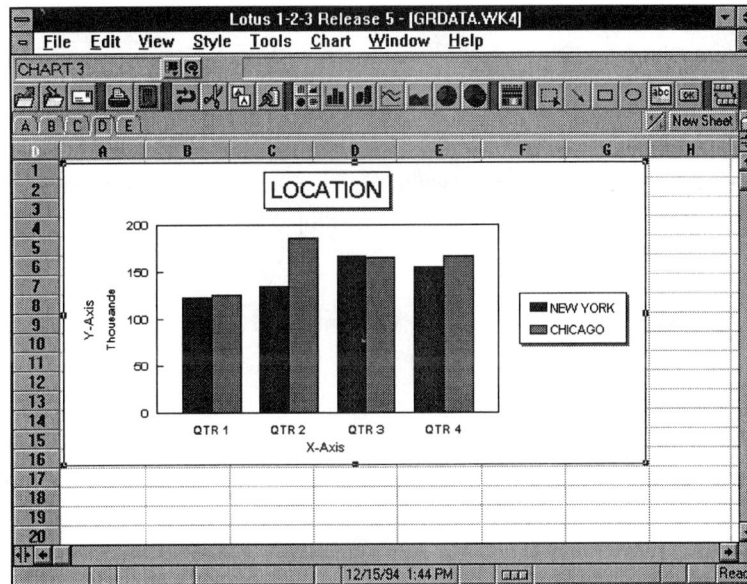

Figure 7 - 5

![icon] 22. Click on the **Draw a chart using the selected range** SmartIcon or choose **TOOLS/Chart** from the Menu Bar.

23. Click on Worksheet Tab **E**.

24. By holding down the left mouse button, select the area in the worksheet where you want your chart to appear. Select the approximate range **A1..G16**.

25. Release the left mouse button and your chart will appear.

Your charting results will look like Figure 7 - 6.

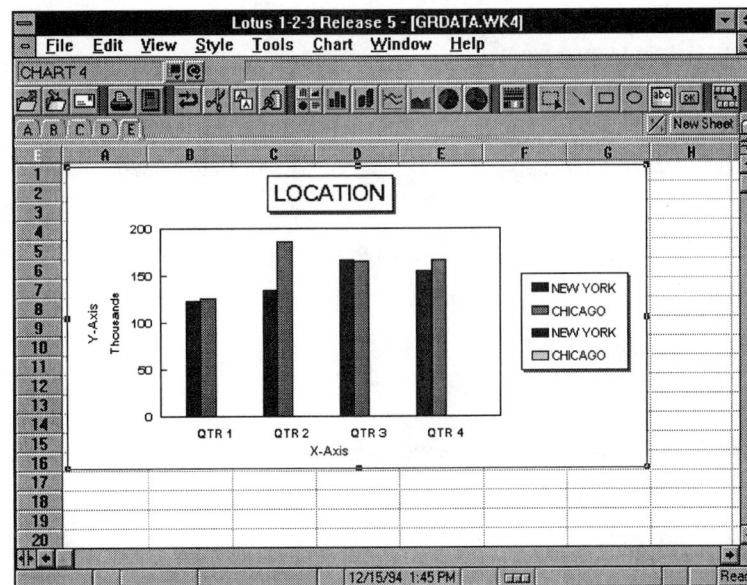

Figure 7 - 6

Again an automatic bar chart is created. Later, you will change this chart to a mixed chart. This chart may look strange now because it appears that only part of the selected data was plotted.

26. Return to sheet **A** and look at the data in **A:A21..A:E25**. The values in rows **22** and **23** are in the hundreds of thousands. The values in rows **24** and **25** are in percentages. Thus, *Lotus* had to try to plot one chart containing both numbers in the hundreds of thousands and percentages against the same vertical axis. In doing so, the percentages are so small in relation to the other data that they cannot be seen. Again, you will fix the appearance of the chart later.

27. **Save** your file as **GRDATA1**. DO NOT CLOSE your file.

SELECTING AND CHANGING THE CHART TYPE

When you created the automatic charts in Activity 7.1, *Lotus* plotted bar charts for you. Now you are going to learn how to change from a bar chart to other chart formats.

As described earlier, *Lotus* provides many different types of charting formats. After a chart is created, you can easily change the chart type.

To change the chart type:

- Click on the empty background area of the chart to select it. When a chart is selected, or active, there are small black squares, known as handles, around the outside frame of the chart.

- Choose **CHART/Type** from the menu choices that appear on your Menu Bar when a chart is active, or click on the **Select a chart type** ▦ SmartIcon which appears when a chart is active.

- Under **Types**, choose a Chart Type.

- Choose one of the **Styles** for the Chart Type.

- Under **Orientation** you can choose to display the chart in **Horizontal** format or in **Vertical** format. There is no orientation option for pie or radar charts.

- If you want to display **data values** under the chart, choose the **Include table of values** check box. This is not an available option for Pie, XY, HLCO, or Radar charts.

Shortcut: If you know the type of chart you want to create, you can use one of the SmartIcons to change the chart type. These SmartIcons will appear when a chart is active.

▦	Vertical bar chart	▦	Vertical area chart
▦	3D vertical bar chart	●	Pie chart
▦	Vertical line chart	◕	3D Pie chart

Activity 7.2: Changing the Chart Type

1. Use **FILE/Open** to choose the file **GRDATA1** if the file is not already open.

2. Click on Worksheet Tab **C**. You want to make this chart a **3D Pie Chart**.

3. Move your mouse pointer to a position on the white background area of the chart. It will change to an arrowhead with a solid black square below it. Click on the chart to make it active.

A chart is active when you see the small black squares around the outside frame.

Problem Solver: *If the handles are on a particular object within the chart rather than on the outside frame of the chart, simply make sure the mouse pointer is on an empty part of the white background area of the chart and click again.*

Notice that the Menu Bar choices and SmartIcons have changed somewhat now that the chart is active.

4. Choose **CHART/Type**.

5. In the **Types** area of the **Type** dialog box, click on **3D Pie**.

6. There are two pictures of **3D pie** charts in the **Type** dialog box. These represent two style choices: a pie chart with slices arranged by size in clockwise order or counterclockwise order. Click on the picture for **clockwise**.

7. Click on **OK**. Your chart is now displayed as a **3D pie chart**. Your results should look like Figure 7 - 7.

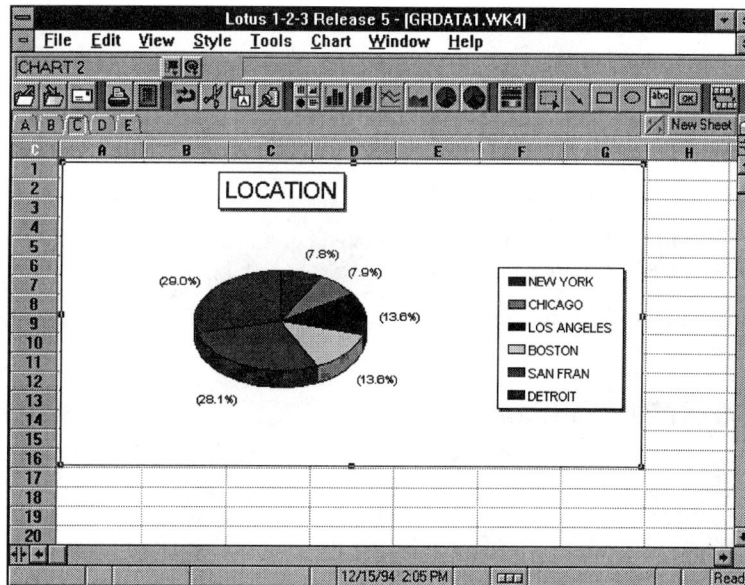

Figure 7 - 7

8. Click on Worksheet Tab **D**. You want to make this chart a **3D area chart**.

9. Click on the background area of the chart to make it active.

10. Choose **CHART/Type**. Click on **3D Area**.

   Two style options appear.

11. You want to chart the data so the data series appear front to back rather than stacked on top of one another. The first picture, the one you want, should already be selected. If it is not, click on it.

12. Choose **OK**. You now have a **3D area chart** displayed. Your results should look like Figure 7 - 8.

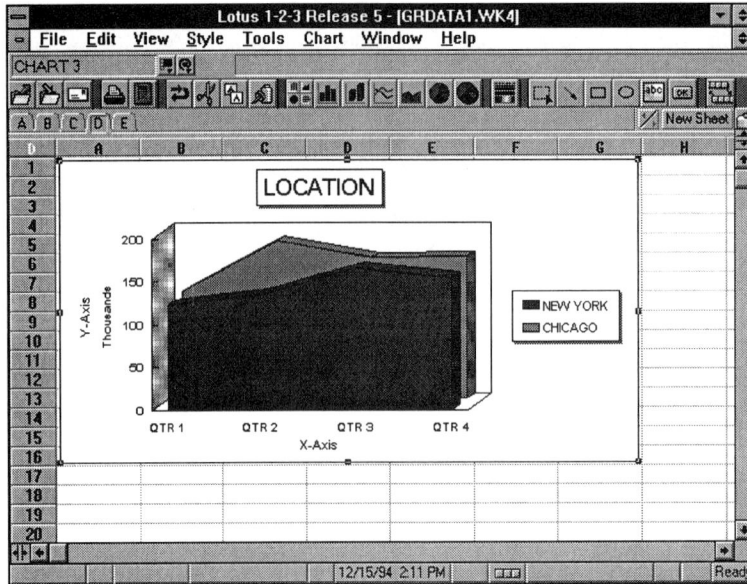

Figure 7 - 8

13. Click on Worksheet Tab **E**. You want to make this chart a mixed chart.

14. Click on the background area of the chart to make it active.

15. Click on the **Select a chart type** SmartIcon. Click on **Mixed**.

    Six style choices appear.

16. You want to chart the data so it is a mixed bar and line chart. The first picture, the one you want, should already be selected. If it is not, click on it.

17. Choose **OK**. You now have a mixed chart displayed. Your results should look like Figure 7 - 9.

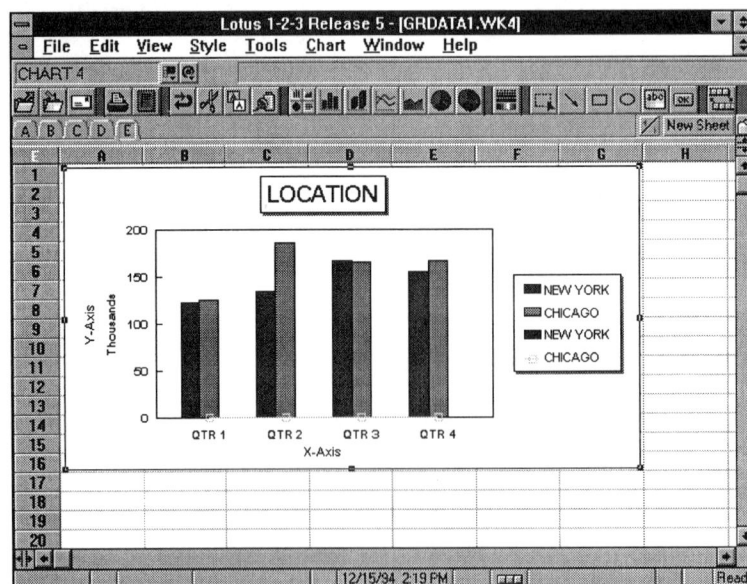

Figure 7 - 9

Your mixed chart still appears strange. You will correct this later.

18. **Save** your file as **GRDATA2**.

RENAMING THE WORKSHEET TABS

In Lesson 6, you learned how to add sheets to your current worksheet file. In this lesson, you are using multiple sheets labeled **A** through **E**. It would be easier to remember, however, what is stored in each sheet if you could assign more descriptive names to the sheets. Next, you will change the names of the tabs so each tab has a unique identifier.

To change the name of the worksheet tab:

- Double click on the tab.
- Type the new name.
- Press **ENTER**.

Activity 7.3: Changing the Names of the Worksheet Tabs

1. Use **FILE/Open** to choose the file **GRDATA2** if the file is not already open.

2. Move your cell pointer back to the beginning of the file, sheet **A**, cell **A:A1**. Double click on Worksheet Tab **A**. Your cursor is now placed in the Worksheet Tab space and the label **A** disappears. You can now type the new name for your tab. This tab will be called **DATA**.

3. Type: **DATA**. Press **ENTER**.

4. Double click on Worksheet Tab **B**. This tab will be named **BAR Chart**. Type the name: **BAR Chart** and press **ENTER**.

5. Double click on Worksheet Tab **C**. This tab will be named **PIE Chart (or 3D Pie Chart, if you prefer)**. Type the name: **PIE Chart** and press **ENTER**.

6. Double click on Worksheet Tab **D**. This tab will be named **3D AREA Chart**. Type the name: **3D AREA Chart** and press **ENTER**.

7. Double click on Worksheet Tab **E**. This tab will be named **MIXED Chart**. Type the name: **MIXED Chart** and press **ENTER**.

8. Now it is easier to identify the components of the worksheet. Your worksheet will now look like Figure 7 - 10.

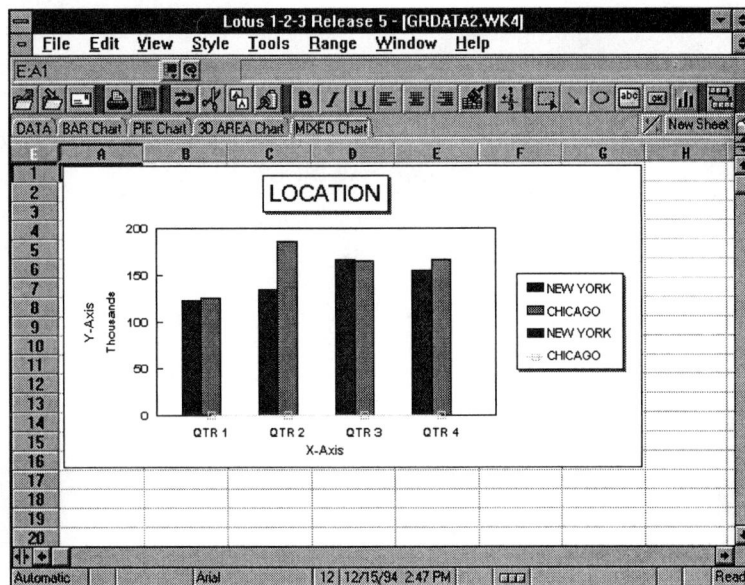

Figure 7 - 10

9. **SAVE** your file again as **GRDATA2.**

ENHANCING YOUR CHARTS

It was reasonably simple to create a chart. Now you want to enhance selectively the appearance of your charts by changing/adding titles and subtitles, adding a footnote, changing the appearance of frames and fonts, adding a second Y-axis, and adding an axis title.

Changing/Adding a Chart Title

A chart may have up to four titles: a title and subtitle (located at the top of the chart), an X-axis title, and a Y-axis title.

To add titles to your chart:

- With the chart active, choose **CHART/Headings**.

- Enter what you want to appear as the title of the chart in the **Line 1** text box of the **Title** area of the **Headings** dialog box, or, if the title appears in the worksheet, type the cell location. Click on **Cell** if the name of the title appears in a worksheet cell.

- Again enter the data or the cell that contains the information you want to appear in the subtitle of the chart (**Line 2** of the the **Title** area of the **Headings** dialog box.).

- Choose whether you want the titles placed in the top **Left, Center, or Right** of the chart.

- Enter any information you want to appear in footnotes in the chart in the **Note** area of the **Headings** dialog box. Again, if the data appears in a cell, click on **Cell**. You may also choose the placement of footnotes.

- When finished, choose **OK**.

Shortcut: Double click on the title of the chart. The **Headings** dialog box appears. Enter the data you want to appear in the headings according to the instructions above.

Activity 7.4: Adding Titles to Charts

1. Use **FILE/Open** to choose the file **GRDATA2** if the file is not already open.

2. Click on the tab, **BAR Chart**. You want to change the title of our chart. Double click on the word **LOCATION**. The **Headings** dialog box appears.

3. Your insertion point is now placed in the **Line 1** text box. The **Line 1** text box also is showing that the contents of cell **A: A5** is the first heading on the chart. Press the **DELETE** key to erase this heading. Type: **ADVANTAGE CORPORATION**.

4. Click on **Cell** to remove the **X** in the **Cell** check box. Our title will not be a cell location.

5. Click in the **Line 2** text box. Type: **1994 Sales Results**.

6. Leave the placement as **Center** for both titles.

7. Under **Note**, click in the **Line 1** text box. Type the following: **Quarter 4 Sales in Detroit were down due to a strike**.

8. Change the placement of the footnote to **Right**.

9. Choose **OK**.

   Your chart should now look like Figure 7 - 11.

10. Click on the tab, **PIE Chart**.

11. Double click on the word **LOCATION**. The **Headings** dialog box appears.

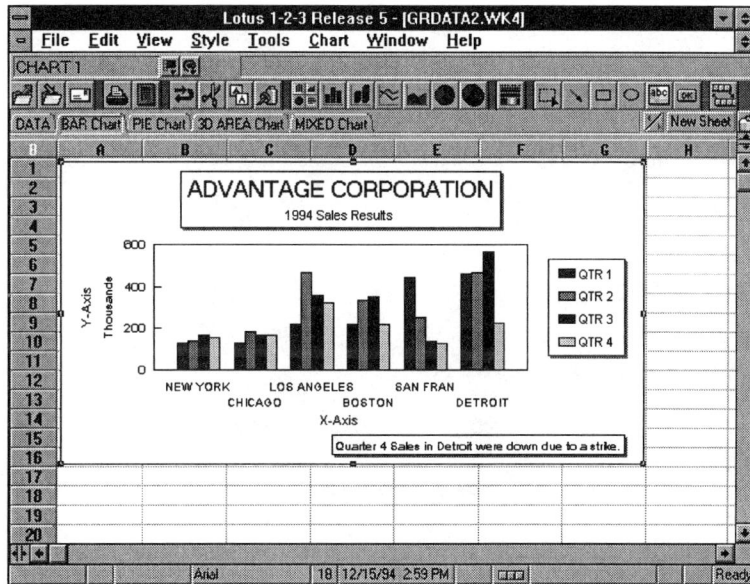

Figure 7 - 11

12. Add (or change) the following titles for your 3D Pie chart:

    Title Line 1: **ADVANTAGE CORPORATION**

    Title Line 2: **First Quarter Operating Results**

    Make sure the titles are **centered**. Make sure the word **Cell** is **not** selected.

    Your 3D Pie chart will now look like Figure 7 - 12.

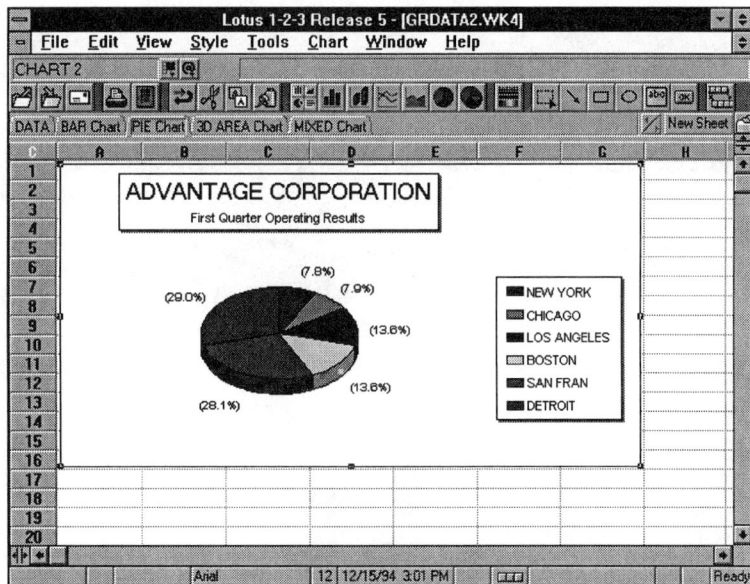

Figure 7 - 12

13. Click on the tab, **3D AREA Chart**.

14. Double click on the word **LOCATION**. The **Headings** dialog box appears.

15. Add (or change) the following titles for your 3D Area chart:

Title Line 1: **ADVANTAGE CORPORATION**

Title Line 2: **New York & Chicago Operating Results**

Make sure the titles are **centered**. Make sure the word **Cell** is **not** selected.

Your 3D Area chart will now look like Figure 7 - 13.

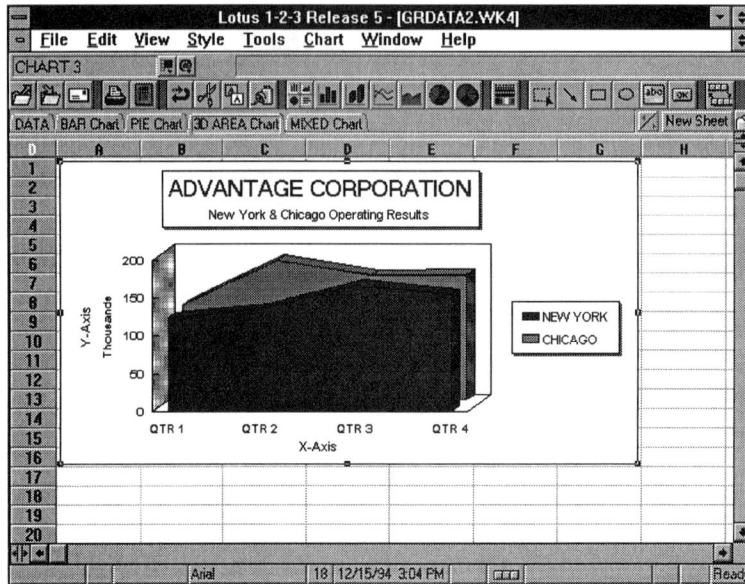

Figure 7 - 13

16. Click on the tab, **MIXED Chart**.

17. Double click on the word **LOCATION**. The **Headings** dialog box appears.

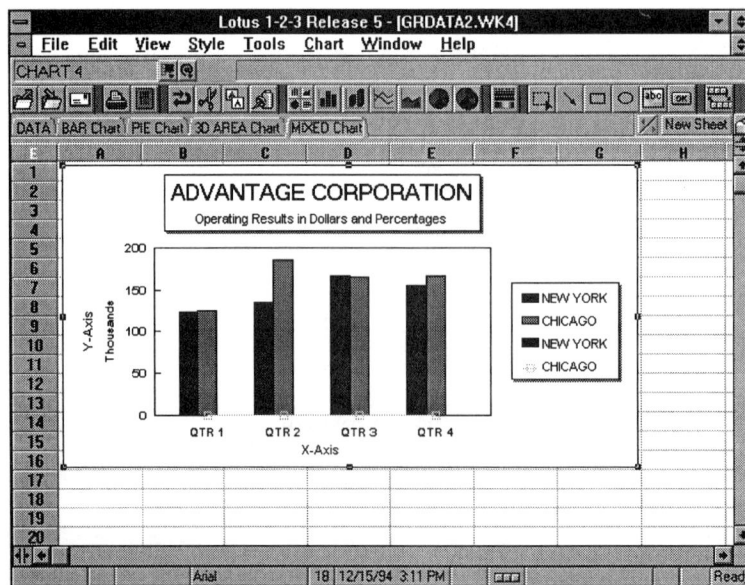

Figure 7 - 14

18. Add (or change) the following titles for your Mixed chart:

    Title Line 1: **ADVANTAGE CORPORATION**

    Title Line 2: **Operating Results in Dollars and Percentages**

    Make sure the titles are **centered**. Make sure the word **Cell** is **not** selected.

    Your Mixed Chart will now look like Figure 7 - 14.

19. **SAVE** your file as **GRDATA3**.

Changing Frames and Fonts in Your Chart

Lotus automatically places a frame around the outside of your titles, your legend, any footnotes, and your entire chart. You may choose to change the appearance of any of these frames. You may also change the fonts of the text within those frames.

To change the frame:

- Click anywhere on the empty background of the area within the frame surrounding the element you want to change.

- With your mouse pointer resting somewhere on the same background area within the frame, click the right mouse button.

- Choose **Lines & Color** from the Quick Menu that appears.

- At the bottom of the **Lines & Color** dialog box, **Designer Frame** should have an **X** next to it. Click on the [ ] next to **Designer Frame**. A choice of **16** different frames appears. Click on a frame you like. A **Sample** now appears in the right side of the **Lines & Color** box.

- Choose **OK**.

To change fonts:

- Click on the element of the chart you want to change.

- With your mouse pointer resting somewhere on the selected element, click the right mouse button.

- Choose **Font & Attributes** from the Quick Menu that appears.

- The **Font & Attributes** dialog box appears.

- Choose a typeface and the size you want.

- If desired, choose **Bold**, **Italics**, and/or **Underline**.

- Choose **OK**.

Activity 7.5: Changing Frames and Fonts Within Your Chart

1. Use **FILE/Open** to select the file **GRDATA3** if the file is not already open.

2. Click on the tab, **BAR Chart**. You want to change some of the frames in different parts of the chart, and the fonts for the title and subtitle of the chart.

3. Click on the white background of the area within the frame surrounding the title and subtitle. This makes the frame active.

4. With your mouse pointer resting somewhere on the background area within the frame surrounding the title and subtitle, click the right mouse button. Choose **Lines & Color** from the Quick Menu that appears.

5. Click on the arrow to the right of **Designer Frame**. Select the last frame in the third row.

6. Click on **OK**.

7. Click on the white background of the area within the frame surrounding the legend. This makes the frame active.

8. With your mouse pointer resting somewhere on the legend background, click the right mouse button. Choose **Lines & Color**.

9. Click on the arrow to the right of **Designer Frame**. Select the last frame in the third row.

10. Click on **OK**.

11. Click on the white background of the area within the frame surrounding the entire chart. This makes the frame active.

12. With your mouse pointer resting somewhere on the chart background, click the right mouse button. Choose **Lines & Color**.

13. In the **Edge** area of the **Lines & Color** dialog box, click on the arrow to the right of **Line Width**. Make the width of the box surrounding the chart slightly thicker. Select the second or third line.

14. Choose **OK**.

15. Click on the title **ADVANTAGE CORPORATION** to make it active.

16. With your mouse pointer resting somewhere on the title, click the right mouse button and choose **Font & Attributes**.

17. Change the **Face** to **Times New Roman**. Change the **Attributes** to **Bold** and **Italics**.

18. Choose **OK**.

19. Change the face of the **Legend** (on the right), the **X-axis labels**, and the **Y-axis labels**. You can choose whatever typeface you like.

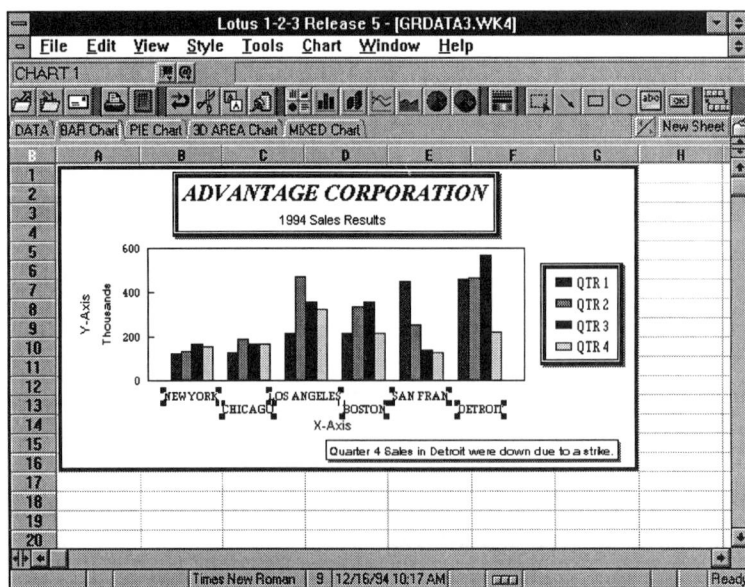

Figure 7 - 15.

All the legend labels will be selected when you click on just one of them; the same is true of the axis labels. When you choose the new font, all the labels for that element will change together.

20. You may change the typeface for any of the other labels in the chart. Don't forget to start by clicking on the label you want to affect to make it active, and then keep your mouse pointer on a selected label when you click the right mouse button.

When you are finished, your chart might look similar to Figure 7 - 15.

21. You can also experiment with changing fonts and frames on your **3D Pie**, **3D Area**, and **Mixed charts**.

22. **SAVE** your file as **GRDATA4**.

Enhancing The Appearance Of The Mixed Chart

In its simplest form, the Mixed chart allows you to have two different types of charts overlaying each other. In addition, *Lotus* allows you to have a second Y-axis. Thus, the values plotted against the two Y-axes do not have to fall within the same scale. In the Mixed chart you created, the values plotted against the left axis currently correspond to both dollars in thousands and to percentages. *Lotus* is not yet providing a separate, correct scale for our second Y-axis; that is why you cannot see the percentage data. You will adjust your Mixed chart so that the values plotted against the left Y-axis correspond to dollars in thousands, and the values plotted against a new right Y-axis correspond to percentages. Next, you will improve the appearance of your mixed chart by defining the second Y-axis.

Defining the second Y-axis:

- Make sure the chart is active.

- Choose **CHART/Ranges**.

- Select the data series to be plotted on the second Y-axis and click on the **Plot on 2nd Y-Axis** check box for each one.

- Choose the **Mixed type** (**Line**, **Area**, or **Bar**).

- Choose **OK**.

Activity 7.6: Enhancing the Mixed Chart

1. Switch to the **Mixed chart** and select the entire chart to make it active.

2. Choose **CHART/Ranges**.

3. Under **Series**, select **C - NEW YORK**. Click on **Plot on 2nd Y-Axis**.

4. At **Mixed type** list box, click on the down arrow and select **Line**.

5. Returning to **Series**, select **D - CHICAGO**. Click on **Plot on 2nd Y-Axis**.

6. Make sure **Line** is still selected as **Mixed type**.

7. Choose **OK**.

8. Now you will see that you have two lines representing the operating results in percentages plotted against the right Y-axis. These lines are placed on top of the bars showing the operating results in thousands of dollars plotted against the left Y-axis. See Figure 7 - 16.

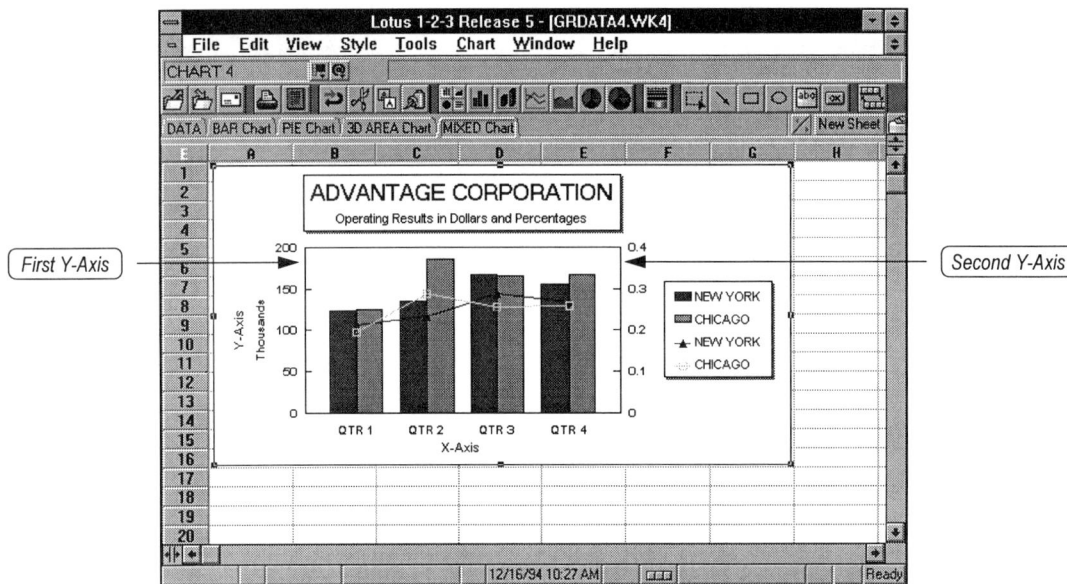

Figure 7 - 16

Adding a title for the second Y-axis:

- Make sure the chart is active.

- Click on any label on the second Y-axis.

- With your mouse pointer resting on one of the selected labels, click the right mouse button to activate the Quick Menu, and select **2nd Y-Axis**.

- Type in a Title for the **2nd Y-Axis**.

- Change the scaling if you want.

- Choose **OK**.

Changing the Number Format of the Scaling of the second Y-Axis

- Make sure the chart is active.

- Click on any label on the second Y-Axis.

- With your mouse pointer resting on one of the selected labels, click the right mouse button to activate the Quick Menu, and choose **Number Format**.

- In the **Format** box, choose a number format. If appropriate, choose a number for **Decimal Places**.

- Choose **OK**.

Activity 7.7: Adding a Title for and Changing the Number Format of the Scale of the second Y-Axis

1. Make sure the **Mixed chart** is active.

2. Click on any value on the second Y-Axis. (The values are on the right side of the chart)

3. With your mouse pointer resting on one of the selected values, click the right mouse button to activate the Quick Menu, and choose **2nd Y-Axis**.

4. Type in a title for the **2nd Y-Axis: Percentages**.

5.   Choose **OK**.

6.   With the **2nd Y-axis values** still selected, rest your mouse pointer on one of the selected labels, click the right mouse button to again activate the Quick Menu, and choose **Number Format**.

7.   In the **Format** box, choose: **Percent**. For **Decimal Places**, scroll to: **0**.

8.   Choose **OK**.

Your chart should now look like Figure 7 - 17.

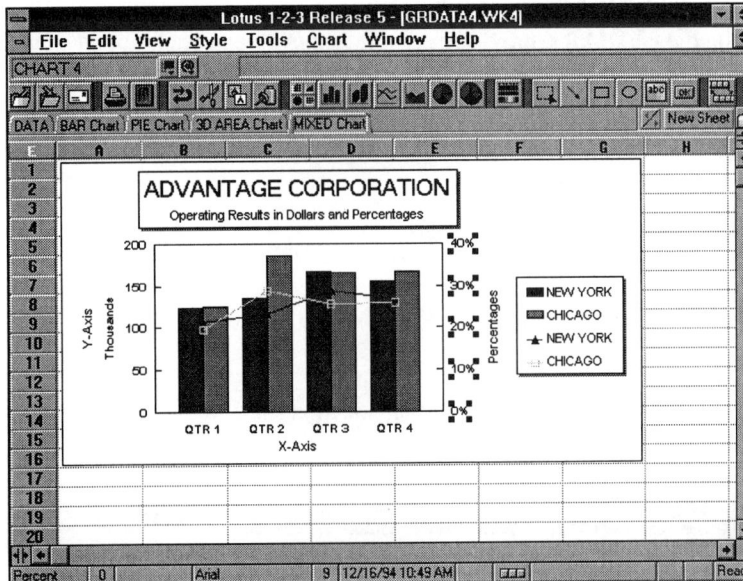

Figure 7 - 17

NAMING CHARTS

Lotus automatically names charts starting with the name **CHART 1**. Since this name is not very descriptive of the contents of the chart, you probably want to name your chart something more appropriate. Once a chart is named, you can easily search for and find the chart even if you do not use a separate worksheet for each chart.

Naming charts:

•   Make sure the chart is active.

•   Choose **CHART/Name**.

•   The **Name** dialog box appears.

•   Press the **DELETE** key to erase the default name (**CHART X**) and type the new name.

•   Click on the **Rename** button.

•   *Lotus* replaces the default chart name with the new chart name in the Selection Indicator at the top left of the screen.

Finding named charts:

•   From the Menu Bar choose **EDIT/Go To** or press the **F5** key.

•   The **Go To** dialog box will appear.

- The **Type of item** you are searching for is a **Chart**. Make sure **Chart** appears in the **Type of Item** text box. If it does not, use the **Type of Item** drop-down list box to choose it.

- A list of charts in the file will appear. Select the chart you are searching for.

- Click on **OK**.

- Your cursor is moved to the chart selected.

Activity 7.8: Changing the Names of the Charts

1. Use **FILE/Open** to choose the file **GRDATA4** if the file is not already open.

2. Click on the tab, **BAR Chart**. Click on the empty white background of the bar chart itself to make it active. Look at the Selection Indicator. *Lotus* still thinks the name of the chart is **CHART 1**. You did change the chart tab, but you did not give your chart a name. Now you will change the name of the chart to **BAR**.

3. Make sure the chart still is active.

4. Choose **CHART/Name**.

5. The **Name** dialog box appears.

6. Press the **DELETE** key to erase **CHART 1** and type the new name: **BAR**.

7. Click on the **Rename** button.

8. *Lotus* places the new chart name in the Selection Indicator at the top left of the screen. See Figure 7 - 18.

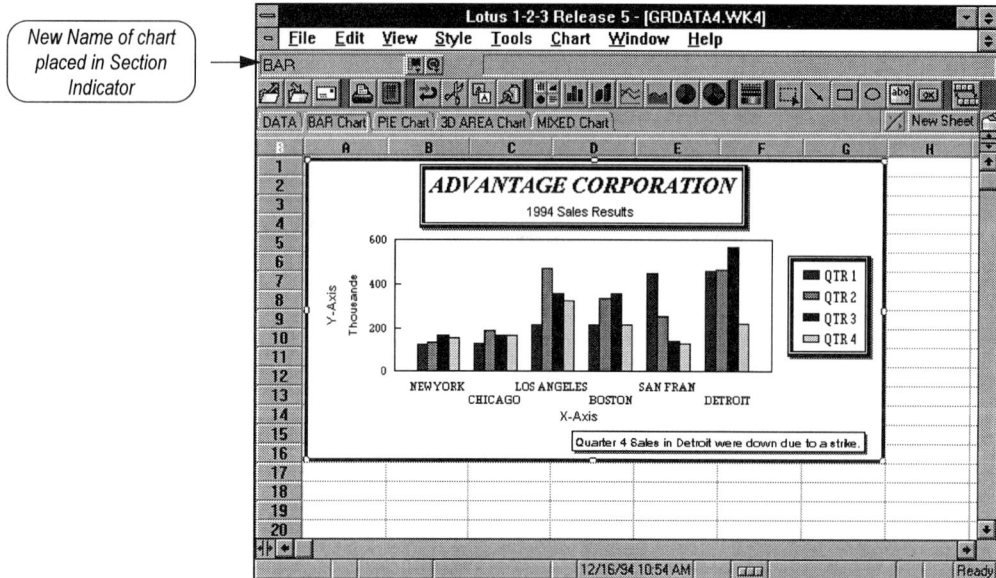

Figure 7 - 18

9. Click on the tab, **PIE Chart**. Click on the empty white background of the 3D pie chart itself to make it active.

10. Choose **CHART/Name**.

11. Press the **DELETE** key to erase **CHART 2** and type the new name: **PIE** (or 3D Pie if you prefer).

12. Click on the **Rename** button.

13. Repeat this process to name the **3D AREA** and **MIXED** charts.

14. To move back to a chart once it is named, press **F5**.

15. Make sure the **Type of Item** is **Chart**.

16. Click on **BAR**. Click on **OK**.

    *This places you back at the **BAR Chart**, with the chart itself active.*

17. **SAVE** your file as **GRDATA5**.

PRINTING CHARTS

You can print charts at the actual size on the page or you can enlarge the chart to fill the entire page. Printing a chart is very simple and very similar to printing the worksheet.

Printing a Chart

To print a chart, first make sure the chart is selected and:

- Click on the [icon] **Display the Print dialog box** SmartIcon or
- Choose **File Print**.
- When the **Print** dialog box appears, choose **Page Setup**.
- Click on the drop-down arrow to the right of the **Size box**.
- Your choices are: **Actual Size, Fill Page,** or **Fill page but keep proportions**.
- To get a full page chart, choose **Fill Page**.

    *The **Fill page but keep proportions** option centers the chart on the printed page but retains the proportions.*

- Under **Orientation**, you can choose **Portrait** or **Landscape**. **Portrait** will print your chart down the page, **Landscape** will print your chart across the page.
- Click on **OK**.
- In the **Print** dialog box, choose **OK**.

Activity 7.9: Printing the Charts

1. Use **FILE/Open** to choose the file **GRDATA5** if the file is not already open.

2. If you are not at the **BAR Chart**, press the **F5** key and move to the **BAR Chart**.

    *Do not forget to choose **Chart** as the **Type of item** if it is not already selected.*

3. Make sure the **BAR Chart** is active.

4. From the menu choose **FILE/Print**.

5. When the **Print** dialog box appears, choose **Page Setup**.

6. Click on the drop down arrow to the right of the **Size box**.

7. Your choices are: **Actual Size, Fill Page,** or **Fill page but keep proportions**. Since you want a full page chart, choose **Fill Page**.

8. Under **Orientation**, choose **Landscape**.

9. Click on **OK**.

10. To make sure you like how the charts looks before printing, choose **Preview**.

11. Your **Print Preview** should look like Figure 7 - 19.

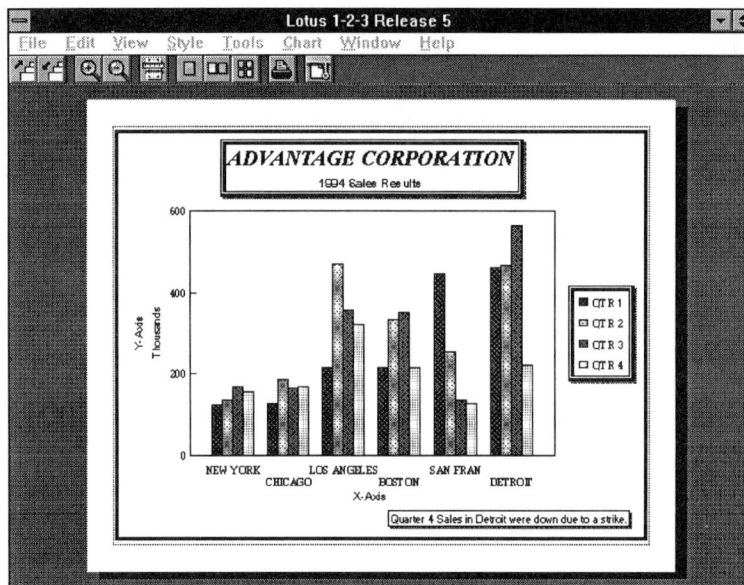

Figure 7 - 19

12. **Close** the **Preview** menu by clicking on the **Close the Print Preview window** SmartIcon..

13. Click on the **Print the current selection** SmartIcon.

14. Click on **OK**.

15. Press the **F5** key and move to the **Mixed Chart**.

16. Make sure the **Mixed Chart** is selected.

17. From the Menu Bar choose **FILE/Print**.

18. Choose **Page Setup**.

19. Print the **Mixed Chart** as a **Fill Page** (full page) chart printed in **Portrait Orientation**.

20. If you want to choose any of the other charts for printing, follow the steps above.

21. **Save** your file as **GRDATA5** and **Close** your file.

SUMMARY

In this lesson you have learned how to create different types of charts, how to add enhancements to these charts, and how to print the results. Although it is not required, many worksheet users place charts in separate sheets behind the data and change the name of the worksheet tab to reflect the chart name. Now lets practice your charting skills by working through the Independent Projects.

KEY TERMS

3-D Area	Designer Frame	Radar
Automatic Chart	Fonts	Second Y-Axis
Bar	Headings	Tools Chart
Chart	High-Low-Close-Open	Worksheet Tabs
Chart Frame	Line	X-Axis
Chart Names	Mixed	Y-Axis
Chart Title	Pie	
Data Series	Printing	

INDEPENDENT PROJECTS

Independent Project 7.1: Charting Data in the Worksheet

In this exercise, you will practice charting data in your worksheet. The file with which you will be working contains a common size Income Statement for a three-year period of time. You are going to plot the sales, cost of sales, expenses, taxes, and net income for a three-year period. Your completed chart will look like Figure 7 - 20.

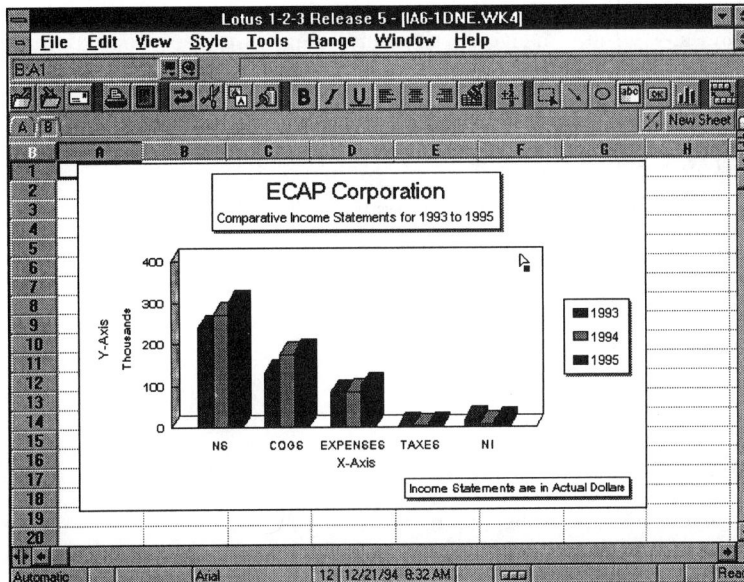

Figure 7 - 20

1. Select **FILE/Open**.

2. The file you want to open is **IA7-1**.

3. Place your cursor in cell **A30**. You want to select the range of cells **A30..D35**. Using the mouse, click on **A30** and drag the mouse to select the range.

4. Click on the **Chart** icon.

5. You need to select where the chart will be placed. We will place the new chart in a separate sheet. Click on the **New Sheet** icon. Your cursor is placed in the new sheet.

6. When your cursor is placed in the new sheet, select the range where you want to place your chart. Select a range approximately the size of the screen.

7. To change the chart type, click on the **Chart Type** icon. Click on **3-D Bar**. Select the first picture.

8. Click on **OK**.

9. Double click on the chart title (it now says **Title**). We will enter the name of the company and a description of the chart.

10. Enter the following:

    Line 1: **ECAP Corporation**

    Line 2: **Comparative Income Statements for 1993 - 1995**

Placement: **Center**

Note 1: **Income Statements Are in Actual Dollars**

Placement: **Right**

11. Click on **OK**.

12. From the menu, select **CHART/Name**. The name of this chart will be **3DBAR**. Click on **Rename** to change the name of the chart.

13. To print the chart, select **FILE/Print Preview**. Make sure you are previewing the **Selected Chart 3DBAR**.

14. Click on **Page Setup**. Change the size to **Fill Page but keep proportions**. Change the orientation to **Landscape**.

15. Click on **OK**.

16. Click on **OK**.

17. If the chart picture is acceptable, click on the **Print** icon.

18. Click on **OK**.

19. **FILE/Save** your file as **IA7-1DNE**.

20. **Print** your worksheet.

21. **FILE/Close** your file.

Independent project 7.2: Creating More Charts in 1-2-3 for Windows

In this exercise, you will practice creating charts in your worksheet. The worksheet file we will be using contains billing and salary information for consultants within your firm. When you are done, your chart should look like Figure 7 - 21.

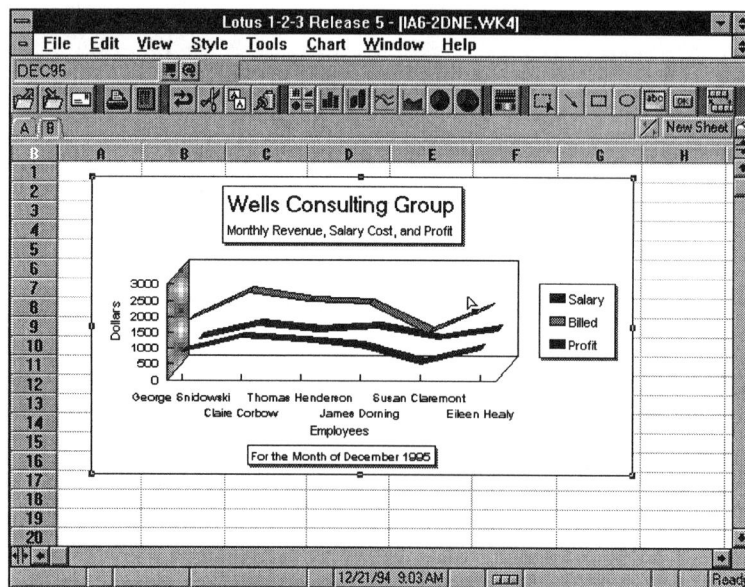

Figure 7 - 21

1.   Select **FILE/Open**.

2.   The file you want to open is **IA7-2**.

3. Place your cursor in cell **A4**.

4. Select the range of cells **A4..D10**.

5. Click on the **Chart** icon.

6. We will place the new chart in a separate sheet. Click on the **New Sheet** icon.

7. Select the range where you want to place your chart. Select a range approximately the size of the screen.

8. To change the chart type, click on the **Chart Type** icon. Click on **3-D Line**. Select the first picture.

9. Click on **OK**.

10. Double click on the chart title (it now says **Employee)**. We will enter the name of the company and a description of the chart.

11. Enter the following:

    Line 1: **Wells Consulting Group** (Make sure **Cell** does not have an **X**)

    Line 2: **Monthly Revenue, Salary Cost and Profit**

    Placement: **Center**

    Note 1: **For the Month of December 1995**

    Placement: **Center**

12. Click on **OK**.

13. Double click on the label **X-axis**. Change the X-axis title to **Employees**.

14. Double click on the label **Y-axis**. Change the Y-axis title to **Dollars**.

15. From the menu, select **CHART/Name**. The name of this chart will be **DEC95**. Click on **Rename** to change the name of the chart.

16. To print the chart, select **FILE/Print Preview**. Make sure you are previewing the **Selected Chart DEC95**.

17. Click on **Page Setup**. Change the size to **Fill Page but keep proportions**. Change the **Orientation** to **Landscape**.

18. Click on **OK**.

19. Click on **OK**.

20. If the chart picture is acceptable, click on the **Print** icon.

21. Click on **OK**.

22. **FILE/Save** your file as **IA7-2DNE**.

23. **Print** your worksheet.

24. **FILE/Close** your file.

Independent Project 7.3: Creating More Charts Within a Lotus Worksheet

In this exercise, you practice creating charts within a *Lotus* worksheet. This worksheet contains clothing sales and expenses within your department store. In this activity, you will create two charts: one for the sales, and one for the expenses. When you are done, your sales chart will look like Figure 7 - 22.

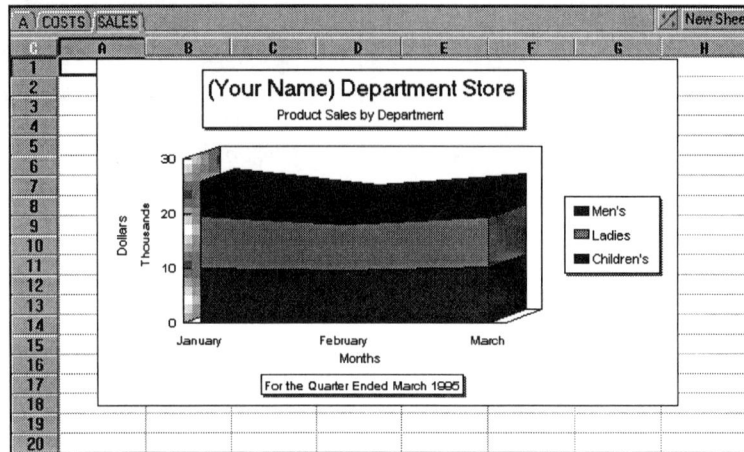

Figure 7 - 22

1. **Open** the file **IA7-3**.

2. Place your cursor in cell **A5**.

3. Select the range of cells **A5..D8**.

4. Click on the **Chart** icon.

5. Place the new chart in a separate sheet.

6. Select a range in the new sheet approximately the size of the screen.

7. To change the chart type, click on the **Chart Type** icon. Click on **3DArea**. Select the second picture.

8. Click on **OK**.

9. Double click on the chart title.

10. Enter the following:

    Line 1: **(Your Name) Department Store** (Make sure Cell does not have an X)

    Line 2: **Product Sales by Department**

    Placement: **Center**

    Note 1: **For the Quarter Ended March 1995**

    Placement: **Center**

11. Click on **OK**.

12. Double click on the label **X-axis**. Change the X-axis title to **Months**.

13. Double click on the label **Y-axis**. Change the Y-axis title to **Dollars**.

14. Select **CHART/Name**. The name of this chart will be **SALES**.

15. Double click on Worksheet Tab **B**.   Type a new name for the sheet, **SALES**. Press **ENTER**.

16. Make the chart active by clicking anywhere on the chart.

17. To print the chart, select **FILE/Print Preview.** Make sure you are previewing the **Selected Chart SALES.**

18. In **Page Setup,** change the size to **Fill Page but keep Proportions.**   Change the **Orientation** to **Landscape**.

19. Click on **OK**.

20. Click on **OK**.

21. If the chart picture is acceptable, click on the **Print** icon.

22. Click on **OK**.

23. Click on Worksheet Tab **A**.

24. Select the range of cells **A12..D17**.

25. Click on the **Chart** icon.

26. Place the new chart in a separate sheet.

27. To change the chart type, click on the **Chart Type** icon. Click on **3DArea**. Select the second picture.

28. Click on **OK**.

29. Double click on the chart title.

30. Enter the following:

    Line 1: **(Your Name) Department Store** (Make sure Cell does not have an X)

    Line 2: **Expense Categories excluding Cost of Goods Sold**

    Placement: **Center**

    Note 1: **For the Quarter Ended March 1995**

    Placement: **Center**

31. Click on **OK**.

32. Change the X-axis title to **Categories**. Change the Y-axis title to **Dollars**.

33. Double click on the **Legend**. Change the legend to be **January**, **February**, **March** rather than Data **A**, **B**, and **C**.

34. Select **CHART/Name**. The name of this chart will be **COSTS**.

35. Change Worksheet Tab **B** to **COSTS**. Press **ENTER**.

36. Make the chart active by clicking anywhere on the chart.

37. To print the chart, select **FILE/Print Preview**.

38. In **Page Setup,** change the size to **Fill Page but keep proportions**. Change the **Orientation** to **Landscape**.

39. Click on **OK**.

40. Click on **OK**.

41. If the chart picture is acceptable, click on the **Print** icon.

42. Click on **OK**.

43. **FILE/Save** your file as **IA7-3DNE**.

44. **Print** your worksheet.

45. **FILE/Close** your file.

Independent Project 7.4: Creating a Mixed Chart

In this exercise, you will create a mixed chart from the data in a worksheet that contains Budgeted versus Actual Sales Results for a Sporting Goods Store. When you are done, your chart might resemble Figure 7 - 23.

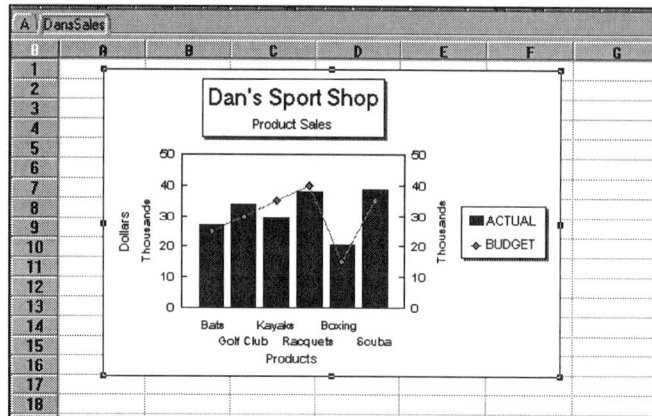

Figure 7 - 23

1. **Open** the file **IA7-4**.

2. Select the range of cells **A8..C14**.

3. Click on the **Chart** icon. Place the new chart in a separate sheet.

4. Change the **Chart type** to **Mixed**.

5. Select **CHART/Ranges**. Select **Series B- Budget**. Select **Plot on 2nd Y-Axis** and select the **Mixed Type** to **Line**.

6. Change the chart title to **Dan's Sport Shop**.

7. Change the X-axis title to **Products**.

8. Change the Y-axis title to **Dollars**.

9. Name the chart **DANSSALES**.

10. Create a new name for the Worksheet Tab: **DANSSALES**.

11. **Print** the chart.

12. **Save** your file as **IA7-4DNE**.

13. **Print** your worksheet.

Lesson 8 Database Basics

Objectives

In this lesson you will learn how to:

- Define a database table
- Sort a database on one sort key
- Sort a database on multiple keys

- Use the fill command
- Use Fill by Example.

PROJECT DESCRIPTION

In your new position, worksheet files were given to you, but you often have a need to reorganize the data. You would like to be able to sort information within the worksheet quickly. Therefore, you take out you *Lotus* reference manual and determine how to sort data.

Lotus 1-2-3 Release 5 - [DATA1.WK3]								
A		**B**	**C**	**D**	**E**	**F**	**G**	**H**
10	Antonio, Erin	F	58	1	01/02/73			
11	Bartholemew, Phyllis	F	49	1	11/16/84			
12	Boyenga, Gladys	F	24	1	02/19/82			
13	Cruz, Elinor	F	33	1	06/26/85			
14	Dixie, David	M	56	1	09/28/82			
15	Finch, Robert	M	55	1	02/01/69			
16	Finley, Maude	F	37	1	06/25/72			
17	Harrison, Wilbert	M	22	1	02/17/82			
18	Keith, Mildred	F	23	1	09/01/82			
19	King, John	M	34	1	01/20/76			
20	Kupferberg, Eli	M	44	1	02/27/82			
21	O'Leary, Shawn	M	26	1	02/02/79			
22	Paige, Carol	F	38	1	07/27/77			
23	Ringrose, Millicent	F	26	1	10/02/82			
24	Rinko, Carlo	M	29	1	12/05/73			
25	Smith, Alphonso	M	62	1	02/21/82			
26	Winkowsin, Ruth	F	38	1	08/24/76			
27	Black, Edward	M	33	2	07/02/76			
28	Dailey, Larry	M	49	2	03/12/82			
29	Dalton, William	M	53	2	04/05/75			

Figure 8 - 1

WHAT IS A DATABASE TABLE

A **database** is a collection of related data organized in a manner that allows for easy access, retrieval, and use of that data. You can create a **Database Table** in *Lotus*, which is a range of data organized in such a way that you can easily sort the data, retrieve data from the database, and print it. In Lesson 3, you moved data by using the technique of cutting and pasting. It was

161

mentioned that although this method did allow you to reorganize data, there is a better way to accomplish the same task, known as sorting. In this lesson, we will first retrieve a file containing a database table and sort the data. Later in this lesson, we will look at how we can use *Lotus* commands to easily create our own database table.

SORTING DATA

Before sorting the data in our database, there are some terms you must be familiar with. Figure 8 - 2 illustrates the terminology. A **record** is all the information about one item in a database table. Each **record** must be a separate row. In our example, all of the information about each employee is a record. Each record contains a series of **fields**. A **field** contains a specific piece of information within a record. Each column in a database table represents a separate field. The **fields** in our illustration are *employee, sex, age, division,* and *hire date*. Each field contains information about an employee record.

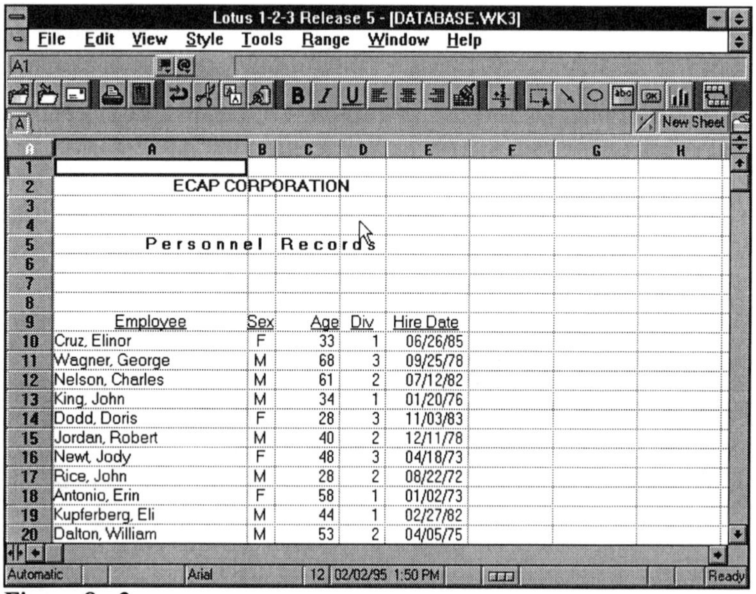

Figure 8 - 2

The data in the database table are much easier to work with if they are organized in a sequence that is meaningful. Can you imagine how difficult it would be to find a phone number in the phone directory if the data was not organized alphabetically? *Lotus* will permit you to **sort** the data in the worksheet by the contents of the fields. You may choose to sequence the data in either **ascending** or **descending** order.

SORTING A DATABASE

When you start a sorting operation, you must specify the records to be sorted, the field or fields on which to sort, and the sort order (ascending or descending). The field you select to sort on is called the **sort key**.

To sort a database on one sort key:

• Select the range of data to be sorted.

The range of data is to include all data to be sorted <u>but not the column headings</u>. Make sure you include all of the fields in each record. Failure to include all fields will result in sorting only a part of each record.

- From the menu select **RANGE/Sort**.

- Enter the *field* to sort by in the **Sort by** text box. The field to sort by is entered as a cell address. You need only enter the address of any cell in the field you wish to sort by. The only cell you cannot use is the cell containing the column heading.

- Click on either **Ascending** or **Descending**.

- Choose **OK**.

Activity 8.1: Sorting Data in the Database on One Sort Key

1. **Open** the file **DATABASE**.

2. Select the range of data to be sorted. The range of data to be sorted is **A10..E55**. This is all of the data in the database **not** including the column headings.

3. From the Menu Bar select **RANGE/Sort**. The **Sort** dialog box appears. We want to sort the data in the database alphabetically by last name.

4. In the **Sort By** area, the *field* to sort by will be the **A** column (Employee). The **Sort by** box should show **A10**. If it does not, use the **Range Selector** on the right of the **Sort by** text box to select cell **A10**. Click first on the **Range Selector**, then point to and click on cell **A10**. You will be returned automatically to the **Sort** dialog box.

   You do not have to select the entire A column: the first cell in the column is acceptable.

5. Make sure **Ascending** is selected. If it is not, click on **Ascending** to indicate we want this in alphabetical order. Your **Sort** dialog box looks like Figure 8 - 3.

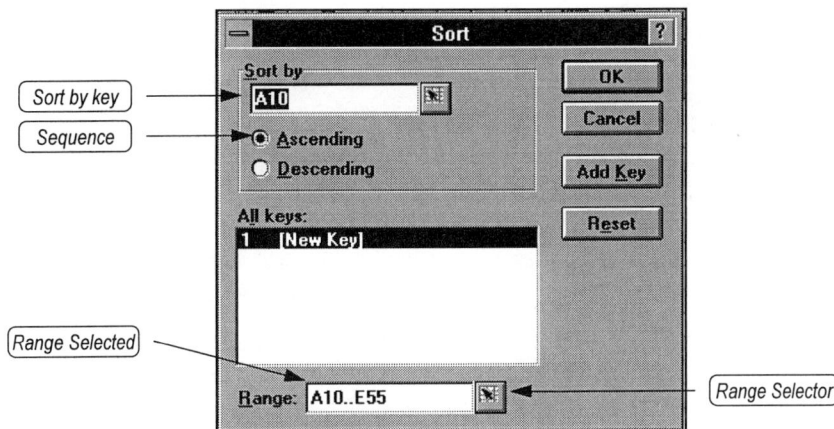

Figure 8 - 3

6. Choose **OK**. Your database is now sorted in alphabetic sequence.

   If you did this correctly, the first record in your database should now be:

   Albert, Joel   M   29   3   12/16/77.

   *If your results are different, click on the **Undo the last command or action** SmartIcon This will return your database back to its original sequence. Start over again at the beginning of the activity.*

   Your sorted database should look like Figure 8 - 4.

7. **Save** your file as **DATA1**.

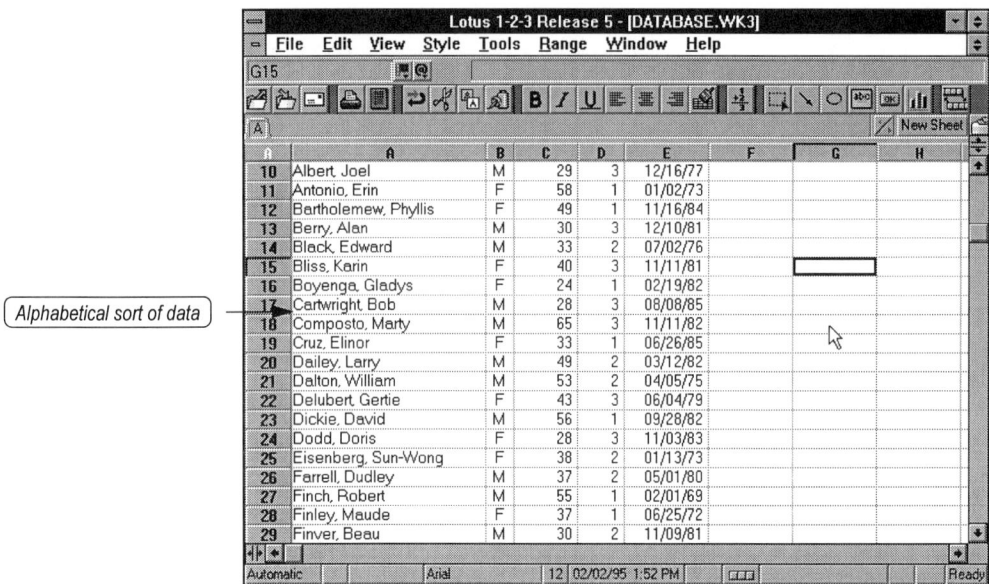

Figure 8 - 4

Sorting a Database on More Than One Sort Key

You may sort a database by over **200** fields, or sort keys.   A multiple sort key sort uses more than one field of data to sort the records. To understand why you would need to sort by more than one field, think back to our telephone directory example. Since many people have the same last name, the phone directory needs to be sorted first by city, then by last name, then first name, etc.

To sort by more than one sort key:

- Select the range of data to be sorted.

  Make sure the range of data includes all data to be sorted but not the column headings.

- From the menu select **RANGE/Sort**.

- Click on the **Reset Command** button [**Reset**] to clear all previous sort instructions.

- Enter the address of any cell in the *field* to sort by in the **Sort by** text box, or use the **Range Selector** to point and click on any cell in the sort field (except the cell containing the field label).

- Click on either **Ascending** or **Descending**.

- Click on the **Add Key** command button [**Add Key**].

- Enter the second *field* to sort by in the **Sort by** text box.

- Click on either **Ascending** or **Descending**.

- Continue this process until you select all the sort fields.

- Choose **OK**.

  Lotus will begin by sorting the data in your database table by the first key, then by the second key, etc.

Activity 8.2: Sorting Data in the Database on Two Sort Keys

1. If it is not already open, open the file **DATA1**.

2. Select the range of data to be sorted. The range of data to be sorted is **A10..E55**. This is all of the data in the database not including the column headings.

   The range may still be selected from the previous activity, if you did not close the file.

3. From the Menu Bar, select **RANGE/Sort**. The **Sort** dialog box appears. We want to sort the data in the database not only by division, but also within each division, alphabetically by last name.

Reset

4. Click on the **Reset** button. This will clear the settings from your prior sort.

5. To the right of **Sort by** text box, click on the **Range Selector**. This will place your mouse pointer back into the worksheet. Click on cell **D10** to indicate to *Lotus* that we want to sort first by *division*.

6. Make sure **Ascending** is selected. If it is not, click on **Ascending**.

Add Key

7. Click on the **Add Key** command button.

8. The second sort key will be the *last name*. In the **Sort by** text box, use the **Range Selector** to select **A10**.

9. Make sure **Ascending** is selected. *(Your **Sort** dialog box now looks like Figure 8 - 5.)*

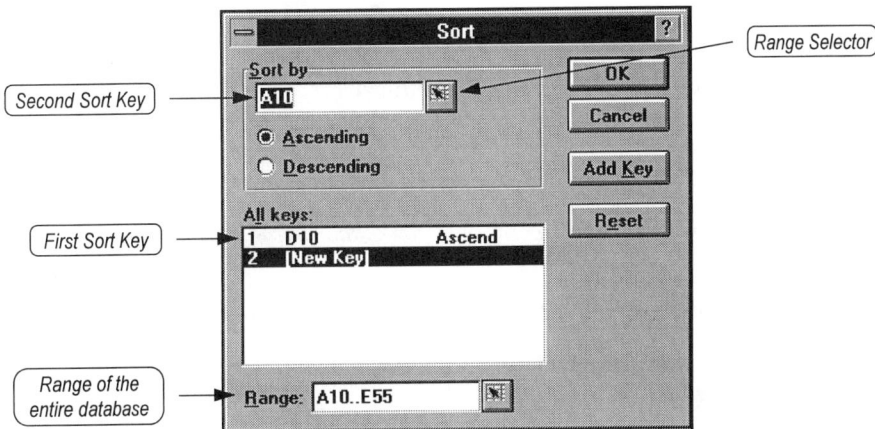

Figure 8 - 5

10. Choose **OK**. Your database is now sorted by division and in alphabetic sequence within each division. Your results should look like Figure 8 - 6.

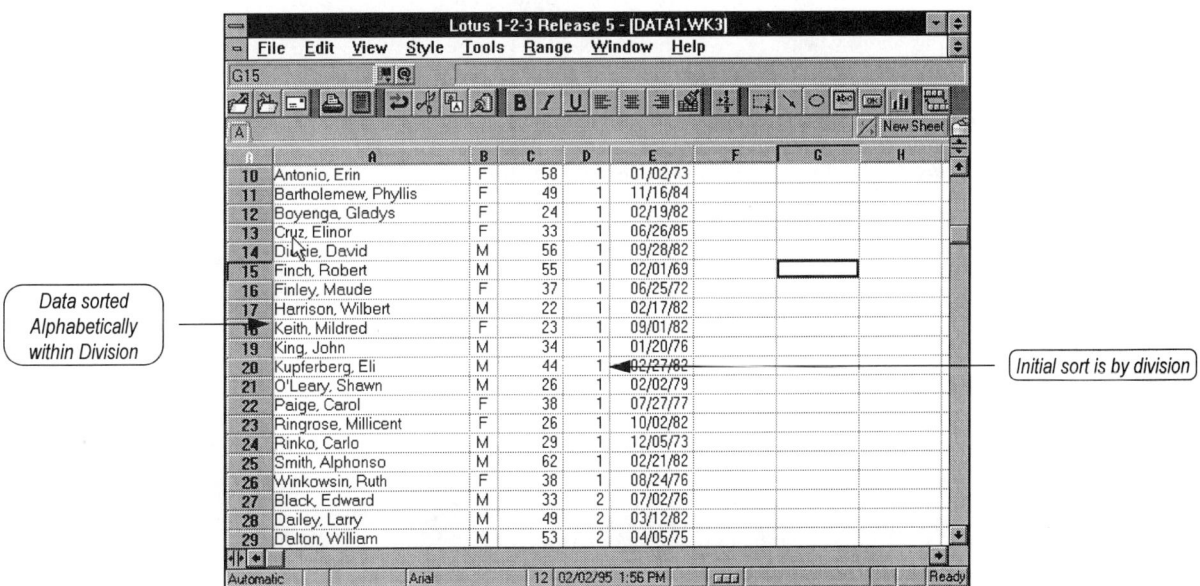

Figure 8 - 6

11. **Save** your file as **DATA2**.

12. **Close** your file.

USING THE FILL COMMAND

The **RANGE/Fill** command can be used to add sequence numbers, dates, times, or percentages to records in a database. When you sort data in a database, you change the sequence of the information. Sometimes, if the original sequence is not alphabetic or numeric, it might be difficult to return it to its original sequence. This is one example where the **RANGE/Fill** command might be helpful. It can also be used whenever you need to add a series of consecutive numbers in a column or row. For example, you might choose to create an interest table. Rather than typing in all the interest percentages, you can use the **RANGE/Fill** command will perform this task if you tell it what rate to start with, what rate to end with, and the increments (intervals) by which to increase.

To use the Fill command:

*   Select the range (column, row, or both) that you want filled.

*   Select **RANGE/Fill**.

*   In the **Fill** dialog box, enter the **Start** value, the **Increment** value, and the **Stop** value.

    *You do not have to enter the **Stop** value. Lotus will stop at the ending value or the end of the range, whichever comes first.*

*   The default **Interval** is linear, but you will also notice that you can choose time frames for intervals.

*   Click on **OK**.

Activity 8.3: Using the Range Fill Command

1. You should have an empty worksheet on your screen from the last activity. If not, close the file **DATA2** and/or any files that currently are open. We are going to create a series of consecutive numbers in column **A** that could identify, for example, store numbers.

2. In the blank worksheet, we need to select the range we want filled. We are going to select the range **A5..A20**. This column will contain a series of store numbers, starting with **100**.

3. Select **RANGE/Fill**.

4. In the **Fill** dialog box, type the **Start** value: **100**.

5. The **Increment** value is **1**. You do not have to change this.

6. The **End** value will be **115**, but *Lotus* will stop at the end of the range before it gets to the default value of **8191**. Therefore, we can leave the default number of **8191**.

7. The **Interval** will be **Linear**.

8. Select **OK**.

9. Now your store numbers are placed in the **A** column from **A5..A20**. Your results will look like Figure 8 - 7.

10. Type the label in cell **A4**: **STORE #**.

11. Save your file as **FILL**.

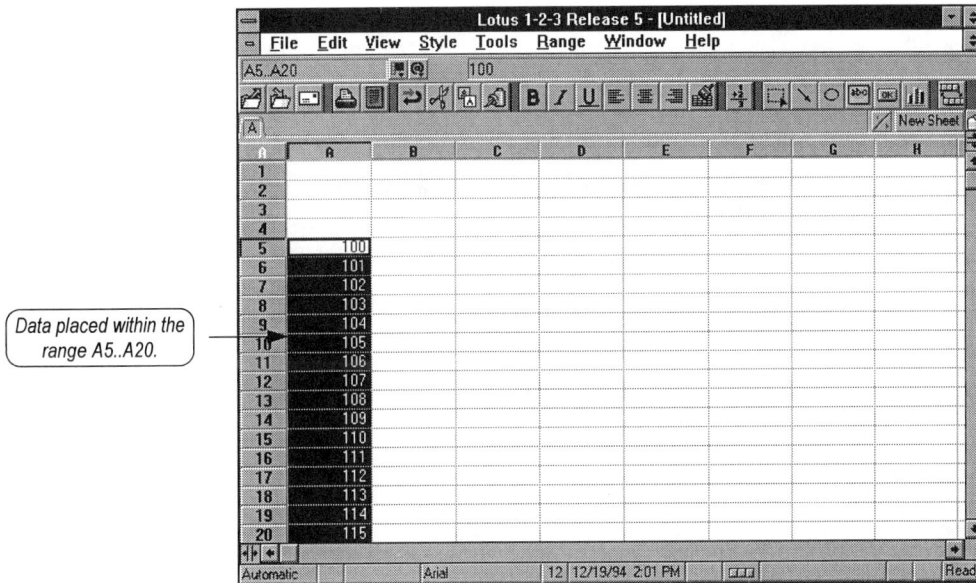

Data placed within the range A5..A20.

Figure 8 - 7

USING THE FILL BY EXAMPLE COMMAND

Lotus can automatically enter data in a range if the range is to have a specific sequence to it. Using *Lotus*, we can enter days, months, years, quarters, etc., into a column or a row. To create the sequence, determine where the first entry will be and enter that first entry into that cell. Then select the range of data to be filled starting with your first entry. Then select either **RANGE/Fill by Example** or click on the **Complete a sequence in a selected range** SmartIcon ⌗ from the **Editing** SmartIcon set. The range will be automatically filled.

To use the Fill by Example command:

- Type the first entry in the cell of your choice.

- Select the range of data to be filled. Be sure to start the range with the cell containing the first entry.

- From the menu select **RANGE/Fill by Example** or click on the **Complete a sequence in a selected range** ⌗ SmartIcon.

Activity 8.4: Using Fill by Example

1. **Open** the file **FILL** if it is not already open.

   We are going to add labels for some of the columns in this worksheet to identify the months. Then, data could be entered into the worksheet for, for example, monthly sales figures by store for a chain of retail stores.

2. In cell **B4**, enter the label, **JAN**. Right align the label.

3. Using the mouse, select the range **B4..M4**. This range will contain all of the labels for the months, starting with **JAN**.

   Note: You could have entered the word January. We chose JAN because we wanted shorter labels. Also, since we started by having the label JAN right aligned, all of the labels that will be filled in will also be right aligned.

4. Select **RANGE/Fill by Example**.

5. Now the abbreviations for the months are placed in the range you selected and are right aligned.

   Your results will look like Figure 8 - 8.

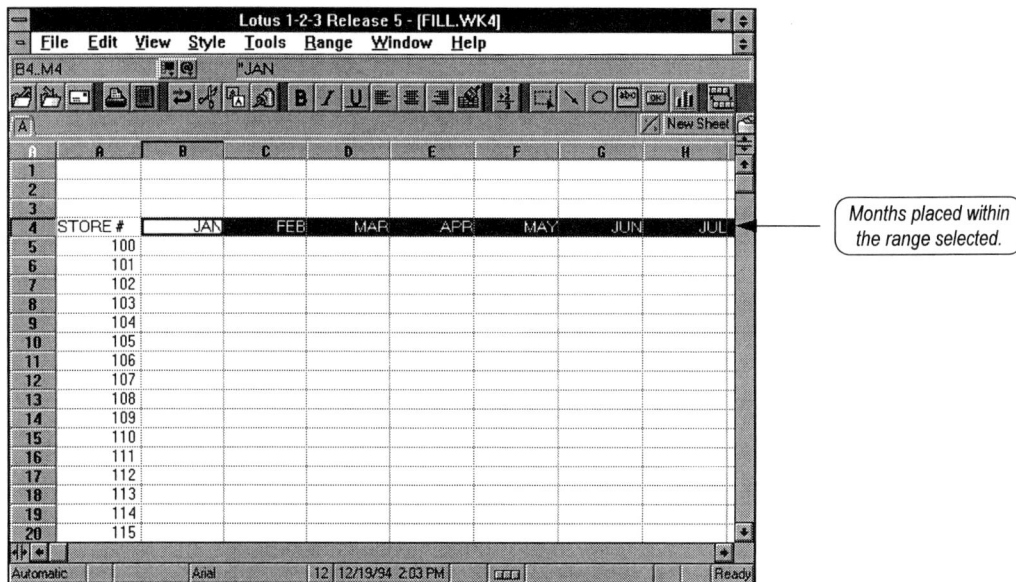

Months placed within the range selected.

Figure 8 - 8

6. Now you are ready to enter the data into your worksheet.

7. **Save** your file as **FILL2**.

8. **Close** your file.

SUMMARY

In this lesson you briefly explored the concepts of database tables, sorting data in databases, and using Data Fill and Fill by Example to add numbers or labels to a column or row. You can practice sorting data within a worksheet by completing the Independent projects.

KEY TERMS

Ascending	Fill	Record
Database	Fill by Example	Sort Key
Database Table	Increment	Sorting
Descending	Interval	Start Value
Field	Range Selector	Stop Value

INDEPENDENT PROJECTS

Independent Project 8.1: Sorting Data in the Worksheet

In this exercise, you will practice sorting data in your worksheet. The file with which you will be working contains information on various investments you have made. You are going to sort the data in the worksheet. Your completed worksheet will look like Figure 8 - 9.

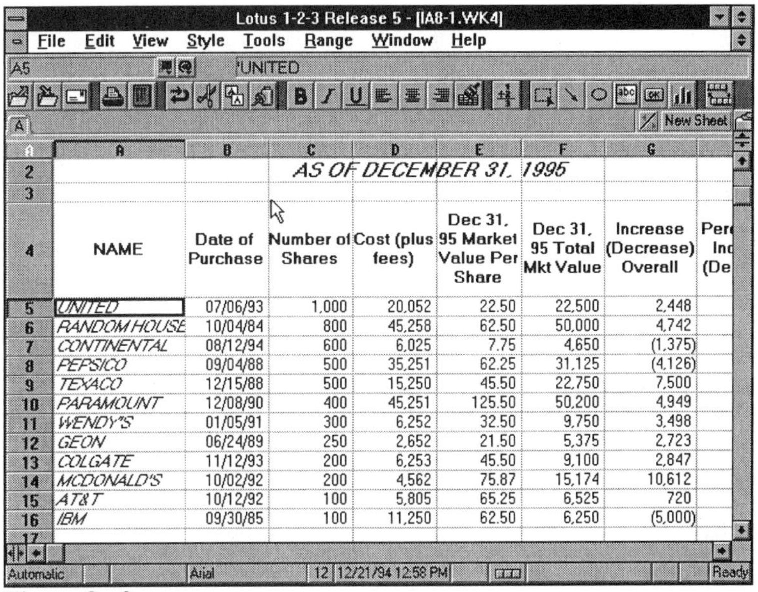

NAME	Date of Purchase	Number of Shares	Cost (plus fees)	Dec 31, 95 Market Value Per Share	Dec 31, 95 Total Mkt Value	Increase (Decrease) Overall	Per Inc (De
UNITED	07/06/93	1,000	20,052	22.50	22,500	2,448	
RANDOM HOUSE	10/04/84	800	45,258	62.50	50,000	4,742	
CONTINENTAL	08/12/94	600	6,025	7.75	4,650	(1,375)	
PEPSICO	09/04/88	500	35,251	62.25	31,125	(4,126)	
TEXACO	12/15/88	500	15,250	45.50	22,750	7,500	
PARAMOUNT	12/08/90	400	45,251	125.50	50,200	4,949	
WENDY'S	01/05/91	300	6,252	32.50	9,750	3,498	
GEON	06/24/89	250	2,652	21.50	5,375	2,723	
COLGATE	11/12/93	200	6,253	45.50	9,100	2,847	
MCDONALD'S	10/02/92	200	4,562	75.87	15,174	10,612	
AT&T	10/12/92	100	5,805	65.25	6,525	720	
IBM	09/30/85	100	11,250	62.50	6,250	(5,000)	

AS OF DECEMBER 31, 1995

Figure 8 - 9

1. Select **FILE/Open**
2. The file you want to open is **IA8-1**.
3. Place your cursor in cell **A5**. First, you need to select the range of cells to sort. The range is **A5..H16**.
4. From the menu, select **RANGE/Sort**.
5. You want to sort the data alphabetically. Therefore the sort key will be the **A** column. In the **Sort by** area, use the **Range Selector** to select cell **A5**.
6. Make sure **Ascending** is selected.
7. Click on **OK**.
8. Your investment portfolio is now in alphabetic sequence.
9. Now you want to sort the same portfolio differently. The sequence you want is by the number of shares from high to low. If you have multiple stocks that you own the same amount of share, then those are to be placed in alphabetic order.
10. Select the range of cells to sort. The range is **A5..H16**.
11. From the menu, select **RANGE/Sort**.
12. Select **Reset** to reset the prior sort keys.
13. You want to sort the data by the number of shares from High to Low. Therefore the sort key will be the **C** column. In the **Sort by** area, use the **Range Selector** to select cell **C5**.
14. Make sure **Descending** is selected.
15. Click on **Add Key**.
16. Your secondary sort is alphabetical. Therefore the sort key will be the **A** column. In the **Sort by** area, use the **Range Selector** to select cell **A5**.
17. Make sure **Ascending** is selected.
18. Click on **OK**.
19. Your results should look like Figure 8 - 9.

20. **FILE/Save** your file as **IA8-1DNE.**
21. **Print** your worksheet.
22. **FILE/Close** your file.

Independent Project 8.2: Sorting a Database

In this exercise, you will practice sorting data in the worksheet. The worksheet file we will be using contains billing information for employees within your firm. When you are done, your worksheet should look like Figure 8 - 10.

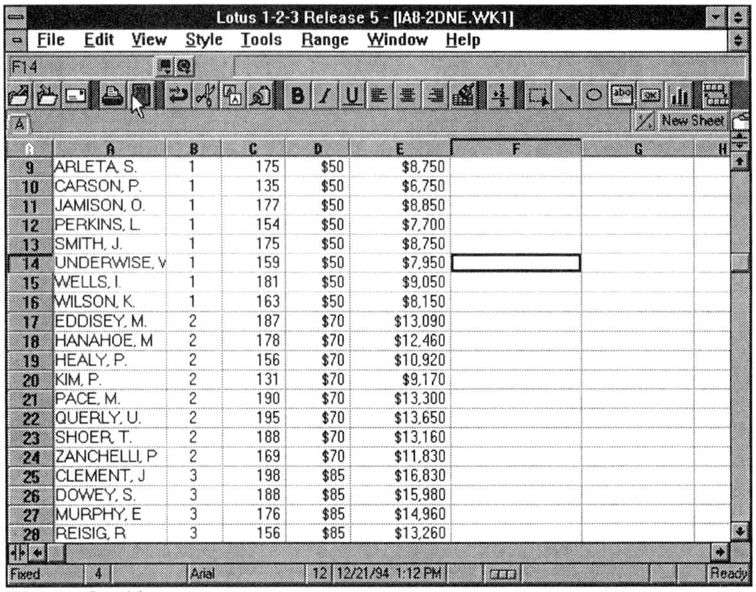

	A	B	C	D	E
9	ARLETA, S.	1	175	$50	$8,750
10	CARSON, P.	1	135	$50	$6,750
11	JAMISON, O.	1	177	$50	$8,850
12	PERKINS, L.	1	154	$50	$7,700
13	SMITH, J.	1	175	$50	$8,750
14	UNDERWISE, V	1	159	$50	$7,950
15	WELLS, I.	1	181	$50	$9,050
16	WILSON, K.	1	163	$50	$8,150
17	EDDISEY, M.	2	187	$70	$13,090
18	HANAHOE, M	2	178	$70	$12,460
19	HEALY, P.	2	156	$70	$10,920
20	KIM, P.	2	131	$70	$9,170
21	PACE, M.	2	190	$70	$13,300
22	QUERLY, U.	2	195	$70	$13,650
23	SHOER, T.	2	188	$70	$13,160
24	ZANCHELLI, P	2	169	$70	$11,830
25	CLEMENT, J	3	198	$85	$16,830
26	DOWEY, S.	3	188	$85	$15,980
27	MURPHY, E	3	176	$85	$14,960
28	REISIG, R	3	156	$85	$13,260

Figure 8 - 10

1. Select **FILE/Open**.
2. The file you want to open is **IA8-2**.
3. Select **RANGE/Sort Reset**.
4. You want to sort the data in the worksheet as follows:

   By level   **Ascending** sequence

   By name   **Alphabetic** sequence
5. Select the range of cells to sort. The range is **A9..E30**.
6. Select **RANGE/Sort**.
7. The first sort key will be the **B** column. In the **Sort by** area, use the **Range Selector** to select cell B**5**.
8. Make sure **Ascending** is selected.
9. Click on **Add Key**.
10. Your secondary sort is the **Last Name**. The sort key will be the **A** column. Make sure **Ascending** is selected.
11. Click on **OK**.

12. Your worksheet is now in the sequence you want.

13. **FILE/Save** your file as **IA8-2DNE**.

14. **Print** your worksheet.

15. **FILE/Close** your file.

Independent Project 8.3: More Sorting

In this exercise, you practice sorting data within a *Lotus* worksheet. This worksheet contains student grades in a Financial Accounting Class. When you are done, your worksheet will look like Figure 8 - 11.

	A	B	C	D	E	F	G
6	Ross, Judith Ann	Act	N	99	100	89	96.00
7	Cesare, Anthony	Act	Y	97	95	94	95.33
8	Warr, Stacey	Act	Y	100	94	92	95.33
9	Zangrandi, Patricia A.	Act	Y	99	93	92	94.67
10	Gentile, Joseph	Act	Y	89	87	89	88.33
11	O'Hara, Breda M.	Act	Y	89	82	87	86.00
12	Weisse, Raymond	Act	Y	90	73	85	82.67
13	Hickey, Mary G.	Act	N	85	78	83	82.00
14	Russell, David Richard	Act	Y	88	65	91	81.33
15	Gherardi, Denise	Act	N	94	70	77	80.33
16	Westrick, Nancy I.	Act	N	90	69	77	78.67
17	Amaya, Jaime	Act	Y	81	70	75	75.33
18	Castello, Christopher L.	Bus	N	92	90	91	91.00
19	Guiffrida, Grace	Bus	N	99	63	83	81.67
20	Pagliuca, Carolyn S.	Bus	Y	89	53	77	73.00
21	Delaive, Andrew William	Bus	N	52	40	67	53.00
22	Zinicola, Joseph M.	Bus	N	67	24	59	50.00
23	Riggio, Tina Lynn	Fin	N	80	63	73	72.00
24	Vogler, Tammy	Fin	Y	68	71	65	68.00
25	Sheil, Danean	Fin	N	86	26	55	55.67

Figure 8 - 11

1. **Open** the file **IA8-3**.

2. Select **RANGE/Sort Reset**.

3. You want to sort the data in the worksheet as follows:

   By Major   **Alphabetic** Sequence

   By Final Avg.   **Descending** sequence

4. Select the range of cells to sort.

5. Select **RANGE/Sort**.

6. Enter the sort keys as defined in step 3.

7. Your result should look like Figure 8 - 11.

8. **FILE/Save** your file as **IA8-3DNE**.

9. **Print** your worksheet.

10. **FILE/Close** your file.

Appendix:
Featured Reference

The following table contains a summary of the main features presented in the lesson. As you know, most features in Lotus can be performed in a variety of ways. Many of the menu bar commands can also be selected from The Quick Menus. Listed mouse shortcuts involve the use of the buttons on the Standard and Formatting Toolbars and other mouse techniques. Shortcut keys are keystrokes of function keys. Many features require that the text be selected prior to executing the command. If you need more detail on using these features, the table contains a reference to the lesson describing its use.

Features	Menu Bar Commands	Mouse Shortcut	Shortcut Keys	
Alignment	STYLE/Alignment	Center Icon Align Left Icon Align Right Icon	CTRL + E CTRL + L CTRL + R	2
Bold	STYLE/Fonts & Attributes	Bold Icon	CTRL + B	2
Borders, add, change or remove	STYLE/Lines & Colors			2
Center across Columns	STYLE/Alignment		CTRL + E	2
Charts, changing type	CHART/Type	Chart Type Icon		7
Charts, creating	TOOLS/Chart	Chart Icon		7
Clear cell contents	EDIT/Clear	Click on Cut Icon	DELETE	1
Clear contents and format	EDIT/Clear,Both			2
Column Width	STYLE/Column Width	Drag right column header border (or double click border to Fit To Widest Entry		1
Column, Select		Click on column header		1
Comma Format	STYLE/Number Format	Format Selector on Status Bar		2
Copy cell contents to adjacent cells	EDIT/Fill	Drag fill handle		3
Copy cell contents to nonadjacent cells	EDIT/Copy EDIT/Paste	Copy button Paste button; or Point to selection, press **CTRL** and drag to new location	CTRL + C CTRL + V	3
Currency Format	STYLE/Number Format	Format Selector of Status Bar		2
Delete Rows/Columns	EDIT/Delete			3
Edit cell contents		Double-click on cell	F2	1
Exit Lotus	FILE/Exit		ALT + F4	I
Font	STYLE/Fonts & Attributes			2
Font Size	STYLE/Fonts & Attributes			2
Footers	FILE/Page Setup, Header/Footer			3
Formulas, displaying on worksheet	STYLE/Number Format, Text			4

Features	Menu Bar Commands	Mouse Shortcut	Shortcut Keys	
Font Style	STYLE/Fonts & Attributes	Bold, Italic, Underline Icon	CTRL + B CTRL + I CTRL + U	2
Functions, Insert		@ Function Selector		4
Gridlines, remove from printout	FILE/Page Setup, Gridlines			2
Headers	FILE/Page Setup, Headers/Footers			2
Help on a specific topic	HELP/Search for Help on			I
Help, contents	HELP/Contents		F1	I
Help, context sensitive		Help Icon	F1	I
Insert Rows (Columns)	EDIT/Insert , Columns or Rows			3
Italics	STYLE/Fonts & Attributes	Italic Icon	CTRL + I	2
Move cell contents	EDIT/Cut EDIT/Paste	Cut Icon Paste Icon; or Point to selection and drag	CTRL + X CTRL + V	3
New File, create	FILE/New			I
Open a file	FILE/Open	Open Icon	CTRL + O	I
Page Setup for printout	FILE/Page Setup			2
Percent Format	STYLE/Number Format	Format Selector on Status Bar		2
Preview printout	FILE/Print Preview	Print Preview Icon		2
Print	FILE/Print	Print Icon	CTRL + P	1,2, 4
Row, Select		Click on row header		1
Save a file, using a different name	FILE/Save As			2
Save a file, using same name	FILE/Save	Save Icon	CTRL + S	1
Sequence, Create	RANGE/Fill by Example	Fill By Example Icon		8
Sort data	RANGE/Sort			8
SUM function		@ Function Selector		3
Underline	STYLE/Fonts & Attributes	Underline Icon	CTRL + U	2
Undo	EDIT/Undo	Undo Icon	CTRL + Z	1
Worksheet, change from sheet to sheet		Click on new tab	CTRL + PAGE DOWN (UP)	6
Worksheet, rename sheets		Double-click sheet tab		7

Index

First published in Great Britain 2024 by Farshore
An imprint of HarperCollins*Publishers*
1 London Bridge Street, London, SE1 9GF
www.farshore.co.uk

HarperCollins*Publishers*
Macken House, 39/40 Mayor Street Upper,
Dublin 1, D01 C9W8, Ireland

BEANO

BEANO.COM

A Beano Studios Product © DC Thomson & Co Ltd. (2024)

Written by Mara Alperin

ISBN 978 0 00 861650 2
Printed in UK
001

Stay safe online. Any website addresses listed in this book are
correct at the time of going to print. However, Farshore is not
responsible for content hosted by third parties. Please be aware that
online content can be subject to change and websites can contain
content that is unsuitable for children. We advise that all children
are supervised when using the internet.

MIX
Paper | Supporting
responsible forestry
FSC™ C007454

This book contains FSC™ certified paper and other controlled
sources to ensure responsible forest management.

For more information visit: www.harpercollins.co.uk/green

BEANO

POCKET PUZZLES

CONTENTS

Once upon a time, in the not so faraway place of Beanotown, there lived an 11-year-old boy called Marmaduke Bunkerton III. But to his friends, he was known as Lord Snooty.

Lord Snooty had everything a young lord could desire: a castle to live in, a butler named Parkinson, a fabulous art collection and loads and loads of cash.

But there was one thing he was missing . . .

WI-FI.

There would be no video games to play, no You-Hoo channels to watch and no group chats with mates to send top-hat emojis to.

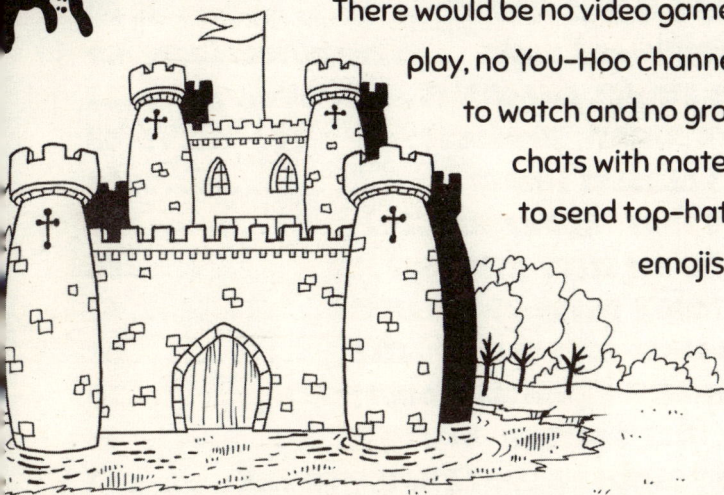

What was a young lord to do with his spare time without Wi-Fi?

Lord Snooty puzzled and puzzled over it, until at last the answer came to him...

Puzzling, puzzling ... wait a minute, that's it! Puzzles! That will keep me occupied! And I have a noble idea of how to get some!

PUZZLE CONTEST!
Grand Prize = £1,000

Are you bitter about boredom, but passionate about puzzles? If so, please submit your best puzzle to Lord Snooty at Bunkerton Castle, by Friday morning! The creator of the funnest puzzle will win £1,000!

Sorry folks – only residents of Beanotown can enter. Let's take a look at some entries! – The Ed

DENNIS'S PONGY PUZZLE

Only the keenest detective can solve my puzzle to work out one of Beanotown's biggest mysteries: who farted?

Anyone could have done it (it might have even been me)! But here are three clues to help you cross out the suspects, until only one is left ...

CLUE 1: The farter can't be in the same row or column as Mrs Creecher – no one would dare try that!

CLUE 2: The trumper can't be someone who is next to a bugle, as that would have covered up the sound.

CLUE 3: The tooter can't be someone who is next to a flower, as that would have covered up the smell (eww).

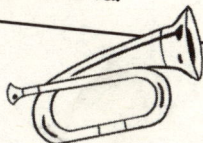

You know, creating new puzzles is hard work. It's nothing to sniff at – in fact, you should probably hold your nose instead for this puzzle, because it has a bit of a pong ...

It was _____ who farted!

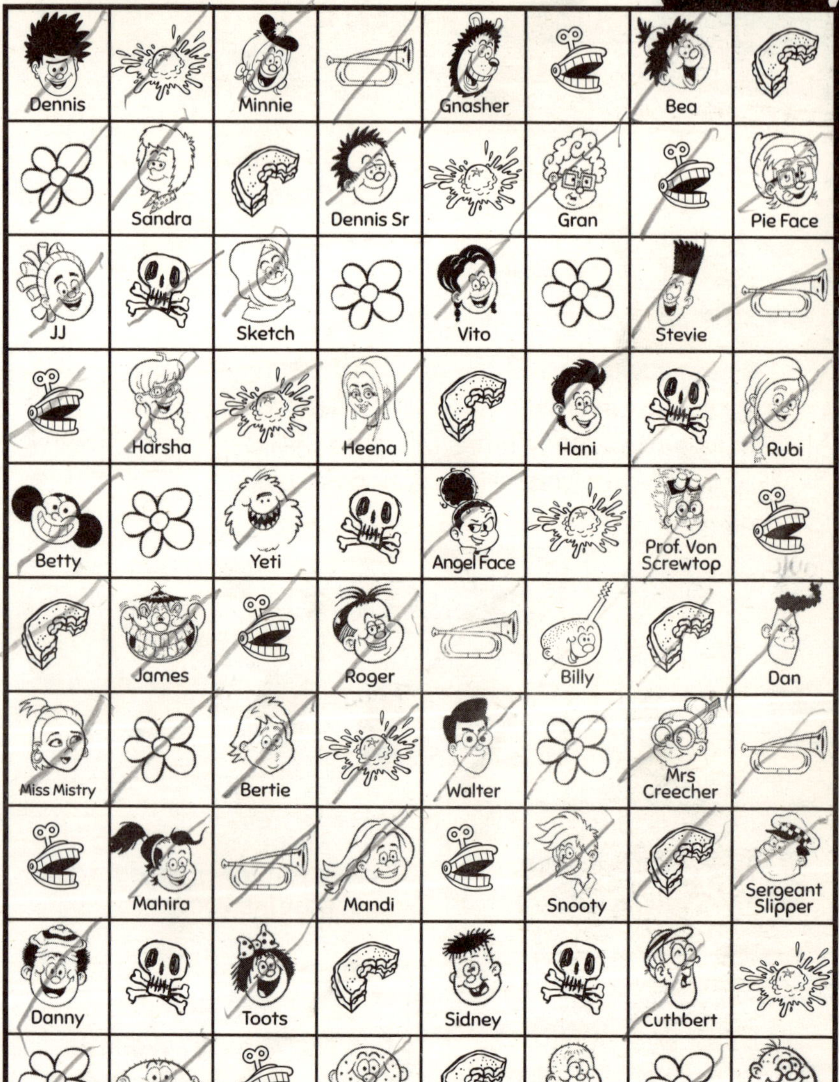

Answer on page 74

MINNIE'S MATHS RIDDLE

Now I have a new excuse for being late – I was too busy making this maths puzzle. You can't blame me, but you CAN blame maths!

Class should start when I'm ready for it to start. But Miss Mistry seems to think otherwise. Would you like to know how many times this term I've been late? Just follow the simple instructions below ...

5   28
16
21   3

25   14
8   26

17   4
27
22   9

STEP 1: Put an X over all the multiples of 2.

STEP 2: Put three lines through all the multiples of 3.

STEP 3: Scribble as hard as you can over all the multiples of 5.

STEP 4: Now circle the only number remaining – that's the answer!

Minnie has been late ⎣7⎦ times this term!

GNASHER

GNASHER'S SAUSAGE WORDSEARCH

Sausages are perfect when they're plain, or tasty with toppings. Can you search for my favourite sausages and condiments in the puzzle below?

```
B Z R E L I S H S C B E K B A
P H S R J G U G H P H S K W N
U P B R G Z P I K W P E X T I
H E P H B O P K V A D E D L G
C T X N D O D W G Z O H I Q R
T S R M L K A T I V X C J C O
E P K A R A C W O M J D H K E
K Z T J G E Z K U H M O E Y G
T A I T S R U W T A R B G H D
X S A L A M I X Q I Y K L R H
M Q M U U D Y B Z L V N A K H
K F R N D F I O T E H T M B U
G N I S S E R D H O S P Z N M
H S X G R A Z Q P U K M R O N
J T W P G V O N M D F U L Q R
```

BRATWURST

CHIPOLATA

CHORIZO

HOTDOG

SALAMI

CHEESE

DRESSING

KETCHUP

MUSTARD

RELISH

Answer on page 75

FIND BEA'S DIRTY NAPPY

Did you know that just one week's worth of Bea's whiffy nappies can weigh the same as three warthogs on a wagon*?

But lucky for you, there's only one stinky nappy here. You just have to find where it is ...

Answer on page 75

I helped Bea make a putrid, pongy puzzle. You might have to put a peg on your nose while you play!

*Actually, I have no idea whether this is true, or Dennis made it up ... but do you want to be the one to check it? Besides, it makes scents! –The Ed

DENNIS SENIOR'S PAPER CLIP PUZZLE

This puzzle wasn't supposed to be about paper clips! I was trying to make a 'Cool Dad's Fun Shed' puzzle, but I spilled a box of Perkins Plentifully Patterned Paper Clips all over it . . . Arrrgh!

How quickly can you count all the paper clips in this pile?

There are _____ stripy paper clips.

There are _____ spotty paper clips.

There are _____ plain paper clips.

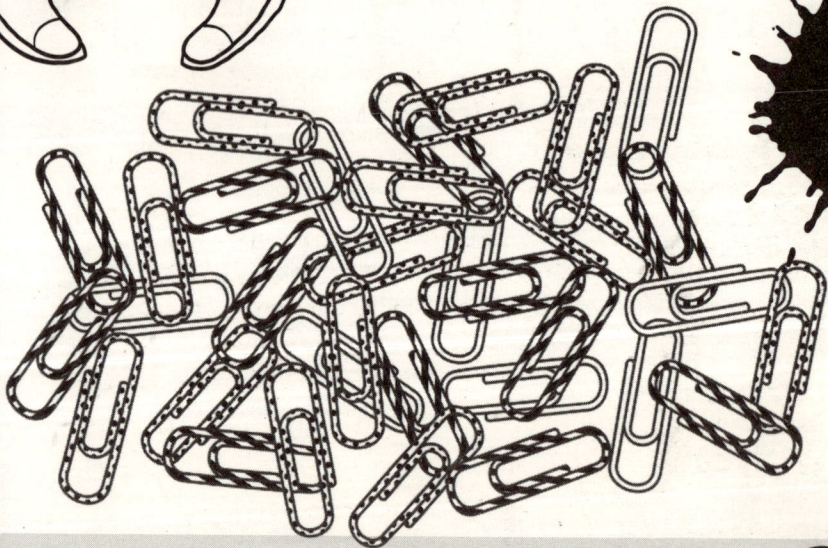

Answer on page 76

SANDRA'S NIGHTTIME ART MISSION

Last night, a painting went missing from Wilbur Brown's knock-off art collection. He's not sure which painting, though. He doesn't even like art – he just thinks that owning it will make him look richer. He's tasked me with figuring out what's missing. I don't know why he thinks I'll know ... Can you work out which painting ~~I stole~~ was taken, using the clues?

THE I-SCREAM

THE GREAT SHAVE OFF KANAGAWA

I have no secret ninja skills. I'm sure I know nothing about the whereabouts of a priceless piece of art. And I definitely have an alibi. Who's asking?

CLUE 1: The artist was hangry when painting this artwork, having skipped breakfast that morning.

CLUE 2: The artist felt like painting outside that day.

CLUE 3: The subject of the painting was having a really bad day until Ice Ice Betty's van parked nearby.

THE MONA PIZZA

STARCHY NIGHT

Sandra ~~stole~~ borrowed this painting:

_____

GRAN'S JUMPERS

I've knitted so many jumpers for my grandson Dennis, but one of them went a little bit wrong. Can you pick out the odd jumper from the jumble of jumpers below?

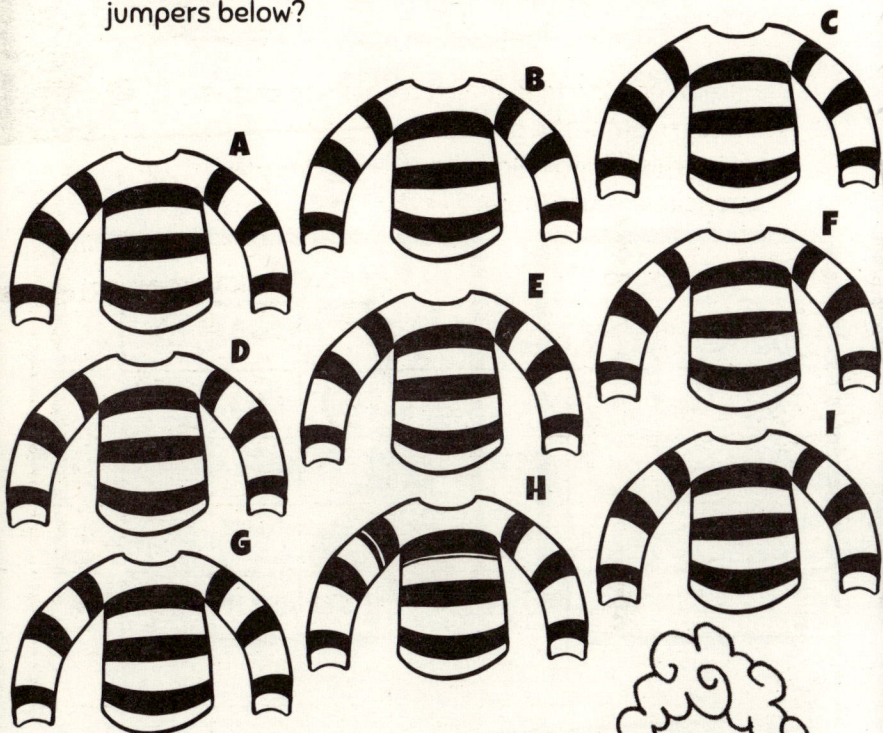

A B C D E F G H I

I do love knitting – when I'm not too busy zooming around on my motorcycle, that is. In fact, maybe Lord Snooty should give knitting a go if he's really that bored. I bet his butler would love a new pair of socks!

JJ'S BUNKERTON CASTLE DASH

Even if my puzzle isn't the best one, I'm going to be the first to Bunkerton Castle to hand mine in!

Help me race to Bunkerton Castle to be the first to enter the contest! Use this key to follow the quickest route there...

down left up right

START

FINISH

PIE FACE'S EASY-AS-PIE PUZZLE

I have three empty pie crusts and nine fillings. I want to put three fillings in each pie, but I'm not sure which ones go together. Can you use the notes below to work out what I should put in each pie?

CHEESE, **CHOCOLATE** and **CURRY SAUCE** all start with the letter 'C', so they each need to go into different pies. That's just the way it is with pie sometimes!

PEARS pair nicely with **SPINACH**, but not with **CHEESE**.

You can't put **YOGURT** and **CURRY SAUCE** into the same pie – it would be too soggy.

Olive Sprat recommended mixing **APPLES** and **CURRY SAUCE**. I think I might try it ...

Olive Pratt told me her favourite pies have **SPINACH** and **CHOCOLATE** in them. How ins–PIE–rational!

Gnasher likes **SAUSAGE** but not **CURRY SAUCE**. I'd better make one that he will eat!

Hmm, there's an ingredient missing in one of my pies ... oh, yes, I know what could go in it: **LEEKS**!

BONUS: Circle the pie that looks the yummiest and I'll enter it into next month's pie-baking contest! Do you think I'll win?

FILLINGS:

Apples   Leeks
Cheese   Pears
Chocolate   Sausage
Curry sauce   Spinach
               Yogurt

I'm filling pretty good about my chances for winning Lord Snooty's contest AND the Olives' pie-baking contest next month!

VITO'S WHOPPING WORDSEARCH

Making the world a better place is no small task ... and neither is this wordsearch! How quickly can you find these important words?

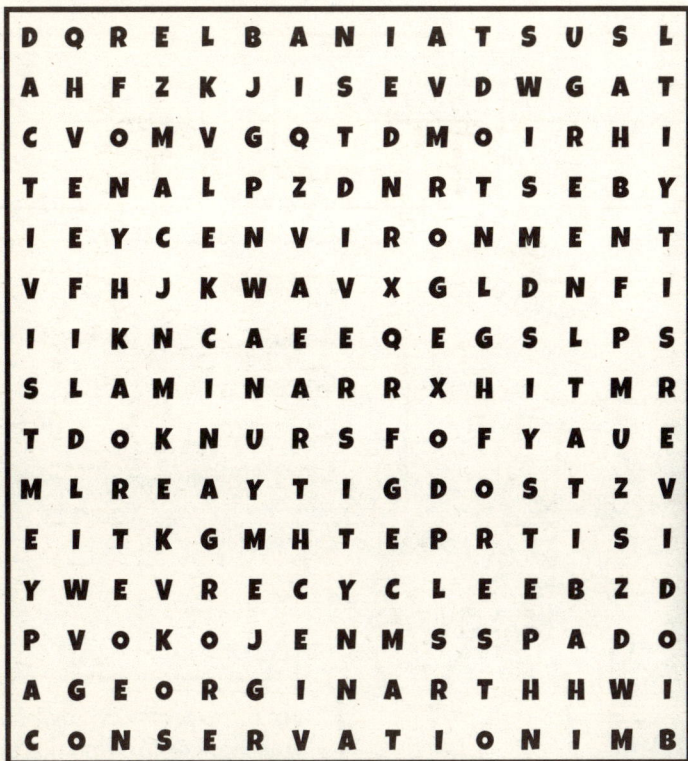

Answers on page 78

```
D Q R E L B A N I A T S U S L
A H F Z K J I S E V D W G A T
C V O M V G Q T D M O I R H I
T E N A L P Z D N R T S E B Y
I E Y C E N V I R O N M E N T
V F H J K W A V X G L D N F I
I I K N C A E E Q E G S L P S
S L A M I N A R R X H I T M R
T D O K N U R S F O F Y A U E
M L R E A Y T I G D O S T Z V
E I T K G M H T E P R T I S I
Y W E V R E C Y C L E E B Z D
P V O K O J E N M S S P A D O
A G E O R G I N A R T H H W I
C O N S E R V A T I O N I M B
```

ACTIVIST
ANIMALS
BIODIVERSITY
CONSERVATION
DIVERSITY
EARTH
ENVIRONMENT
FOREST

HABITAT
GREEN
ORGANIC
PLANET
RECYCLE
SUSTAINABLE
WILDLIFE

SKETCH'S DOT TO DOT

There are many dots to connect, but if you start by drawing the drawbridge, it will come together in no time...

With £1,000, I could buy the best new tablet for my drawings! And I have a feeling Lord Snooty will like this puzzle...

21

MANDI'S MOTIVATION MIX-UP

I like to write down inspirational quotes like these. They sometimes help me get through tough days!

There's been a mix-up with these three quotes I've written down. Can you piece them back together?

Never underestimate a teacher with

Use your fear ... it can take you to

that defines us, but

It isn't what we say or think

jets in their hands and

the place where you store

feet. – Minnie Makepeace

what we do. – Jane Austen

your courage. – Amelia Earhart

1_____

_____

2_____

_____

3_____

_____

MAHIRA'S FOOTBALL FUN

I'm very good at puzzles – almost as good as I am at football! And did you know that you can rearrange all the letters in the word 'FOOTBALL' to spell 'LOAF BOLT'?

How many words can you find from the letters in my favourite word, **F-O-O-T-B-A-L-L**? I've given you five clues to get started...

1. A hammer, saw or spanner is a _ _ _ _ _

2. A baby horse is a _ _ _ _ _

3. Where Professor Von Screwtop performs his science experiments is in a _ _ _ _

4. Most sticks will do this if you throw them in water _ _ _ _ _ _

5. Walter Brown will do this if you tie his shoelaces together when he's not paying attention! _ _ _ _ _

What other words can you make from just those letters?

_ _ _ _ _ _   _ _ _ _ _ _   _ _ _ _ _ _

_ _ _ _ _ _   _ _ _ _ _ _   _ _ _ _ _ _

_ _ _ _ _ _   _ _ _ _ _ _   _ _ _ _ _ _

_ _ _ _ _ _   _ _ _ _ _ _   _ _ _ _ _ _

Answers on page 79

HARSHA'S PRANKSTER CROSSWORD

Can you show off your pranking powers by solving this tricky crossword? You have to start by crossing your eyes and shouting out your favourite word.

Just kidding. It's a crossword puzzle. You know what to do!

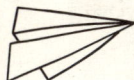

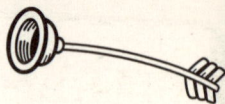

1. If you hide this thing that's used to wipe your bum, you'll put your parents in a stinky mood: _ _ _ _ _ _ _

2. Why put water in balloons when you can fill them with a sticky green goo-like substance called: _ _ _ _ _

3. This sort of powder makes you scratch your head trying to work out who pranked you: _ _ _ _ _ _ _

4. Whoopee! This popular prank feels as soft as a pillow, but it's as loud as a trump! It's a whoopee _ _ _ _ _ _ _

5. These red fruits that go splat are all that! (And they're definitely not vegetables, even if they wish they were.)

_ _ _ _ _ _ _ _

6. If you leave this rubber reptile under your little brother's pillow, it's simply hiss-terical: _ _ _ _ _

7. The next time someone asks for a spoonful of sugar for their tea, you could give them this look-alike, best-mate-of-pepper seasoning by 'accident': _ _ _ _

8. Sneakily wake your sibling up ten minutes before their _ _ _ _ _ , and tell them that they're late for school. They'll be so panicked, that they won't even check the time to see that they're actually early!

I'm great at puzzling when I'm not pranking and plotting!

HEENA'S EMOJI CODE

Can you crack my code? Each emoji stands for a different letter. What does my message below say?

★ A	B	C	D	E	F	G	H	☆ I
J	↗ K	L	M	N	♡ O	P	Q	R
S	T	✳ U	V	# W	X	Y	Z

_ _ _ _ _ _ _ _ _ _ _ _ _ _ _ '_ _ _ _ _ _

_ _ _ _ _ _ _ _ _ _ _ _ _ _ _ _ _,_ _ _ _ _ _ '_ _

_ _ _ _ _ _ _ _ _ _ _ _ _ _ _ _ _ _ _ _

_ _ _ _ _ _ _ _ _ _ _ _ !

_ _ _ _ _ _ _ _ _ _ !

I'm so tired of my little brother snooping! But he'll never work out what I'm saying now, ☺♡☺

HANI'S MAZE

Can you find your way through this maze without crossing paths? Watch out for the slime – if you slip across some of that, you'll have to go back to the beginning and start over. Be sure to collect all of the sweets – your tummy will thank you!

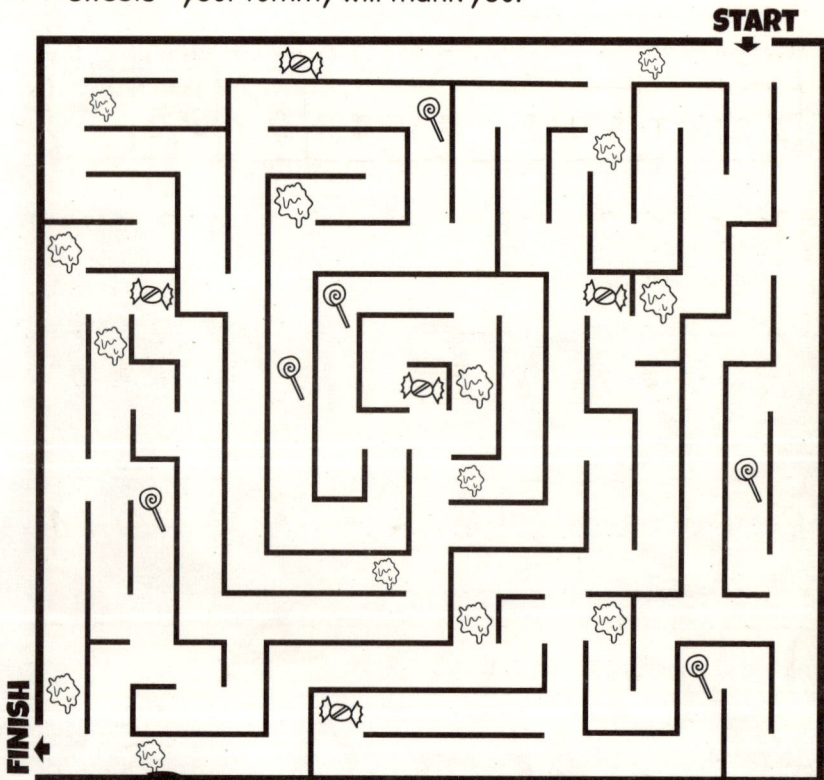

START

FINISH

Lord Snooty can't play computer games at home? THAT IS THE SADDEST THING I'VE EVER HEARD IN MY ENTIRE LIFE! I'm going to make a puzzle that looks like a computer game to help him feel better!

27

DANGEROUS DAN'S DECODER PUZZLE

Imagine you needed to hack into the enemy's computer by using a cypher to decode their password. I've never done this, by the way. I certainly didn't do it last Tuesday, when I was ... erm ... busy doing homework.

Start at the letter that's circled and write in every third letter. Keep going round until you've used up all the letters ... and revealed the secret password!

Answer on page 80

[TOP SECRET]

The password is:

_ _ _ _ _ _ _ _ _ _ _

28

CALAMITY JAMES'S DENTAL DILEMMA

At first, I couldn't think of a good puzzle, so I went for a walk to clear my mind. Upon leaving the house, I promptly tripped over my untied shoelaces and fell into the path of a runaway piano. Just my luck!

I was at St Somewhere Hospital afterwards, worried that I'd run out of time to come up with a puzzle, when an idea hit me (literally – the X-ray machine fell on my head, cracking a bunch of my teeth). I'm now on the way to the dentist for some fillings. Can you count all the cracks in my teeth?

Total:

____

Answer on page 81

STEVIE'S SPOT THE DIFFERENCE

Look at these two nearly identical scenes from my latest You-Hoo video. Can you find the ten differences between pictures A and B? Colour in a star each time you spot one!

A

Lord Snooty, man, I'm so bummed you can't watch anything on You–Hoo without Wi-Fi. So I made you a puzzle from your favourite channel – my channel! (Why wouldn't that be your favourite?)

B

RUBI'S INVENTION INVENTOR

This is the best puzzle in the book because there's no wrong answer! Instead, my latest invention is an inventor that invents inventions! Use the idea generator on the next page and then draw your hilarious new invention below.

My invention: _Helien power I art clover_

Rubidium Von Screwtop, boldly going where no puzzle inventor has gone before...

FIRST LETTER OF YOUR NAME

A = All–speed
B = Brainwave–powered
C = Clockwork
D = Delicate
E = Electric
F = Frozen
G = Gravity–defying
H = Helium–powered
I = Itchy
J = Jelly–filled
K = Karate–chopping
L = Loud
M = Majestic
N = Noisy
O = Oversized
P = Pongy
Q = Quirky
R = Robotic
S = Slobbery
T = Troublesome
U = Upside–down
V = Vacuum–powered
W = Wailing
X = Large
Y = Yodelling
Z = Zappy

MONTH OF YOUR BIRTH

JANUARY: Sloth
FEBRUARY: Hairball
MARCH: Burp
APRIL: Gnome
MAY: Fart
JUNE: Juice
JULY: Energy
AUGUST: Sleep
SEPTEMBER: Banana
OCTOBER: Slug
NOVEMBER: Egg
DECEMBER: Ghost

FAVOURITE COLOUR

RED: Converter
ORANGE: Magnifier
YELLOW: Catcher
GREEN: Detector
BLUE: Cloner
PURPLE: Repeller
PINK: Alarm

BIGGY'S LIBRARY CODE BREAKER

Hurrah for Homework used to be the least checked-out book at Beanotown Library – only Cuthbert Cringeworthy ever read it! But recently, instead of gathering dust, it's been on our most-borrowed list. Could students be using it to pass secret messages around?

Write out the letters with dots below them to discover the hidden message.

Chapter Six: Homework Heroes Through History

In 1023 CE, a young Viking named Borgar the Boring set a new Viking World Record when he did homework for forty-seven hours straight. This pummelled the previous record set by Halgar the Humdrum (which was only thirty hours and sixteen minutes, because Halgar had to stop and run to the loo).

Borgar the Boring filled twenty-one stone tablets with geometric equations, and then spent the remainder of the time composing tedious essays by carving ancient runes into iron plinths. Some of his most-ignored essays included:

- Viking horned helmets – is there a point?

- A mundane meditation on Viking mould and mildew

- The causes and effects of Viking long-boat traffic jams

F y o u r e a d t h i s i t __ __ ____ ____

____ ____ _____ _____!

BETTY'S ICE CREAM PAIRS

Why sit back and chill when you can solve this sweet puzzle? There are loads of ice creams below, but I can say for sherbert that only two of them are a perfect pair! Can you make a match before they all melt?

Circle the matching ice creams.

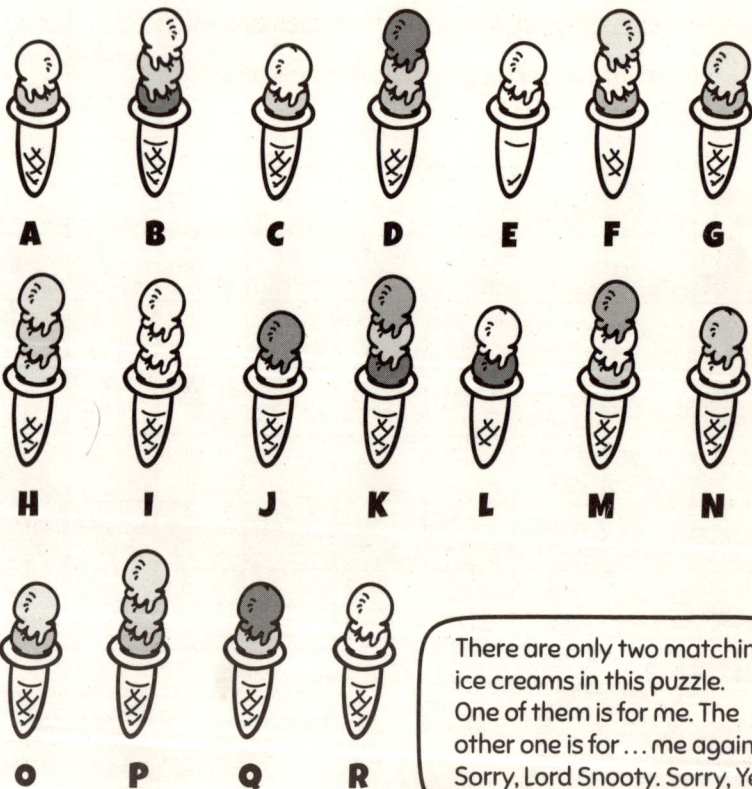

A B C D E F G

H I J K L M N

O P Q R

There are only two matching ice creams in this puzzle. One of them is for me. The other one is for ... me again. Sorry, Lord Snooty. Sorry, Yeti!

ERIC'S BANANAS MAZE

Bananaman LOVES bananas. But do you know what not even he likes to eat? Bad bananas! Can you find your way through this banana maze, only moving up and down, and avoiding all the dark unripe and overripe ones, and banana skins until you find Bananaman?

START

FINISH

If you're bored, Lord Snooty, I know a certain fruit-based superhero, who can help with that!

| bad | bad | bad | good |

36

BILLY'S RAPID ROUTE RACE

The directions may be mixed up, but can you work out the quickest route to Bunkerton Castle? First, solve the maths puzzles. The one that equals 1 is the first direction, the one that equals 2 is the second direction, and so on! But be careful – any that equal 0 are wrong turns!

1._____
2._____
3._____
4._____
5._____
6._____

$(3 \times 2) - 6 =$ __

Turn left by the lighthouse.

$(15 \div 5) + 3 =$ __

Dash across the drawbridge.

$(11 - 9) \times 2 =$ __

Race towards the railway station.

$4 + 1 + 3 - 7 =$ __

Zoom past Beanotown Zoo.

$(7 \times 2) - 14 =$ __

Go west when you pass WilburCorp.

$(2 \times 2) + 1 =$ __

Head south towards the school.

$(6 \times 2) - 9 =$ __

Turn left before the library.

$(9 \div 3) - 1 =$ __

Go west towards Widl.

$2 + 5 - 1 - 6 =$ __

Swim across Lake Mess.

Answers on page 83

ROGER'S FART DODGERS MAZE

I'm the best at dodging, but even I need help escaping this one! The Olives' dodgy stew has had explosive consequences! Can you help me find a route out of the school, avoiding all the farts in the way?

CANTEEN

SCHOOL EXIT

VERY HEAVY WEIGHT INDEED

MRS SPLINT'S INJURY SOLVER

As the school's nurse, I've had all manner of injuries come through my door. But just when I think I've seen it all, Calamity James gets admitted to the sick bay – again! Use the key below to colour in the grid, and find out what fell out of the sky and hit him on the head this time.

	1	2	3	4	5	6	7	8	9	10
A										
B										
C										
D										
E										
F										
G										

BLACK
C9

GREEN
B8, B9, C8, C10, D8, D9, D10, E8, E9, F2, F3, F4, F5, F6, F7, G2, G3, G6, G7

BROWN
A4, A5, B3, B4, B5, B6, C2, C3, C4, C5, C6, C7, D2, D3, D4, D5, D6, D7, E1, E2, E3, E4, E5, E6, E7

Answers on page 4

ANGEL FACE'S CASE OF THE MISSING CAKE

Someone swiped the last slice of cake at my birthday party – rude! – leaving behind nothing but chocolatey crumbs and some footsteps. I've narrowed it down to four suspects. Follow their footsteps to catch the culprit!

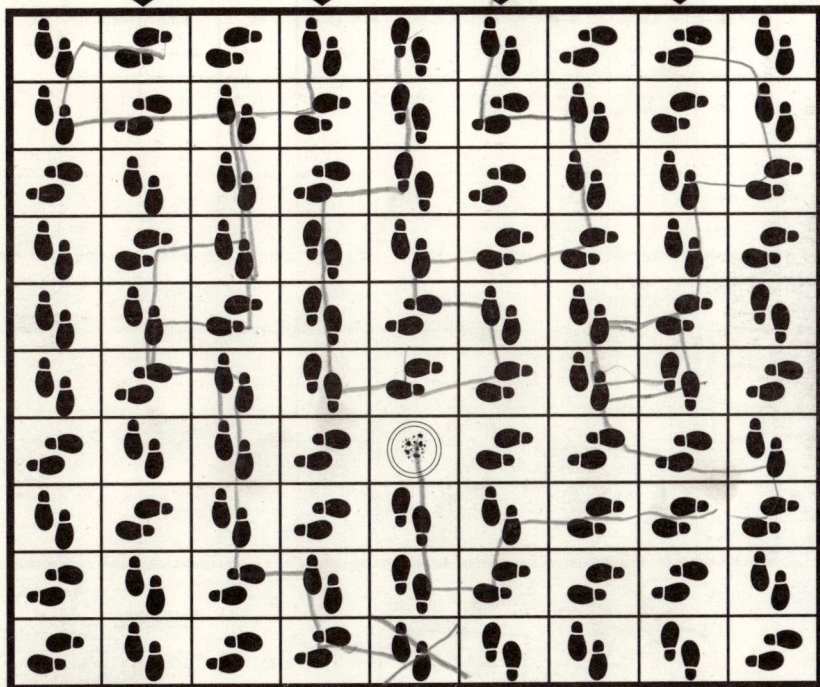

I don't normally share my case notes from my Investigations Agency unless there's something in it for me ... like a grand prize for a puzzle!

I like helping Angel Face with her cases. She writes in code sometimes, and I'm getting pretty good at it too. What could be better than a coded puzzle with a joke at the end?

JENNY'S MORSE CODE

The answer to this joke is written out in Morse code! Can you use the guide below to crack it and write your own?

A	B	C	D	E	F	G	H	I
•—	—•••	—•—•	—••	•	••—•	——•	••••	••

J	K	L	M	N	O	P	Q	R
•———	—•—	•—••	——	—•	———	•——•	——•—	•—•

S	T	U	V	W	X	Y	Z	
•••	—	••—	•••—	•——	—••—	—•——	——••	

JENNY'S JOKE :

How can you tell if a vampire has a cold?

•• —   ••• — •— •—• — •••

__ __ _____ _____

—•—• ——— ••—• ••—• •• —•

__ _____

Try writing your own jokes in Morse code for your friends!
– The Ed

WALTER'S SEARCH AND SNITCH

When Dennis and his friends break the rules – which they often do – they deserve to be punished. In fact, it's better to just go ahead and put them in detention now. It will save you time later. Find all 21 kids misbehaving in the school canteen. Draw a big X over all of their faces.

Why would I be jealous of Lord Snooty and his silly old 16-bedroom castle? I'm much smarter than he is, and my dad is the mayor of Beanotown.

Answers on page 86

BERTIE'S DOT TO DOT

Connect the dots to reveal the most important, awe-inspiring, generous person in Beanotown. Can you guess who it is?

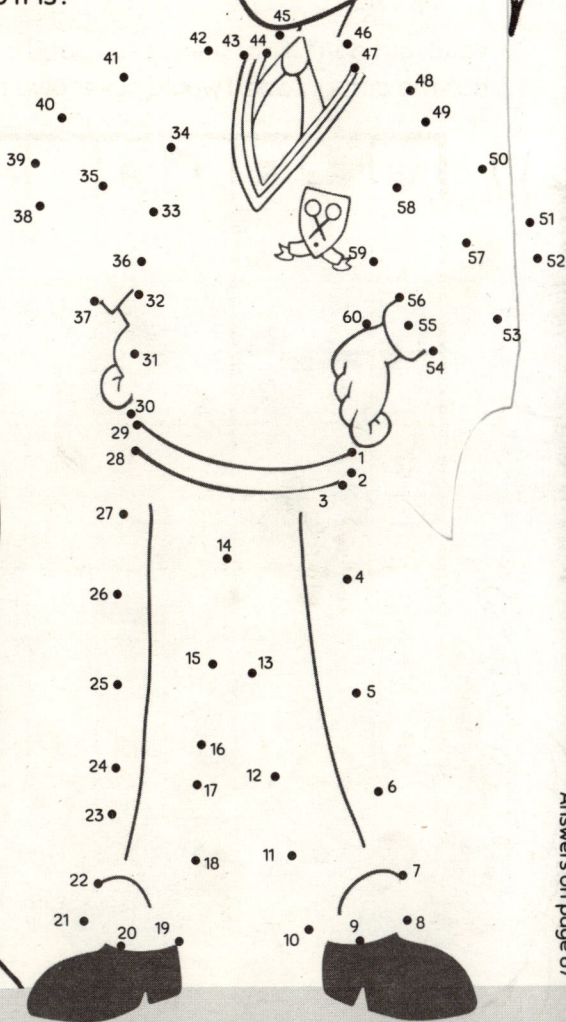

Isn't he marvellous?

Answers on page 61

WILBUR'S VAULT-CRACKING SUDOKU

Solve the number puzzle below by filling in the missing numbers. All numbers 1–9 must appear once in each box, but never in the same column or row.

Three numbers have a star on them. Put those numbers in order from smallest to biggest to crack the code to the vault. But don't start feeling too good about yourself – it's not the actual code. I would never give that up!

★	6	5	1	9			7	8
			6	3	5	4	1	
	1	9		7	8	5		
	4	2	3	★	6	7		
8	5			4	7	9	3	
	3		5	8		6		
	8			2			5	★
5	7		8		1		9	3
2		1	7		3	8	6	4

The code to the secret vault is:

___ ___ ___

47

MRS CREECHER'S PRANK SPOTTER

Bash Street has many rules, which I read to the students every Monday morning, and yet somehow, they keep on getting broken, along with my windows! Can you spot the twenty times rules have been broken at school this week? I'll clearly have to read the rules out again next Monday...

Answers on page 88

MISS MISTRY'S SUBJECTS CROSSWORD

Can you solve the clues in this crossword puzzle to figure out what we're learning about in class this week?

1. Dennis is plotting something today. But that's OK – he's just plotting points on a graph, because we're studying ...

2. It's *past* time for us to start learning about the Egyptians, the Vikings and the Romans in this lesson.

3. Minnie claims her homework was stolen by invisible space koalas. Her acting was so good, I almost believed her. If only we had been studying this.

4. I never *leaf* out a lesson on plants ... and I have an outer space lesson too, but I need to *planet*. What subject are these lessons from?

5. It's time to *brush* up on drawing and painting in my favourite lesson.

6. In this lesson, we'll study maps (because we'd be lost without them!).

WHELAN'S PICTURE PUZZLE

This puzzle is for my adoring fans, who attend all of my Super Epic Turbo Cricket matches. If Lord Snooty isn't a fan of me yet, he will be once he's finished my puzzle. Can you number these mixed-up strips, so they create a complete picture?

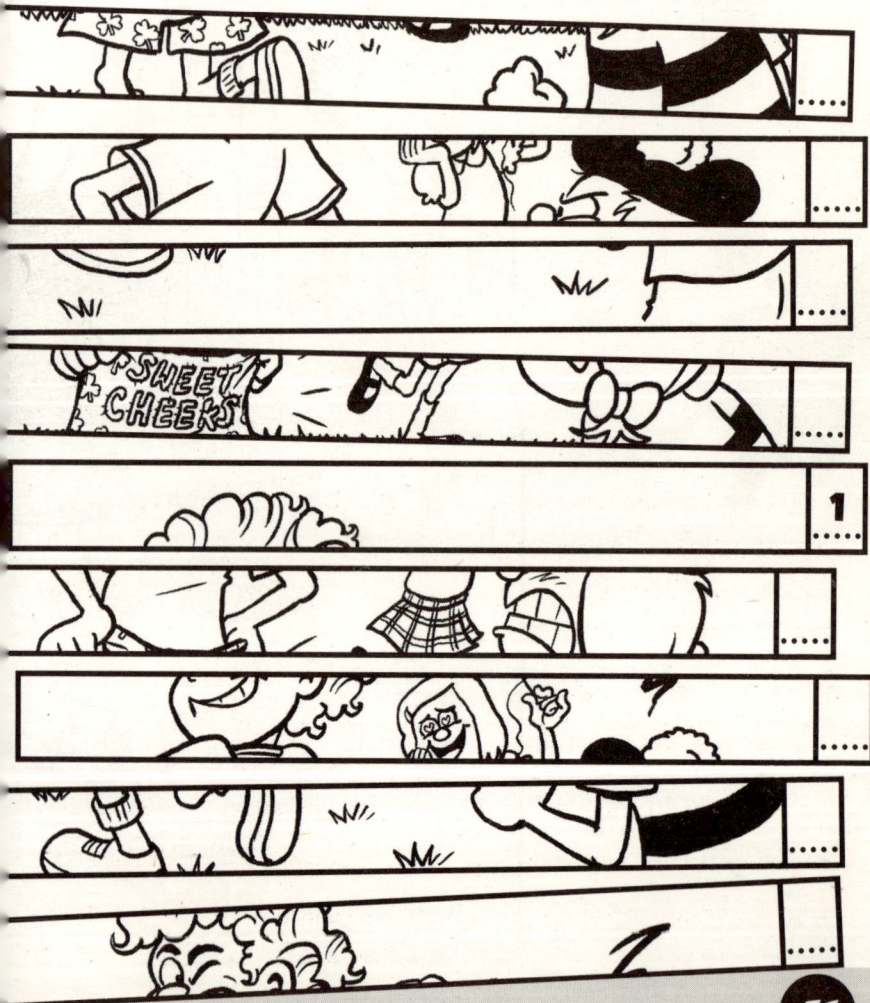

LORD SNOOTY'S BOGEYMAN HUNT

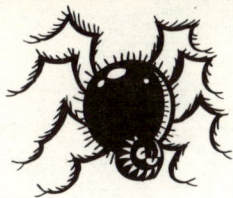

Minnie told me that the bogeyman isn't real ... but if that's the case, then why do I keep hearing horrible moans, piercing shrieks and drip–drip–dripping inside my castle at night?* I'm sure there's something creepy hiding – can you find all four bogeymen?

When I saw how much fun everyone was having creating their puzzles, I wanted to come up with one too!

SNOOTY HOME

*There's actually an eerie-sistable boomic called *Dennis & Gnasher: The Bogeyman of Bunkerton Castle* that answers this question and more ... – The Ed

53

SMIFFY'S ROCK SCRAMBLE

Kevin is the perfect pet pebble pal. Except when he wanders off at the beach and I can't find him. But maybe you can help spot Kevin? He's the only rock that I can look deep into the eyes of and know that he'll never take me for granite.

KEVIN

PLUG'S MIRROR MYSTERY

When I stare into the mirror, I see a magnificent, beautiful reflection looking back. But can you work out which reflection is mine? (The others are ever so slightly less dazzling – but still blamazingly gorgeous.)

DANNY'S TREASURE QUEST

Imagine you're a pirate searching for treasure out at sea. All you have is this ancient scroll of clues. Can you follow them to work out where the treasure is buried?

1. Start at the 'START'.

2. Go east 3 spaces.

3. Go south 5 spaces.

4. Go west 1 space.

5. Go north 2 spaces.

6. Go east 6 spaces.

7. Go south 4 spaces.

8. Go west 5 spaces.

9. Go south 3 spaces.

10. Go east 3 spaces.

11. Go north 2 spaces.

12. Go east 2 spaces.

13. Go south 4 spaces.

14. Go west 5 spaces.

15. Go south 1 space.

Answers on page 90

	1	2	3	4	5	6	7	8	9	10
A	START									
B										
C										
D										
E										
F										
G										
H										
I										
J										
K										
L										
M										
N										

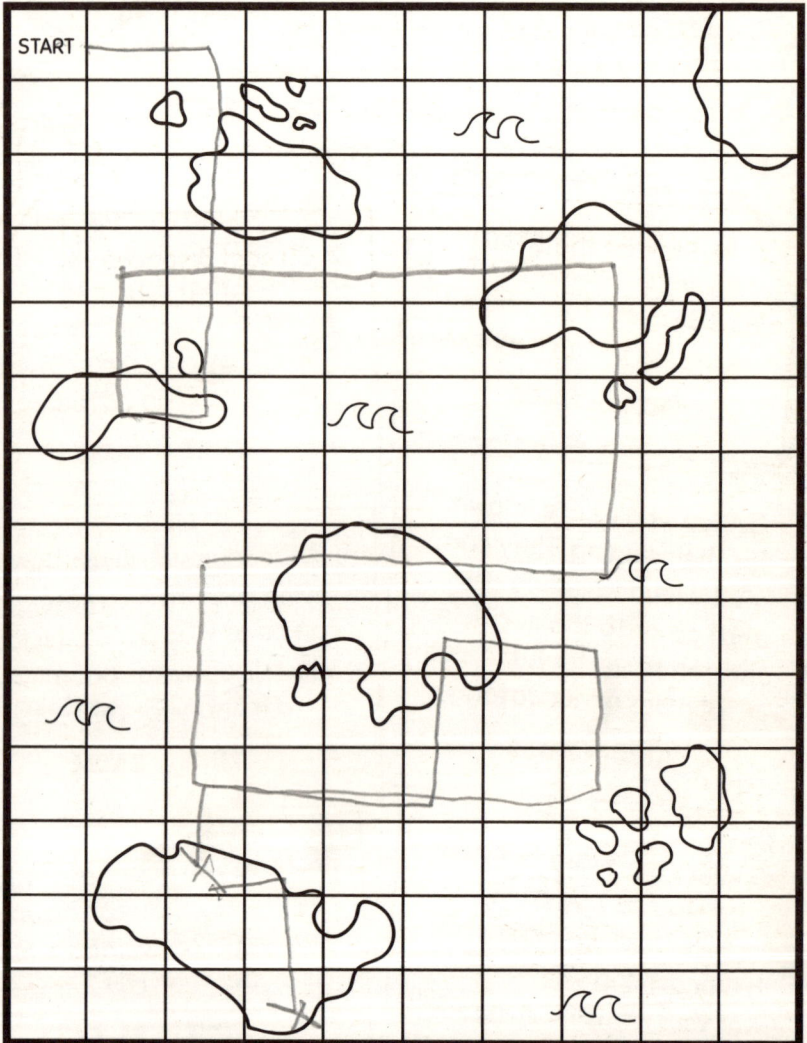

FREDDY'S MUSICAL MAYHEM

Test your musical knowledge in this puzzle! Two of these facts aren't true. Can you figure out which ones are the imposters?

1. The loudest human singer recorded was at 113.8 decibels. That's about as loud as live rock music!

TRUE or **FALSE**

2. The Bermuda dip is a bird who sings so loudly (140 decibels) that its prey becomes frozen on the spot. Luckily for you, they only eat spiders, insects and small rodents.

TRUE or **FALSE**

3. Blue whales are known for their singing. They can make loud whistling calls that go up to 188 decibels and can travel for hundreds of miles underwater.

TRUE or **FALSE**

4. Cicadas sing when they're trying to attract a mate. They can be as loud as 135 decibels, which is about as booming as a military jet take-off.

TRUE or **FALSE**

5. Skunks don't sing, but they can fart as loud as 122 decibels, which is noisier than a thunderclap. You have to cover your ears and your nose!

TRUE or **FALSE**

6. Have you heard of howler monkeys? They can howl as loudly as 128 decibels, which is louder than a chain saw.

TRUE or **FALSE**

CUTHBERT'S MATHS CIRCUIT

Fill in the missing numbers in the grid, in order from 1 to 25, completing the entire circuit using only horizontal and vertical lines. I like to think of this puzzle as a journey through the love of homework.

	18		16	15
20				
1	24		12	11
	25	6		
3	4		8	9

After I give this puzzle to Lord Snooty, I'm going to turn it in to Mr Teacher as extra homework for him to mark.

TOOTS'S BRILLIANT BOWS

Look at the scene below from Beanotown Museum. Can you circle the ten polka-dot bows (not including mine, of course), before it's time for the museum to close?

Answers on page 91

MITTEN OF DOOM

"BILLY" THE WORLD'S FASTEST DINOSAUR

60

SIDNEY'S ANIMAL ANAGRAMS

I've got loads of pets, living up on the roof of Bash Street Towers. Solve these anagrams to figure out which animals I have.

GOD
_____

AGAINU
_____

AGEINU GIP
_____

GENIPO
_____

ARTBIB
_____

EGGEDHOH
_____

UDEWOOLSO
_____

TOGA
_____

PRIDES
_____

EUMOS
_____

Answers on page 92

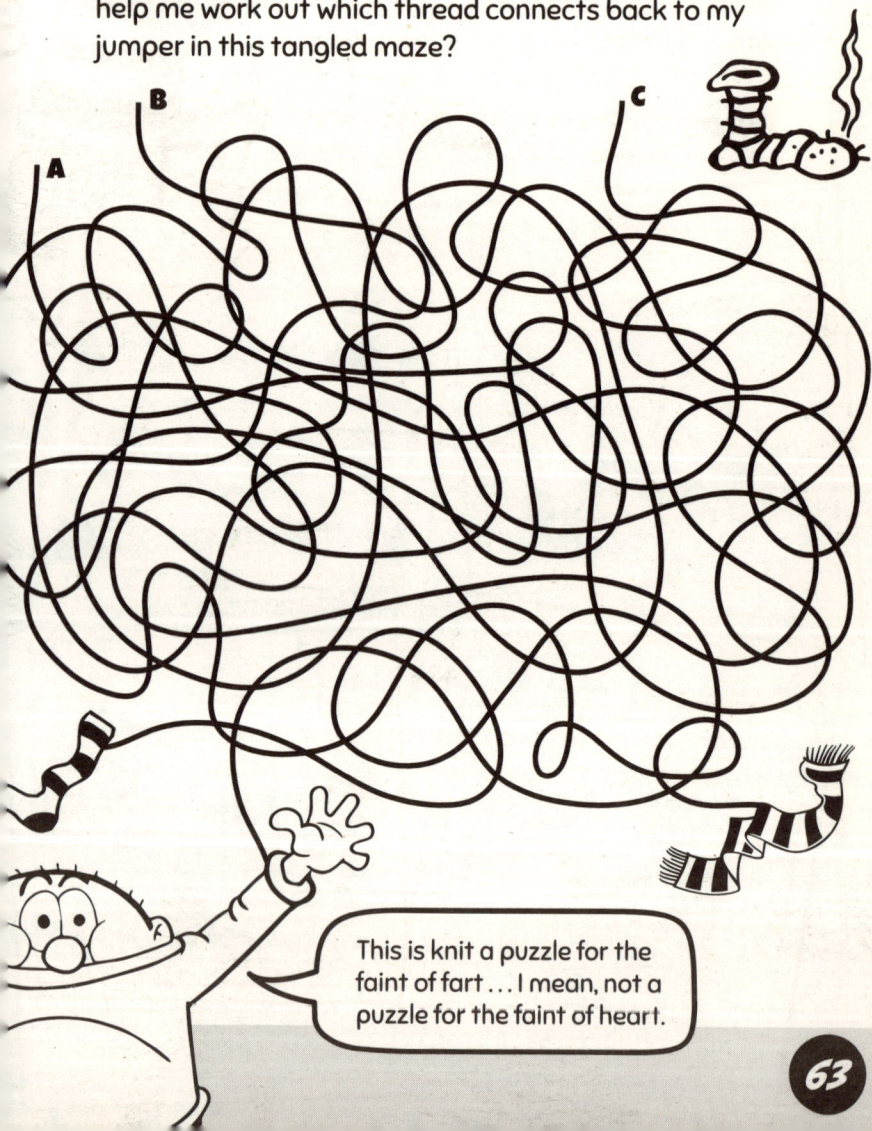

WILFRID'S JUMPER JUMBLE

Luckily, my favourite jumper is so thick that even if it starts to unravel, it will still cover me. But can you help me work out which thread connects back to my jumper in this tangled maze?

A

B

C

This is knit a puzzle for the faint of fart ... I mean, not a puzzle for the faint of heart.

ERBERT'S GLASSES FINDER

Last time I was at Lord Snooty's castle, I lost my glasses. At least, I think I did – I can barely see through my spare pair. Lord Snooty took lots of pictures, so can you search the photographs to figure out where I left them? Please? It should be as easy as A, B, See . . .

SCOTTY'S SPOT THE DIFFERENCE

I've taken two photos of the Bash Street Pups for my wall. Both photos are very similar, but with ten differences. Can you spot all the differences in picture B and help me decide which one to print?

Answers on page 93

THE OLIVES' MYSTERY STEW SUDOKU

We're perfecting a new recipe for our mystery stew. But to trial the recipe, you need to draw in the missing ingredients in each grid. All nine ingredients should appear once in each box, but never in the same row or column.

Answers on page 93

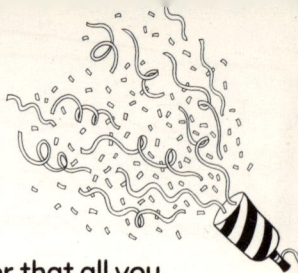

LES PRETEND'S DRESS-UP SCRAMBLE

The next time you're bored, remember that all you need is a few props to mix and match, and you'll never run out of characters to be. Here are some of my disguises – can you unscramble them below?

BROOT

R _ _ _ _

MYUMM

M _ _ _ _

GINK

K _ _ _

NIALE

A _ _ _ _

DRIWAZ

W _ _ _ _

CHIWT

W _ _ _ _

PREESHORU

S _ _ _ _ _ _ _

Answers on page 94

MEBOIZ

Z _ _ _ _

CORK RAST

R _ _ _ S _ _ _

Lord Snooty, you don't need Wi-Fi to have fun! You just need to use your imagination!

RALF'S A-MAZE-ING PUDDLE PUZZLE

Today's mystery stew recipe didn't go down as well as the Olives had hoped – and in the case of some kids, it didn't go down at all! Can you find a route through this maze that cleans up all the puke puddles?

START

Answers on page 94

FINISH

BANANAMAN'S BANANAS WORDSEARCH

This puzzle is full of bananas! Can you find them all? That's right – ten 'BANANAS' are hidden in this wordsearch. They could go across, down, upwards or backwards, so keep your eyes peeled!

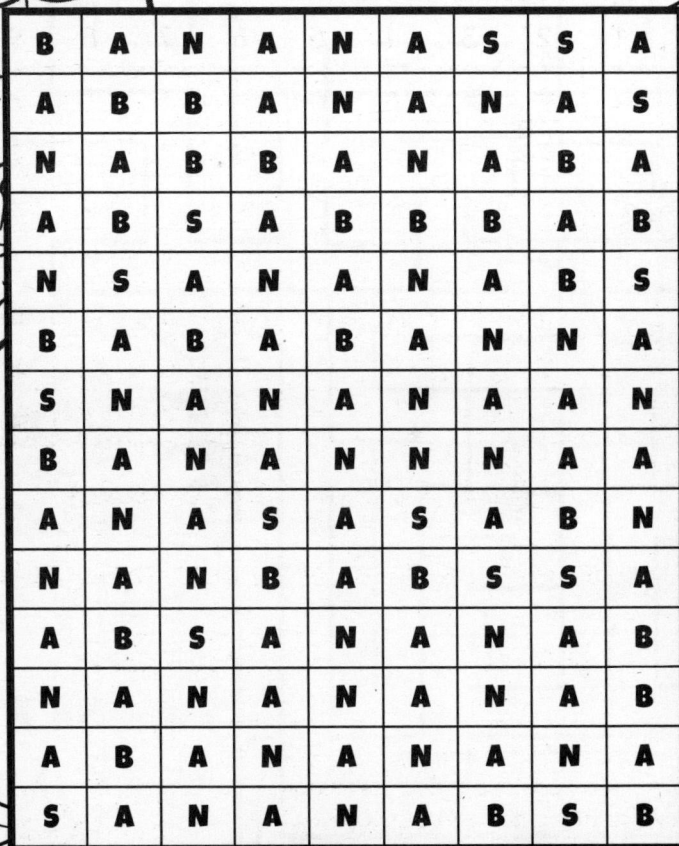

B	A	N	A	N	A	S	S	A
A	B	B	A	N	A	N	A	S
N	A	B	B	A	N	A	B	A
A	B	S	A	B	B	B	A	B
N	S	A	N	A	N	A	B	S
B	A	B	A	B	A	N	N	A
S	N	A	N	A	N	A	A	N
B	A	N	A	N	N	N	A	A
A	N	A	S	A	S	A	B	N
N	A	N	B	A	B	S	S	A
A	B	S	A	N	A	N	A	B
N	A	N	A	N	A	N	A	B
A	B	A	N	A	N	A	N	A
S	A	N	A	N	A	B	S	B

CHIEF O'REILLY'S DETECTIVE PUZZLE

I got honked at the entire way to the police station this morning. Turns out someone had stuck a sticker on my car saying 'Honk if you think my bum stinks!' The cheek! Well, the joke's on them as they dropped a key piece of evidence. It's a bit torn though, so can you use the grid to help me discover the culprit?

	1	2	3	4	5	6	7	8	9
A	K	P	N	A	N	H	S	I	A
B	U	E	M	O	N	R	W	Y	F
C	F	A	C	B	K	D	Z	X	J
D	A	V	E	X	G	B	L	V	T
E	D	S	T	N	P	N	E	M	S
F	Z	T	I	H	B	P	O	Q	A
G	G	Q	J	U	E	L	C	A	W

D9, A6, F3, E9   E1, G8, B3, F9, D5, B2   G9, D1, A7

_ _ _ _   _ _ _ _ _ _   _ _ _

F6, B4, E2, A7, F3, D6, G6, B8   G7, C2, B1, E2, E7, C6   D6, B8

_ _ _ _ _ _ _ _   _ _ _ _ _ _   _ _

E1, G5, E6, B5, A8, E9   B3, E7, A3, F9, C3, G5

_ _ _ _ _ _   _ _ _ _ _ _

Aha! We've solved it. But the image of a grinning girl with a stripy top, bobble hat and halo, saying 'It wasn't me' seems kinda sus …

SERGEANT SLIPPER'S SPOT THE DIFFERENCE

Look at these two pictures taken of a slimy crime scene. Someone is up to no goo ... I mean, someone is up to no good! Can you spot ten differences in picture B? Colour in a glob of slime each time you find one of the differences!

THE SERIOUS MAN

A good police officer always pays attention to clues in the meme of the slime ... I mean, at the scene of the crime.

B

THE MAN

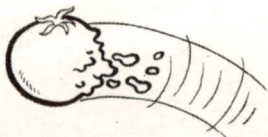

Answers on page 95

ANSWERS

No peeking at the answers until after ~~you've tried the puzzles~~ I've peeked at them first!

PAGE 8 - DENNIS'S PONGY PUZZLE

It was **SIDNEY** who farted!

PAGE 10 - MINNIE'S MATHS RIDDLE

Minnie has been late **17** times this term!

PAGE 11 - GNASHER'S SAUSAGE WORDSEARCH

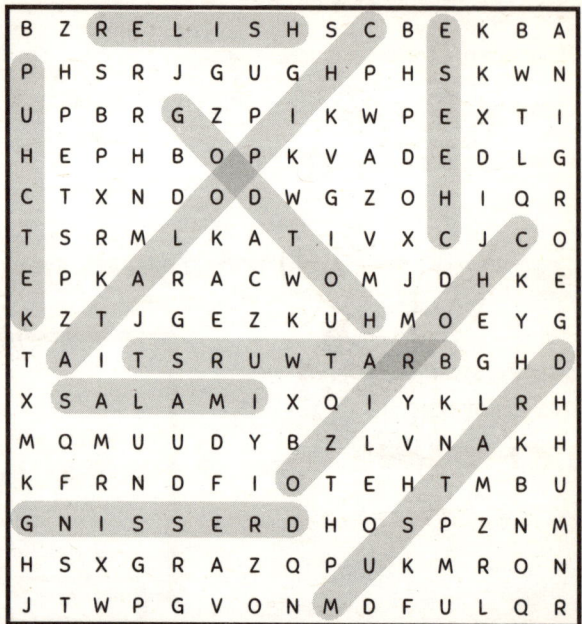

PAGE 12 - FIND BEA'S DIRTY NAPPY

PAGE 13 - DENNIS SENIOR'S PAPER CLIP PUZZLE

There are **12** stripy paper clips.

There are **13** spotty paper clips.

There are **8** plain paper clips.

PAGE 14 - SANDRA'S NIGHTTIME ART MISSION

Sandra ~~stole~~ borrowed this painting:

THE I-SCREAM

THE I-SCREAM

PAGE 16 - GRAN'S JUMPERS

START

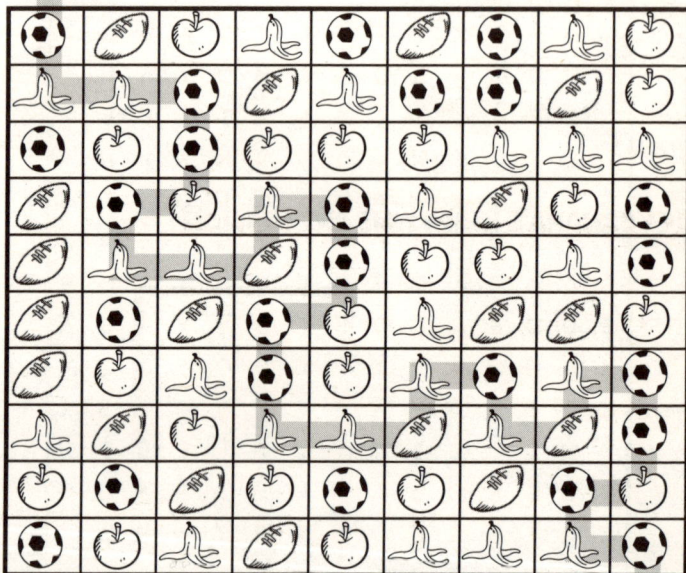

FINISH

**PEAR, SPINACH,
CHOCOLATE**

**LEEKS, APPLES,
CURRY SAUCE**

**SAUSAGE,
YOGURT, CHEESE**

77

PAGE 20 - VITO'S WHOPPING WORDSEARCH

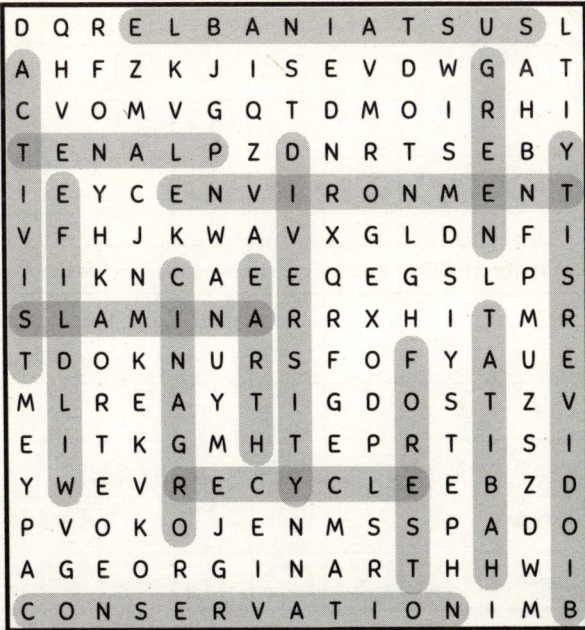

D	Q	R	E	L	B	A	N	I	A	T	S	U	S	L
A	H	F	Z	K	J	I	S	E	V	D	W	G	A	T
C	V	O	M	V	G	Q	T	D	M	O	I	R	H	I
T	E	N	A	L	P	Z	D	N	R	T	S	E	B	Y
I	E	Y	C	E	N	V	I	R	O	N	M	E	N	T
V	F	H	J	K	W	A	V	X	G	L	D	N	F	I
I	I	K	N	C	A	E	E	Q	E	G	S	L	P	S
S	L	A	M	I	N	A	R	R	X	H	I	T	M	R
T	D	O	K	N	U	R	S	F	O	F	Y	A	U	E
M	L	R	E	A	Y	T	I	G	D	O	S	T	Z	V
E	I	T	K	G	M	H	T	E	P	R	T	I	S	I
Y	W	E	V	R	E	C	Y	C	L	E	E	B	Z	D
P	V	O	K	O	J	E	N	M	S	S	P	A	D	O
A	G	E	O	R	G	I	N	A	R	T	H	H	W	I
C	O	N	S	E	R	V	A	T	I	O	N	I	M	B

PAGE 21 - SKETCH'S DOT TO DOT

78

PAGE 22 - MANDI'S MOTIVATION MIX-UP

Use your fear ... it can take you to the place where you store your courage. – Amelia Earhart

It isn't what we say or think that defines us, but what we do. – Jane Austen

Never underestimate a teacher with jets in their hands and feet. – Minnie Makepeace

PAGE 23 - MAHIRA'S FOOTBALL FUN

1. **TOOL**   2. **FOAL**   3. **LAB**   4. **FLOAT**   5. **FALL**

PAGE 24 - HARSHA'S PRANKSTER CROSSWORD

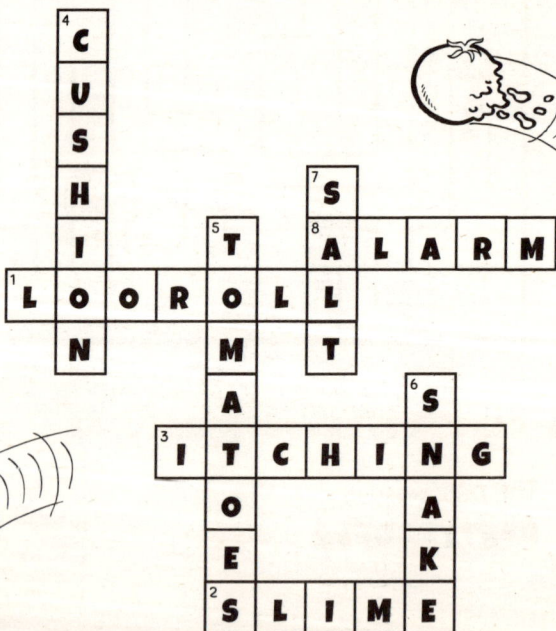

79

MY SIBLINGS THINK I'M TOO OLD FOR PRANKS, BUT I'VE CHANGED THEIR RINGTONES TO FART NOISES!

PAGE 27 - HANI'S MAZE

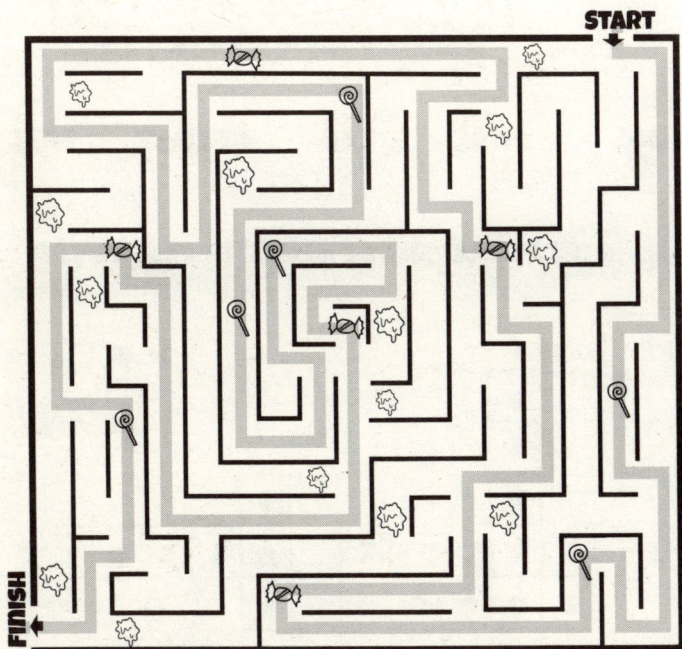

START

FINISH

PAGE 28 - DANGEROUS DAN'S DECODER PUZZLE

The password is:
PARTYPOOPER

James has **38** cracks in his teeth.

IF YOU READ THIS, IT IS YOUR TURN TO PRANK SOMEONE!

PAGE 36 - ERIC'S BANANAS MAZE

START

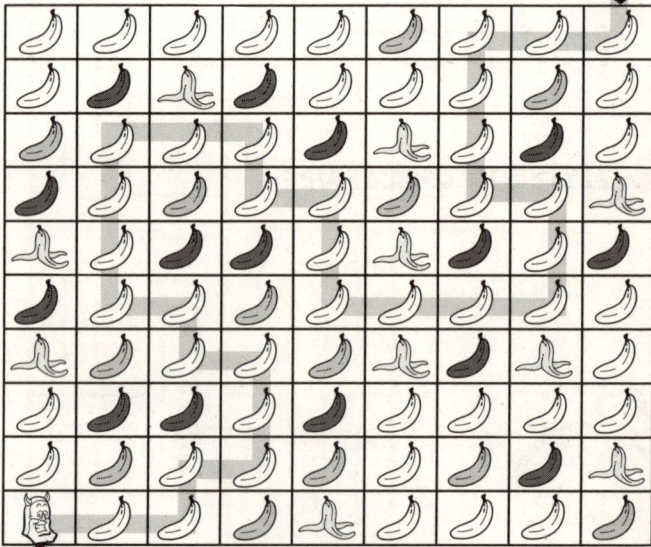

FINISH

PAGE 37 - BILLY'S RAPID ROUTE RACE

1. **ZOOM PAST BEANOTOWN ZOO**

2. **GO WEST TOWARDS WIDL**

3. **TURN LEFT BEFORE THE LIBRARY**

4. **RACE TOWARDS THE RAILWAY STATION**

5. **HEAD SOUTH TOWARDS THE SCHOOL**

6. **DASH ACROSS THE DRAWBRIDGE**

83

PAGE 39 - MRS SPLINT'S INJURY SOLVER

How can you tell if a vampire has a cold?

IT STARTS COFFIN

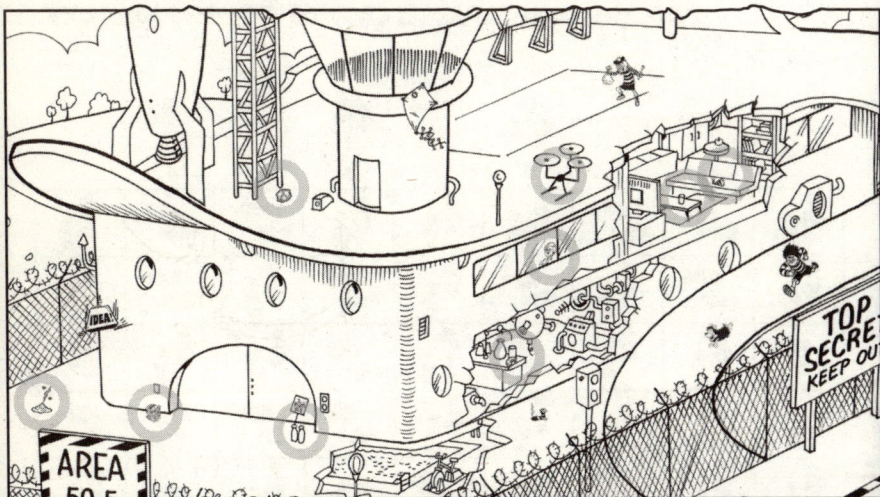

Surprise, surprise. It's
Bertie's best friend, Walter!

PAGE 47 - WILBUR'S VAULT-CRACKING SUDOKU

vault code:
1, 4, 7

4	6	5	1	9	2	3	7	8
7	2	8	6	3	5	4	1	9
3	1	9	4	7	8	5	2	6
9	4	2	3	1	6	7	8	5
8	5	6	2	4	7	9	3	1
1	3	7	5	8	9	6	4	2
6	8	3	9	2	4	1	5	7
5	7	4	8	6	1	2	9	3
2	9	1	7	5	3	8	6	4

87

PAGE 48 - MRS CREECHER'S PRANK SPOTTER

PAGE 50 - MISS MISTRY'S SUBJECTS CROSSWORD

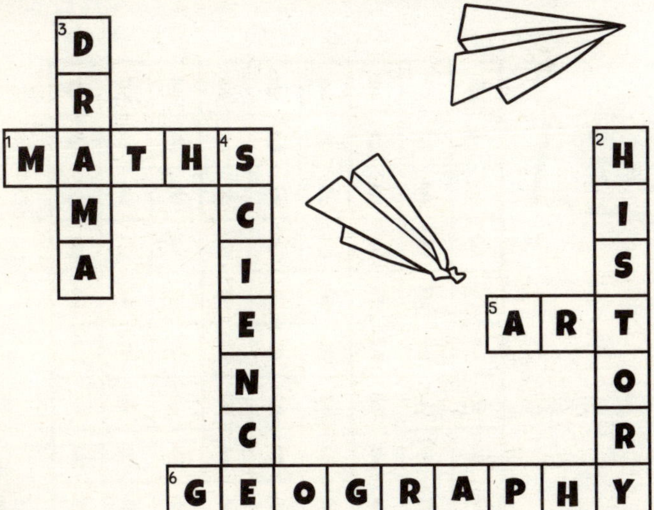

PAGE 54 - SMIFFY'S ROCK SCRAMBLE

PAGE 55 - PLUG'S MIRROR MYSTERY

C

PAGE 56 - DANNY'S TREASURE QUEST

The treasure is buried in **N4**

The imposters are: **2** and **5**

19	18	17	16	15
20	21	22	13	14
1	24	23	12	11
2	25	6	7	10
3	4	5	8	9

GOD
DOG

AGAINU
IGUANA

AGEINU GIP
GUINEA PIG

GENIPO
PIGEON

ARTBIB
RABBIT

EGGEDHOH
HEDGEHOG

UDEWOOLSO
WOODLOUSE

EUMOS
MOUSE

PRIDES
SPIDER

TOGA
GOAT

PAGE 63 - WILFRID'S JUMPER JUMBLE

Thread **B** connects to Wilfrid's jumper

PAGE 64 - ERBERT'S GLASSES FINDER

92

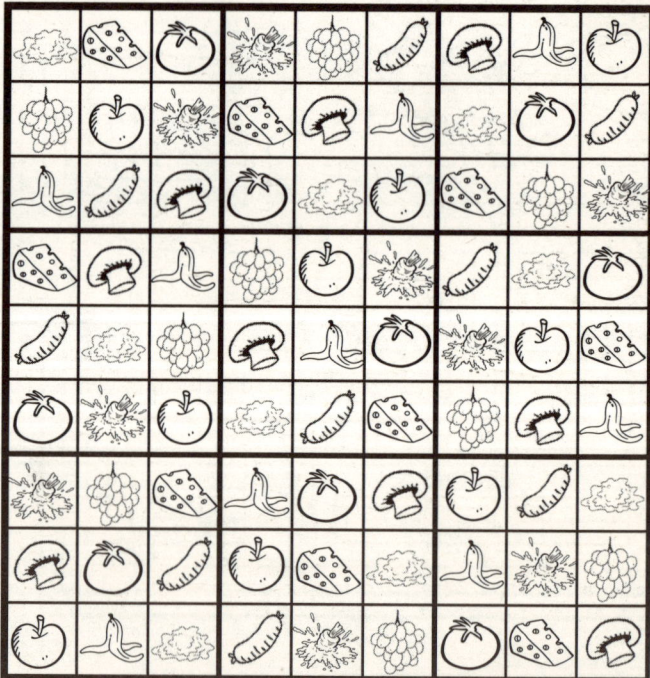

PAGE 67 - LES PRETEND'S DRESS-UP SCRAMBLE

BROOT
ROBOT

MYUMM
MUMMY

GINK
KING

NIALE
ALIEN

DRIWAZ
WIZARD

PREESHORU
SUPERHERO

CHIWT
WITCH

MEBOIZ
ZOMBIE

CORK RAST
ROCK STAR

PAGE 68 - RALF'S A-MAZE-ING PUDDLE PUZZLE

THIS DAMAGE WAS POSSIBLY CAUSED BY DENNIS MENACE

PREVIOUSLY IN BEANOTOWN...

BEANO
BOOK OF FUN
200+ PUZZLES, RIDDLES & GIGGLES!

BEANO
JOKE BOOK
BEANOTOWN'S BEST JOKES!

BEANO
WOULD YOU RATHER?
WITH OVER 200 BRAIN-BENDING CHOICES!

FOR EVEN MORE FUN, HEAD TO BEANO.COM

CONTINUE THE FUN AND LAUGH YOURSEL SILLY WITH THESE HILARIOUS BOOKS